the Buchmann family

from Rosenwiller to St. Louis

A STORY OF TEN GENERATIONS

Rose Marie Buchmann Roach Miller

The Buchmann Family

ISBN 978-1-4357-4655-8
ID: 2998724   www.lulu.com

Dedication

In the 1960s my children were members of the local country club swim team. At one competitive meet Andy, age eight, won the twenty-five yard freestyle race. As he stood on the block to receive his first place blue-ribbon, his fourteen year old sister, Kim, turned to her father and said, "Well, you know he comes from a long line of champions."

This collection of stories is dedicated to those adventurous and courageous "champions" of the Buchmann, Hammer, Grombach and Neutzling families who left their European homes in pursuit of a dream and a brighter future in the United States of America. Every one of them is responsible for ensuring that Andy and the rest of this wonderful family "come from a long line of champions."

Preface and Acknowledgments

When I was a child I believed all families were exactly like mine. Wisdom has come with maturity and now I know that is not the case. I owe my view of the world to my parents, Emile and Leota Buchmann, who brought the four of us up in a home filled with love and laughter. For that I thank them.

This is the story of four European families, **Buchmann** from Rosenwiller, bas Rhin, France, **Hammer** from Leimersheim and Neupfotz in Bavaria, **Grombach** from Mannheim, Germany, and **Neutzling** from Sponheim, Germany. In the years between 1847 and 1885, these families and/or individuals emigrated to the United States, eventually settling in Belleville Illinois and nearby St. Louis Missouri. Our maternal ancestors were the first, Neutzling from Sponheim in 1847 to Pomeroy Ohio and Phillip Grombach to Belleville in 1849. In 1853 our paternal ancestors followed. Michael Hammer sailed from LeHavre France to New York with his mother, Margaretha, and four siblings. The Hammers originally settled in Ft. Thomas Kentucky, then moved to Cincinnati and finally to St. Louis. Henry X Buchmann was the last to arrive in America. He emigrated in 1885, almost thirty years later than the Neutzling family. He went first to Belleville and then to St. Louis.

I am especially grateful to the three who wrote down their own stories. Henry X Buchmann, my grandfather, wrote his "My Memoirs" in 1925 and provided invaluable clues for subsequent Buchmann family research. My aunt, Marie Buchmann, left letters and notes describing her life with Henry X and Drusilla. And my dear sweet mother, Leota Grombach Buchmann, penned remembrances of her early life as a gift for her adored eleven grandchildren.

I am forever indebted to my cousin, Herbert Alois Buchmann, who tracked the Hammer family to Leimersheim and Neupfotz. Herb also gets the credit for much of the genealogical research on the Buchmann and Hammer families.

I am also beholden to my close family. My siblings, Emmy, Jeane and Carl wrote their memories of "growing up Buchmann" and my children, Kim, Rob, Andy and Phil, shared their childhood memories and perceptions. My nephew, David Williams, sent me a copy of a taped interview with his grandmother Leota in which she relates her experiences during the Great Depression of the 1930s. My niece, Jill Williams DeMichele, also contributed stories about "Grandma B."

This project could not have been completed without the enthusiastic assistance of the 'Eighth Generation,' Kim, Rob, Phil, Andy, Caron, Barbara and Michelle who all volunteered their considerable talents in editing, photo editing, layout, design and technical advice.

Many of these stories were written in a "writing down the stories" class taught by my dear friend, Professor Jacqueline Jackson of the University of Illinois at Springfield (formerly Sangamon State University, 1970-1994). She believed in me and was endlessly fascinated by the stories of Henry X and Emile and the four little dancing Buchmanns.

You made it happen, Jackie. Thank you.

And once again, may I remind you:

"I don't know whether it actually happened that way or not, but you can see for yourself that the story is true"

Lakota Tribal Elders

The stories are as I remember them;
however;

"I don't know whether it actually happened that way or not, but you can
see for yourself that the story is true"

Lakota Tribal Elders

For *my parents and my children and my grandchildren*

The dance goes on

Contents

Phillipe BUCHMANN
b. 1743, Rosenwiller
d. 23 May 1821, Rosenwiller
& Anne Marie BECKERT
bp. Rosenwiller
mp. Rosenwiller

Phillippe BUCHMANN
b. 1788, Rosenwiller
d. 23 Mar 1858, Rosenwiller
& Julienne HUCK
b. 1787, Rosenwiller
m. 9 May 1805, Rosenwiller

Xavier BUCHMANN
b. 16 Dec 1812, Rosenwiller
d. 21 Jan 1858
& Brigitte RUDOLFF
b. 24 Jan 1812, Rosenwiller
d. 11 Sep 1835, Rosenwiller
Unmarried.

Louis BUCHMANN
b. 23 Aug 1834, Rosenwiller, Bas du Rhin, Alsace-Lorraine, France
& Marie Anne RICHERT
b. 16 Nov 1834, Rosenwiller, Bas du Rhin, Alsace-Lorraine, France
m. 12 May 1861, Rosenwiller, Bas Rhin, France

Henry Xavier Thomas Louis BUCHMANN
b. 18 Dec 1859, Rosenwiller, Bas du Rhin, Alsace-Lorraine, France
d. 19 Feb 1948, St. Louis, MO
& Drusilla Maria HAMMER
b. 26 Apr 1870, Cincinnati, OH
d. 8 Dec 1958, St. Louis, MO
m. 29 Oct 1889, St. Boniface, St.Louis, Missouri

Edouard Xavier BUCHMANN
b. 17 Oct 1861, Rosenwiller
d. 1919, Amarillo, Potter County, TX, USA
& Mary Louise DOEMKER
b. 7 Feb 1872
d. 4 Jun 1946, La Mesa, San Diego County, CA

Marie Brigitte BUCHMANN
b. 9 Sep 1863, Rosenwiller

Elisabeth BUCHMANN
b. 12 Nov 1864, Rosenwiller

Charles BUCHMANN
b. 2 Nov 1866, Rosenwiller
d. 1869, Rosenwiller

Marie Louise BUCHMANN
b. 20 Oct 1868, Rosenwiller

Charles BUCHMANN
b. 10 Aug 1869, Rosenwiller

Marie Madeleine BUCHMANN
b. 30 Jul 1871, Rosenwiller
d. 30 Jul 1947, Paris France
& VOILLE

Unknown BUCHMANN

Unknown BUCHMANN

Xavier BUCHMANN
b. 16 Dec 1812, Rosenwiller
d. 21 Jan 1858
& Julienne DEMARCK
m. 22 Jan 1840, Rosenwiller

Sophie BUCHMANN

Caroline BUCHMANN
b. 1 Apr 1821, Rosenwiller

Part One

Henry X and Drusilla

Drusilla in 1905

Henry X and Drusilla

The Stories:

It all starts with Henry X

"My Memoirs" written by Henry X in 1925

Memories from Aunt Marie

Paroisse de Rosenwiller

Uncle Floss

It all starts with Henry X

I knew only one of my immigrant ancestors, Henry Xavier Louis Thomas Buchmann, or "Henry X" as he is affectionately known in this chronicle. I remember him as a quiet, proud man with a miraculous grey bushy moustache. Sometimes he and my dad would go to the basement where I suspect they would share a bottle of Grandpa's homemade wine. Cousin Herb remembers that Grandpa had a favorite vendor at the old Soulard Market who would save the ripest Concord grapes for him. Herb also remembers seeing wine casks in the basement that "were taller than Henry X." Henry X and Drusilla celebrated their fiftieth wedding anniversary in October of 1939 at the Bevo Mill in St. Louis. The toast was made with Grandpa's vintage wine. I was only twelve years old at the time but I still remember the tart sting of my first sip of Buchmann wine. Grandpa always told us he bottled the wine in France and brought it with him when he emigrated over fifty years before. It is a romantic, wonderful story but it may not be exactly true. We always wondered how and where he had stored the wine bottles for over fifty years.

In 1925 Henry X wrote 'My Memoirs' probably at the request of his daughter, Marie. He included his parents' lineage and some details of his early family life in France. From that account we learned the family was from the tiny Alsatian village of Rosenwiller canton Rosheim. In 1995, I wrote to the Recorder of the Paroisse de Rosenwiller seeking information about the Buchmann family and Henry X. In what I now realize was an amazing stroke of good fortune, my inquiry was passed along to Monsieur Alfred Engel, Le-Maire - Adjoint (Assistant Mayor) of Rosenwiller. Monsieur Engel responded with a detailed "tableau genealogique" of the Buchmann family with several entries made using a __RED__ typewriter ribbon! Translating the chart and documents into English revealed that Henry X was a full two years older than he knew! Henry X and his father before him were born before the marriage of their parents. Each was "legitime par le marriage"; (made legitimate by the subsequent marriage of their natural parents).

From Monsieur Engel's chart we learned that Henry X was born on December 18, 1859 (not 1861 as appears on all other documents). He was christened "Xavier Thomas Richert," taking his mother's name, as was the custom. Xavier was the natural son of Louis Buchmann, a twenty-five year old farmer from Rosenwiller. Louis Buchmann officially acknowledged paternity. His mother was Marie Anne Richert, also twenty-five years old and a resident of Rosenwiller. There is a note in the margin of the record of his birth that states: "This infant was made legitimate by means of the marriage of his father and mother on May 12, 1861, under the name of Xavier Thomas Buchmann." A brother, Edouard Buchmann, was born on October 17, 1861. Xavier Thomas (Henry X) was the oldest of ten children. Little is known of his siblings except Madeleine who kept in touch with Henry X and his family. Madeleine married a Monsieur Voille and lived in Neully on the Seine River in France.

His younger brother, Edouard, emigrated some years later to the United States and settled in St. Louis, but there was, as far as we know, no contact between the brothers. We have a copy of a marvelous letter written in 1948 in which Madeleine tells her forty-three year old niece, Marie:

> *Your parents, my dear Marie, are certainly pleased to have you with them; remember though, it is a bit late for you to be overly selective in choosing a well-to-do man. That would be much easier when one is 21 or 22 years old. At that age a girl has good potential. When that time is over it becomes more difficult. But one never knows--you certainly can still hope that your Prince Charming will yet come along who will make you happy. As it is, you are your parents' chief source of help.*

We know that Henry X was conscripted into the German Army and was honorably discharged in September of 1883. In April of 1885 he left Antwerp, bound for New York on the Red Star Line ship "Waesland." Henry X was twenty-five years old. Sailing with him were two others from Rosenwiller, Monic [sic] Buchmann, age seventeen, and Remique Uhl, age twenty-two. Both of these passengers were relatives of Xavier but we know nothing further of them.

Xavier tells us he went to Belleville Illinois:

> *to my granduncle which was over 90 years old. I was in Belleville one week my uncle told me I should go to St. Louis which I did on Pentecost Monday with a cousin of my mother's side, Charles Richert.*

We do not know when Xavier Thomas changed his name to Henry Xavier. Why he chose to be known as "Henry Xavier" rather than using his middle name of Thomas is still a mystery today. Our dear grandfather, Henry X, was a man known by many names, Xavier Thomas Richert, Xavier Thomas Buchmann, and finally, Henry Xavier Thomas Louis Buchmann. We are grateful for the life he led and for the records he kept.

COPIE INTEGRALE DE L'ACTE DE NAISSANCE DE RICHERT Xavier Thomas, légitimé
par le père naturel BUCHMANN Louis lors de son
mariage avec RICHERT Marie Anne le 12 mai 1861.

ACTE N°3   ANNEE 1859

RICHERT Xavier Thomas né le 18 décembre 1859 à une heure du matin, fils
naturel de BUCHMANN louis reconnaissant la paternité, âgé de 25 ans, cultivateur,
né à ROSENWILLER, domicilié à ROSENWILLER,
et de RICHERT Marie Anne, âgée de 25 ans, sans profession, domiciliée à
ROSENWILLER.

Mention en marge

Cet enfant a été légitimé par le mariage de son père et mère en date
du 12 mai 1861 , sous le nom de BUCHMANN Xavier Thomas.

REMARQUE.

La date de naissance indiquée dans votre "MEMOIRE" (29 octobre 1861) est
erronée. Le nommé BUCHMANN Xavier Thomas est bien né le 18 décembre 1859, dont
témoigne l'acte ci-dessus.
Aucune naissance n'a été enregistrée à la date du 29 octobre 1861.
Par contre, un frère de Xavier Thomas est né à ROSENWILLER le 17 octobre 1861
sous le nom de BUCHMANN Edouard. De là vient peut-être la confusion?
En ce qui concerne les prénoms présumés de Henry Xavier Thomas Louis, l'acte
de naissance ne comporte que les seuls prénoms Xavier Thomas. Les deux autres lui
ont été attribués sans fondement légal.

Fait à ROSENWILLER, le 08 juin 1995

Le Maire-Adjoint,

Alfred ENGEL

'Liberal' translation of documents from Paroisse de Rosenwiller pertaining to the birth & legitimacy of Henry X

Copy of entire birth record of Xavier Thomas Richert: made legitimate by the marriage of his natural father, Louis Buchmann with Marie Anne Richert, 12 May 1861.

DEED #3, 1859

Xavier Thomas Richert born 18 December 1859 at one hour in the morning, natural son of Louis Buchmann (who) acknowledged the paternity, age 25 farmer of Rosenwiller with residence in Rosenwiller, and Marie Anne Richert, age 25, without profession, residence at Rosenwiller.

(*note in margin*)

This infant was made legitimate by means of the marriage of his father and mother on 12 May 1861 under the name of Xavier Thomas Buchmann.

Remarks:

The birthdate indicated on your "My Memoirs" is wrong. The name Xavier Thomas Buchmann was truly born on 18 December 1859 and this is attested to by the census. No birth is on register for the date 18 December 1861.

On the other hand, a brother of Xavier Thomas was born in Rosenwiller on 17 October 1861 under the name of Edouard Buchmann. Perhaps the confusion?

In the concern supposed first name of Henry Xavier Thomas Louis, the birth certificate only includes the single names Xavier Thomas. The two others were attributed without legal foundation.

Done in Rosenwiller, June 8, 1995 by Alfred Engel, The Assistant Mayor

My Memoirs

I, HENRY XAVIER THOMAS LOUIS BUCHMANN, was born in 1861 in Rosenwiller, canton Rosheim (14 miles SW of Strasbourg, foot of Vosges Mts. near NE tip of France, 1831) Alsace, France at that time. My parents were Louis Buchmann, son of Xavier Buchmann. My mother was Marie Richert, daughter of Francois Joseph Richert and Scholastique (nee Steyer) Richert, all of Rosenwiller canton Rosheim. I went to school at Rosenwiller, made my holy communion in 1873; after school days I helped my parents wherever I could at the house as well as on the land which we owned.

In December 1876, my father put me to a little town about 7 miles from our home to learn the cabinet maker trade by Albert Keckmann, an expert in that line; after two years apprenticeship I was learned out and made my examination with honors to my master, as well as to my parents. My time was expired on the third day of December 1878. I worked for my learning master up to May 1879. I then left his place as my parents needed me for a few weeks at their home. After I was not needed anymore at home I went to work for a Master Charles Grimmat, Barr (18 miles SW of Strassburg) Alsace and worked for him up to August 1880. From there I went to Muehlhausen, Alsace near Swiss border, not far from Basel and Belforth France. I worked there for Master Charles Grollmund. This Master Grollmund was by the way the nephew of our then priest of the parish at home in Rosenwiller.

In 1881 I had to leave this Master Grollmund to prepare for the Army. I was an unwilling soldier, but I was a good soldier. My passbook will show my good behavior in the Army as a

Sergeant. I for once took my mother's teachings which she used to tell us; whenever we did not like to do some certain work, she said you better like to do it because you will have to do it anyway, so it is of no use grumbling. So it was with me in the Army there was no other way so you better do it with love. Therefore I can show my credit for same.

After two years service in the Army I was permitted to go home and help my parents at their home as I was the oldest of ten children, one died when four years old. That year I had to be ready at any time for a call in case I was needed during that year. After the year was expired, I asked for permission to go to America, that was in 1884 in April. I got the permission but with the understanding that I work for the Fatherland (German Army) while in America in case of war.

> *(note by Marie Buchmann, his daughter, "however to circumvent this obligation he applied for his citizenship papers at his first convenience when once in the U.S.")*

I landed in New York the day before Ascension Day (1884) so ten days before Pentecost. I went to Belleville Illinois to my granduncle which was over ninety years old. I was in Belleville one week my uncle told me I should go to St. Louis which I did on Pentecost Monday with a cousin on my mother's side, Charles Richert.

I could not get any work as cabinet maker in St. Louis and being I was the company barber in the Army, so I tried that trade and found a job at Fourth and Spruce Street for a weekly wage of one whole dollar. After three weeks there I left and went to work for a Charles Feb, 2718 Chouteau Ave. There I had a little more, got $3.50, board and wash a week and room. In October 1884 I became the boss of the barbershop at 1012 Geyer Avenue. That was in the fair week or the Veiled Prophet week in 1890. I opened another shop at 830 Geyer, had two shops for a few years and had another, 1820 South Broadway for about eight months. Had three shops at one time, then sold them one by one and kept the one at 830 Geyer Avenue. In 1896 was the cyclone on 27th day of May which destroyed the house the greatest part of it. In 1900 I bought and moved my shop and household furniture into the house east namely 824 Geyer Avenue and was there in business up to July 1924 when we moved to 2303 South 18th Street, which we already had bought two years before (August 1922).

On the 29th day of October 1889, I was married to Drusilla Hammer, daughter of Michael Hammer, cigar manufacturer at 7704 South Broadway, St. Louis MO. Four children were born to us, three boys and one girl; Arthur Michael, Florence Andreas and Emile Henry, the girl, Marie Elizabeth.

In 1897 I became a member of St. Ludwigs Branch, No 46, Western Catholic Union for $1000, Insurance, assessment $1.00 per month. In 1904 they raised the assessment to $1.50 p.m. which was 7 cents short of my proper rate and so everybody else paid short. Therefore in 1916 my assessment was to be $4.56 per $1000 Ins per month. I then transferred $500 in the new rate at $2.28 per month and kept $500 in the old rate at 75 cents per month total $1000. On the first day in February 1925 the rate on the last $500 was put up to $3.30 per month. Then I was doing some little figuring; $2.28 and $3.30 and 55 cents branch dues would bring up my monthly contributions to the WCU to $6.13, which I thought was too much after I already had paid in more than 28 years. So I dropped $500 and kept on $500, this is the reason.

The WCU today are in good condition, but the beginners did not know what rate to put on the members for their insurance according to their respective age. Therefore, those which died early played a lottery, their beneficiaries got money for nothing, or in other words which they were not entitled to, because their rate was insufficient. For instance, if I had paid $1.57 per month I would have paid my proper rate according to my age then and would pay that all my life, but now you see above what happened.

In June 1895 the Boss Barbers' Protective and Benevolent Association was organized with a membership of over 260. I was nominated, elected its Treasurer, which office I held up to December 1909, when I refused reelection as Treasurer on account of some reasons of my own. In 1911 I was elected as

Financial and Recording Secretary and held that office up to December 1919 when we dissolved the Association on account of loss of members by selling their business or by death. In the 24 years of the Boss Barbers' Protective and Benevolent Associations' existence I held office for 23 years, a good record is it not? In December 1917 I was elected Treasurer of the St. Ludwig's Branch #46 Western Catholic Union and up to date I am still their Treasurer. In 1916 we had a membership of over five hundred and fifty.

This writing was written by me at 2303 South 18th Street on the fourth day of February A.D. 1925 at St. Louis Missouri. (signed) Hy. X.T.L. Buchmann. (Henry Xavier Thomas Louis Buchmann) in my 65th year.

NOTE: Went to rest February 19, 1948 at 6:45 a.m. His wife, Drusilla, son Arthur and daughter Marie were at his bedside. He was fortified with the Holy Sacraments of the Holy Mother Church, SS Peter and Paul Church, Reverend Ellebracht administering.

Translation of information from genealogy chart sent by Monsieur Engel (his original notes are in <u>red ink</u>):

BUCHMANN, Xavier Thomas (Henry X)

> Natural birth 18 December 1859 at Rosenwiller
>
> Made legitimate 12 May 1861 through marriage of parents.
>
> Registered on birth certificate under the name of RICHERT. Took the name of Buchmann at the legitimation.

BUCHMANN, Louis (natural father)

> Born 23 August 1834
>
> In the deed of marriage, the date of birth mentioned is 19 April 1834
>
> Natural child of Brigitte Rudolff and Xavier Buchmann. made legitimate by means of Xavier Buchmann and Juliane de Marck marriage.

BUCHMANN, Xavier (grandfather)

> Born 16 December 1812
>
> Natural father of Louis Rudolff who was made legitimate then by the marriage of Xavier and Juliane de Marck on 22 January 1840. Louis Rudolff took the name of Louis Buchmann.

Memories from Aunt Marie

Edited by her niece, Rose Marie

Notes on the Text

Marie Elizabeth Buchmann, "Aunt Marie" to her three nieces and three nephews, was born on a snowy January 25, 1905. She died of Lou Gehrig's disease on March 22, 1989. She never married and was devoted to her parents, taking care of them until their deaths in 1948 and 1958. "Memories from Aunt Marie" was compiled and transcribed by her nephew, Herbert Alois Buchmann, from writing fragments he found on old envelopes and scrap paper among her effects after her death in 1989. He managed to compile her written memories, piecing various bits together to form this story, "Memories from Aunt Marie." It appears that many of the notes were written shortly before her death. She refers to the wedding of her great nephew Craig Buchmann in February of 1989 and speaks also of the death of friends in 1988. In the terminal stage of her disease, Marie knew that her remaining time on this earth was short and apparently attempted to capture some family moments for future generations.

Marie's original punctuation, capitalization, grammar and spelling have been preserved except where minor editing was deemed necessary to provide clarity for the reader. Still, some fragments beg for continuity; some of Marie's notes are repetitive. In some cases the original paragraphs have been combined or condensed. The footnotes were added by the editor in an attempt to clarify and expand Buchmann family lore.

Marie has written a detailed account of life with her aging parents, Henry X and Drusilla, of her education and career as a teacher at the Missouri School for the Blind and, after her parents' deaths, of her final years filled with travel and friends. Many of the earlier stories were probably told to her "in bits and pieces" over the course of her parents' lifetimes.

Henry X Buchmann was born in Rosheim, Alsace in 1861[1] and came to the USA after serving in Germany. He did not enjoy military life and promised himself to go to America immediately after discharge saying he did not like being told "how to cut his hair." He was a cabinetmaker by trade.

About two weeks was spent with relatives in Belleville, Illinois. Uncle Ignace had a large family and died at age of ninety-six and lived near the cathedral in Belleville Illinois. 'Belleville Henry' was the son of Ignace and his son was Walter Buchmann and Anheuser Busch employs his son. Uncle Henry's wife was Aunt Lena. As a child I remember visiting them and Uncle Henry would greet us at the door with, "Did you bring your dinner?" Aunt Lena was a very good cook. We looked forward for a week or more for the trip to Belleville, first needed to get to Mass, then street car to downtown St.Louis, then transfer to Belleville street car. We usually arrived at their home between eleven and eleven-thirty.

Dad stayed in Belleville after coming to America about two weeks. He became a barber after coming to St. Louis. His first shop was at 912 Geyer. Later moved to 9th and Geyer-corner house. I was born at 824 Geyer.

Mr. Stute was a customer and as it goes Dad asked if he knew of a good girl. "Yes, she lived in Carondelet 7600 South

---

[1] Marie is mistaken. Henry X reports in his "MEMOIRS" that his father was Louis Buchmann, son of Xavier Buchmann. The birth date, according to the parish records in Rosenwiller, bas Rhin France, was December 18, 1859. Louis Buchmann and Henry X's mother, Marie Richert, married on May 12, 1861, before the October 17, 1861, birth of their second son, Edouard. Most probably, Henry X was told he was born in December of 1861 and for him that was the truth.

Broadway." Story is Dad courted her about once a week traveling by horse-drawn streetcars-no heat and motorman stood on straw in the winter. He used to tell the story—about 4500 South Broadway is a little hill and sometimes horses could not make the hill so men folks would need to push the streetcars up the hill.

Drusilla Marie Hammer[3] married Henry Xavier Buchmann on October 29, 1889 in St. Boniface Catholic Church in St. Louis, Missouri. Drusilla's parents were Michael Hammer[4], proprietor of a Carondolet cigar store, and Rosina Hammer. [5] Michael and Rosina Hammer had three daughters. Drusilla was born in Cincinnati, Ohio on Feast Day of "Our Lady of Good Counsel" on April 26,1870. Aunt Maggie (Margaret) Hammer Feldmeier was born in Lawrenceburg Tennessee February thirteenth 1872 and was two years old when the family moved to St. Louis. Aunt Sis (Josephine) Hammer Hertling was born in Kentucky January 2, 1877. Rosina, their mother, died [6]when Drusilla was twelve, Aunt Maggie was eleven and Aunt Sis was five. Tante Eva, Michael Hammer's sister, took care of his three daughters, Drusilla, Aunt Maggie and Aunt Sis after her husband, Joseph Severin died. He was wounded in the Spanish American War. He wore a silver plate in his head as a result of being wounded. Henry X and Drusilla had three boys,

---

[3] The "good girl" recommended by Mr. Stute.

[4] Michael Hammer was born September 24, 1835, in Leimersheim Rheinland-Pfalz, Bavaria and emigrated to U.S.A. on the ship, *Carack* on July 5, 1853, at the age of eighteen with his mother, Eva Margaretha Malthaner and four siblings. Michael received his naturalization papers in October 1858. He died January 12 1912, in St. Louis.

[5] Rosina Hammer was born March 17, 1849, in Newport Kentucky; died January 27, 1883, in St. Louis of "consumption" (tuberculosis). Drusilla, the oldest of the three daughters was twelve when her mother died. Michael Hammer's sister, "Tante Eva" (Mary Eva Hammer Severin), took care of the three motherless girls, Drusilla, Margaret and Josephine.

[6] Rosina died in 1883

Arthur Michael Joseph [7], Florence Andreas Joseph [8] and Emile Henry Joseph [9] [10]and one daughter, Marie Elizabeth born January 25 1905 at 5 a.m. and weighed nine pounds. About midnight mother said, "I believe you better get the midwife Mrs. Boosen." Dad replied, "Can't you wait until the morning?" It was very cold 10 below and he needed to walk from 824 Geyer to 11th and Lami, a good mile. There were no phones, cabs or streetcars or buses. I arrived at 5 a.m.

Mom and Dad both liked to have a girl. Midwife asked Mom whether they should fool Dad. Tell him, "Buchmanns can only have boys." Mom went along with that. For three days Dad believed he had another boy and was grumpy-no cigars. Customers told him to watch when I was bathed. Then he whistled and stood me on a chair holding onto the back of the chair. Mother said, "If she gets crooked legs, it is your fault." Cigars were given out then and he was very happy "A Girl."

When I was about two years old I developed diphtheria. Dad asked Mr. Jobst to look at his sick girl. My fever was very high and he advised wrapping me in bacon. Dr. Ehrlich had been

---

[7] Arthur Michael Joseph Buchmann born 28 December 1892 in St. Louis MO.; died 15 March 1967 in Washington, MO.

[8] Florence Andreas Joseph Buchmann born 12 June 1895 in St. Louis MO; died 28 July 1979 in Danville IL.

[9] Emile Henry Joseph Buchmann born 21 August 1899 in St. Louis MO; died 30 July 1960 in San Francisco CA.

[10] All three Buchmann sons apparently carried the baptismal name, Joseph. This is the only instance in the family records where the name Joseph appears.

called and when he returned the fever was gone and the bacon was like fried. Doc was surprised. Syrium [sic] was brand new then and Doc gave it to me. They always said I had but three hours to live. Aunt Maggie's Rose died of diphtheria. She was a little older than I was.

I went to St. Peter and St. Paul School, 8th and Allen, starting at age six in first grade. There were no kindergartens in those days. From first grade I went to third grade, skipping second grade. School was one block down the alley. Rosati-Kain High School at Lindell and Newstead, across from the New Cathedral, was my place of learning for four years. Classes were held in a three-story house. St. Joseph and Notre Dame nuns taught us. Miss Bernard was Superior of the St. Joseph nuns. She was a tall heavyset person whose wimple did not hang down as the other nuns but lay flat on her breast. Almost served as a tray. She was most brilliant, taught English. To recall a poem she would look toward windows and begin reciting. Marvelous.

Graduation from Elementary School was in June 1919. At age nine I began taking piano lessons from Sister Johanna of Notre Dame Sisters and later from Sister Justina. Most of my music education was taken under her tutelage. I was a member of her orchestra which Reverend Stevens sponsored playing the violin. Concerts were given and a big event was playing at the eight o'clock morning Mass on Christmas Day.

Sister Theodosia was Superior of Notre Dame nuns. Later she became Provencial [sic] of her Order. Years and years later when I heard she was ill and at Alexian Brothers' Hospital I visited her. Guess what she remembered my name only calling me "Mary" which is my baptismal name. Mary I changed to the French version "Marie" after High School.

During my Junior year I worked at Woolworth 5 and 10 cent store which was on Broadway in Soulard district and was paid $1.00 for an eight-hour day. Later I received a ten-cent raise. That was big money. The money I made I gave to my Dad but the ten-cent raise Mom begged Dad to give that to me for spending money. A big deal. Proud of getting ten cents for my very own. Since Rosati-Kain was miles from 8th and Geyer, two streetcars were my means of transportation, Olive, Maryland, passed Famous-Barr department store. One day I had taste for chocolate kisses and my spending money burned a hole in my pocket so I bought a pound of them and ate almost the entire pound. Years after that it was difficult for me to even look at kisses (chocolate) without feeling nauseated. During my Grade School and High School years I studied the piano and violin so much so that Sister Justina encouraged me to go to St. Louis Institute of Music to further my music education and become a music teacher. I was given a one-year scholarship to St. Louis Institute of Music in Clayton, Missouri. I continued studying with Sister Justine for about five years after High School working at Speck's restaurant from eleven to three a.m. to pay for my expenses and to give me time to practice two to three hours every day. Later I was in Busy Bee's Tea Room.

After attending St. Louis Institute of Music for a year, I transferred to St. Louis University. There I lost a half year of credit. Determined to finish in four years, I went to summer school and took as many as twenty and twenty-two hours. It was hard work especially at that time as I was playing the piano two afternoons and Saturday mornings at the Public High School for their playground dance classes.

Summer vacations were spent on Public School Playgrounds under direction of Mr. Abeken, a lawyer. Mr. Abeken was very firm, but just. If one did something good, everyone knew about it and the same if one did something wrong, everyone knew about that also. Some playgrounds

Dorothy and I had were in North St. Louis—colored schools. Soon Mr. Abeken feared for us at night so we later had all white schools mostly in south St. Louis. We enjoyed these immensely.

Mr. Abeken was in charge of the big pageants out at the Public School Stadium on Kingshighway near Natural Bridge. Under his guidance, Corine Hackauer, choreographer, and Leona Jansen Garfrerich, music, staged huge pageants of two to three thousand children performing in plays, Robin Hood and Hansel and Gretel, Aladdin and Magic Lamp, etc. The children danced in the Public School Stadium in north St. Louis, Kingshighway and Natural Bridge Road. My part at the Stadium was to assist Miss Leona Jansen, later Mrs. Garfrerich, at the piano. When we practiced at the stadium we who were pianists and dance instructors often times stayed at the stadium until the moon came up. We dare not leave until Mr. Abeken gave us permission to leave. He had us so hoodwinked, but he was good to us.

The St. Louis Symphony accompanied us. It was beautiful. Some members of the Symphony orchestra accompanied the dancers at Leona's direction. I helped Leona by turning pages and giving correct music. It was fun. Dorothy Schultz and I worked many years together. She as dance instructor and I as her pianist. The money I earned during the summer and two afternoons and Saturday mornings as an accompanist helped toward my expenses, carfare, tuition, clothes and incidentals at St. Louis University.

Yes, I graduated from St. Louis University in four years, June 1932 with a cum laude citation. That summer I toured Europe, leaving July 1932 and returned in September of 1932.

I did some private music tutoring. Teaching positions were very scarce at that time. Harris Teacher's College required graduation from their institution for a position in their schools. St. Louis University Dean of Education always told us we would be admitted to teach in the public schools but that was not the case unless we took a year of classes at Harris. I did not want to do that so I was a clerk for a while in Edison Brother's Shoe Company office when I was encouraged to take a temporary kindergarten class at St. Roche School on Waterman. Teacher had surgery. The job lasted nine years; I taught a year in the county.

Missouri School for the Blind had an opening. Board of Education referred me and the superintendent, Dr. Thompson, called me and offered the kindergarten teaching position at his Missouri School for the Blind. The St. Louis Board of Education gave him my name since I placed my transcript on file there. Dr. Thompson asked me to come and teach there immediately but I refused since the Priests and Nuns were good to me and I did not want to leave them in a lurch. I would come if someone would take my place at St. Roche.

On Ascension Thursday that year I visited MSB kindergarten. The sub was white and she placed both her hands on the face of Black Calvin Smith and I got Goosebumps. How could I teach them? Nothing more was said and Dr. Thompson did not send me an application form so that was that. I thought nothing more of it. During that summer going to my playground I met Dr. Thompson on the bus and he sat beside me. I asked him if he had a kindergarten teacher. Reply was "I am holding it for you." That was a surprise. I debated about taking the position. I knew nothing about blind peoples [sic]. He assured me I would make it. First two or three days all you see would be eyes, later the whole child. That became true. So much so that later I even kissed the black children as well as the white on Friday afternoons.

At end of first month I was ready to leave. It was so different from what I was used to at St. Roche's. Here I could not say "SEE" and hold up an object but needed to go to each and every child for them to touch it. Miss Melba Sievert who recently graduated from Washington University was in her first year of teaching. She relied on me and I took her music. It was she who encouraged me to stay throughout the year. Guess what? She left at end of year. Too much homework; in an office at five o'clock you put cover over the typewriter and go home. That's it. Not when teaching. Guess what? I stayed thirty years. The children, teachers and parents along with Al Eberhardt gave me a wonderful retirement banquet at Lemmon's restaurant on Gravois. Each child's voice was recorded on tape and each child's hand drawn on a long scroll of shelf paper. A scrapbook was given me containing cards and letters from parents and teachers. I prize it very very much. As gifts, I received a battery watch, three-piece set of traveling bags, the largest piece has wheels and they always said when I retire they would give me a car. They did —a Ford car radio. My car is a 1949 Plymouth. The highest number of children in my class was twenty-five. The smallest number was eight. I say three sighted children equal one blind child! Principal Mrs. Hubbard said that I had some of the worst children in the State of Missouri.

In my first year (started 9/45) the children were very excited one day when they came down to class after lunch saying, "Theresa lost her eye." I became as excited as they, "Lost her eye? How?" Theresa came to the classroom; she had two eyes. How could she lose one? Of course, it was a glass one. Another child's glass eye was a little small for the socket and if it came out in the classroom and she was at the desk, she would pound on the desk until she was given the eye. What a commotion.

I, Marie E. Buchmann, became the fourth kindergarten teacher at MSB, September 1945. Ms. Bell Bohrens was their first teacher, coming in 1906 and remaining until 1916. Mathie Bohrens followed her sister, Bell Behrens, and she continued teaching kindergarten until 1928 (12 years). Mrs. Reinbeck followed Mattie. She remained seventeen years from 1928 to 1945. I followed Mrs. Reinbeck serving MSB for thirty years, 1945 to 1975.

There were six pupils in my first class; Theresa Backer, now Mrs. Lauer who became a teacher at MSB and on the staff yet in 1988. Joe Cunningham died. Barbara Parker, June Wade, Royce Luvers and Arthur Stafford. Nine pupils were in my last class; Mark Buchanan, Tommy McHugh, Robert Massman, Wendy McGraw, Joan Meyers, Jimmy Sikes, David Tucker, Frank Young and Troy Bagley. In 1955 I had twenty-six children with the help of a teacher's aide. From there my classes reduced in number, twenty, then sixteen until only nine darling youngsters in my final year.

I introduced Braille at this early age by playing with Braille alphabet blocks which I deviced [sic]. I am proud to tell you that my idea was copied by other schools for the Blind. Child learned to stand the block with the groove on top. The colored tacks must face the child. Soon the child noticed some blocks have but one tack on the left, some have two on the top, some have two tacks on left and some have three on left, etc. The names were then given:

> *"A" hole/ or tack on the left*
> *"B" hole 1 & 2 on left*
> *"L" hole 1,2,3 on left*
> *"C" hole 1 & 4 on the top*
> *"P" hole 1,2,3 & 4*

Simple words were introduced first, of course, followed by learning to form their names, addresses and numbers. It was not until after usually Christmas vacation that Braille was attacked seriously. I enjoyed my thirty years at MSB so much so that my first two years of retirement were difficult but now I enjoy it.

We also had pageants at all the playgrounds we visited each week. These were in the evenings during August and the big one was at end of August at Stadium. Mother enjoyed them, sometimes Dad went and Pat Burnett's tenant's daughter joined us. I called her my little sister because I wanted a sister so bad. We are friends to this day. Pat is paralyzed on left side as a result of a stroke but thru determination and therapy she walks with a cane, but left arm is limp almost twenty years now (1989).

I was with the playgrounds from 1929 to 1956 until Mother needed me to be with her. Mother died December 8, 1958 on the Feast of Immaculate Conception, buried on Feast day of Our Lady of Gadualope [sic] December 12th.

In October, before their wedding anniversary (10/29), Dad at age of 84 years was operated by Dr. Lund at Lutheran Hospital for prostate trouble. Doc Tremain, Sr., did best he could to elevate [sic] and correct the problem but failed so suggested surgery. Doc was very slow to suggest "cutting of any kind unless absolutely necessary." He was a wonderful doctor. He treated Margaret Hertling from infancy to his death without charge. Dad spent five weeks in the hospital. I said he should remain there until he could help himself-- less strain on Mother.

Dad was a good patient. He would fall a lot and faint. One time he said of me, "You would raise anyone from the dead." Yes, I screamed in his ears and shook him to get him to come to which he did. I naturally was scared. Henry X died February nineteenth 1948 at age 87 years and two months. He was laid out at Kutis on Gravois in town. Mr. Kutis Sr. said, "He was King even in death" for he had the entire establishment for himself. When we returned from cemetery every available space was taken in the funeral home.

New Year's Eve I worked with Art's Marie at Moolah Temple for their New Year's Eve party. It was fun. Before returning home we went to College Church's First Mass at four a.m. New Year's morning while going to Mass at St. Agnes Church, Salena & Sidney, Mom slipped on small piece of ice and broke her wrist. Mom did not awaken me until late morning. It was early afternoon before Dr. came to the hospital. Because Mom ate and drank a little at my request he postponed the operation to following day. Mom went for therapy three times a week and Dad two times to Dr. Lund. For five days a week (I do not remember length of time) yours truly sat in Drs. offices making a purse (white from hookers on a frame).

November tenth 1949 Mom and I moved to 4977 Tholozon with Arthur and Marie living upstairs. Mom did most of the packing since I was working at MSB. The movers were very happy early in the morning but as days went on, their whistling stopped for many small boxes were used for packing. Mom was most happy in her new home. Art's Marie was home and she had company. Soon Art's Marie decided to be a baker at the Federal Reserve Bank cafeteria in St. Louis. Everything was new—neighbors too—(Back) On 18th Street daily tenants would visit with Mom until she had said, "I'll need to lock my door so I can get my work finished."

Trixy became a member of our family, a brown and black terrier to keep Mom company. He did a good job also in protecting her. He died in the fall of '56 leaving a big void. Another dog was found in Manchester dog pond [sic]. Dr. Tremain suggestion. It was not like Trix but Mom was ready to settle for it when the attendant mentioned "It was spatted."[11] Then Mom refused to take it. Thinking that was wrong.

From our house
To your house

Season's Greetings

Grand-Mother
and
Aunt Marie

Drusilla Buchmann

---

11 *She probably means "spayed"*

Mrs. Hubbard, Principal at MSB and Dr. Robert Thompson, superintendent, both wanted me to go to the AAIB convention in Ohio. I did make arrangements with Art and Marie to care for Mom who was becoming a little hard to handle at times. Senility. The school bus was taken so we stayed overnight at Blind schools in Indianapolis, Maryland, Louisville. There we went thru the Publishing House for Blind. Interesting. We also went to Annapolis and were in time for their Sunday services. Mr. Charpiot—art teacher at MSB—was fascinated with a Cadet holding hands with his little daughter while walking down the aisle. Dan said, "I wish I had a little girl." He never did have a child.

Mom became more and more difficult to handle. I was fortunate to have someone to stay with Mom during the day. At night, I slept with one eye opened. I did that for Dad also. Thanksgiving Day of '58 was last day Mom was up and around. She and I spent that day with Art & Marie and enjoyed it immensely but the following day she remained in bed and from then on grew worse. She died 12/8/58 at 7:30 p.m., Feast of Immaculate Conception. Laid out Kutis Funeral Home on Gravois in the City and buried 12/12/58 Feast of Guadalupe and born on Feast of Lady of Good Counsel.

The following summer I took two courses at Harris Teacher's College—one Art course, Mr. Diehl, ceramics. I took clay home to make a project and was told to mold it on a plate— easier—I did. For me, it did not work so I made a round dish and thought it was great. Following morning showed it to Mr. Diehl before class and he said, "It looks like a dog dish." My feelings were hurt. I worked so hard. Mr. Diehl made a three corner dish out of it. Yes, I still have it and prize it.

In order to satisfy state's requirements I took courses at Harris after school and summer vacation. Then in 1964 went to Florida Convention by express bus while most teachers either flew or by car. An eye course by correspondence was taken and studied while on bus. At lunch and meal stops I scouted the city and ate my lunch on bus. It was fun. After the convention I toured Key West. In one day I saw four State Capitols. Also saw

Jackson's 'Hermitage.' People in the South are more friendly than in North. Noticed it on the busses.

For several summers thereafter I vacationed alone by Greyhound bus and enjoyed it. In '64 convention was in Watertown Mass. At Perkins School for Blind. Flew to Quebec to see St. Ann Beauphe Shrine and St. Joseph's Shrine, Niagara Falls, etc. In 1965 Lucille Scalia joined me to go to Yellowstone National Park, Salt Lake City, Colorado mountains. Beautiful. In 1966 Madelein Tessmer Casper toured with me to Jasper, Ontario. Saw Columbia Glacier and rode an icemobile over huge deep cracks or veins. We had a ball. On to Banff, Lake Louise, Boise, Idaho then to Denver. That route was beautiful. Almost surpassed the Alps that I had seen on 1932 after I graduated from St. Louis University and received my A.B. in Education.

At that time we took Cunard Line to Ireland from New York and cruised for ten days on Atlantic. On that trip I visited ten countries including the Vatican, saw the Pope, saw Lourdes in France, went to Little Flowers Monastery and also saw Dad's sister in Paris. Saw Busch's castle on the Rhine. On the side of the mountains were vineyards. Saw windmills in Holland, the palace at Hague with beautiful Chinese art. I believe we visited every museum and cathedral possible while on tour. In 1975 I retired from MSB, then with Pat Burnett and group of teachers we went to Yugoslavia. Most interesting and quaint, especially Dubrovnik called "Pearl of the Adriatic." Marie Braun invited me to join 'Friendly Neighbors', a seniors group to which I did join and belong today. Thru this organization I took several very interesting tours with Henrietta Eisenhauer, tour director of Security Travel.

Mary Logan, blind teacher from MSB, joined me in the tour to Alaska for two weeks. It was 25th wedding anniversary of John and Henrietta Eisenhauer. We saw Alaska's University Totem Poles, museums, Mt. McKinley. Saw moose in Denali Park, the Alaskan pipeline, etc. Four days were on Rotterdam, a very nice ship. Next year took a cruise to the Caribbean. I had two more cruises after this one with Ray Smith, Tosca Wekking and last one with Ray, Pat Burnett and Ken Buchmann.

These were the big tours, many small tours to Radio City, GraceLand, Las Vegas, spring training Cardinals, Disney World, Golden Goose alongside "Queen Mary" in California. Mr. Hughes built this huge plane. It only flew a few feet off the ground. Can be seen today in the museum next to the huge ship, Queen Mary. We slept on the ship one night. Yes, I prefer the modern ships to the older ones. My last ship was "Homeric" to Bermuda, a beautiful place. In March, I plan to go to Hot Springs Arkansas with Pat Burnett as my roommate. Never been there. In 1975, I toured Yugoslavia with Pat Burnett, Esther Askmeyer, the escort and several teachers from Board of Education. Yes, Margaret Logan and I toured Alaska for two weeks. Four days were enjoyed on the Rotterdam. Following year we cruised the Caribbean on Song of Norway. Then in 1985, I cruised on Capile I to Caribbean. In '86, Ray Smith, Pat Burnett, Kenneth Buchmann, and I had a cruise to Mexico on the "Tropicale." We sailed down the Pacific to Puerto Vayarta [sic] Mazatlan and Cabo San Lucas. Four days in Las Vegas in March, four days at Trout Lodge in Missouri. In April of '86 went to Texas for ten day tour. In May of '88 cruised to Bermuda. Bermuda is beautiful with pastel colored buildings and white roofs so constructed that rainwater was caught. This water was their drinking water.

"Going My Way" moving picture

Mother and I wished to see but Dad did not. He preferred to stay home and read his paper. I did not want him to remain home alone for he was not well. He was very difficult to get to change his mind (The German in him). I needed to shed some tears and beg and beg to get him to say, "I'll go." Guess what? He enjoyed the film so much that he stayed to see it a second time. Dad was more willing to go to see a film after that yet always asked, "Is it as good as Going My Way?"

My Brothers and the Armed Forces

Arthur and Florence left for the army together, I believe in fall of 1918. Arthur in Medical Corps and Florence in Signal Corps. Family picture taken before. Both were preparing to go abroad when word came to halt and wait for further word. Three days later Armistice was declared and they both came home following January 1919. A Happy Day.

Emile did not go in the service, too young. His son, Carl, when of age and married, enlisted in the Marines and stayed in over twenty years. His son, Craig, enlisted in the Navy as a dentist after he graduated from Texas U. Dentist School. He married February eleventh 1989. I understand he can go abroad and take his bride with him. Much of Craig's tuition came from scholarships through swimming contests. Dr. Kenneth Buchmann served his country during Korean War as a recreation director. Kenneth received his D.V.M. degree from the University of Missouri through veteran's administration. Arthur, Marie, Herbert and Kenneth lived at 4977 Tholozon at that time. It was a sad time to watch him walking down Tholozon alone to enter the army. Herbert was exempt due to his poor vision. At present he has but one good eye, no sight in the other eye.

Marie's Memories end on a sad note.

I contracted the Lou Gehrig disease. How I do not know. Learned of the disease in September of '88, the day Ray Smith entered Memorial Home, Grand and Magnolia, and Henrietta learned of the operation for colon cancer on the following Friday. She is great now. Ray died 9/28/88. Marie Brown died 2/4/84. She went for heart surgery and evidently died on the table. I miss her tremendously. We were pals from early grade school years. Later she sang professionally and I played the piano for her.

More Notes from Aunt Marie Buchmann in a letter to Jeanie

Tante was sister of Michael Hammer, their father. She married Mike Severin. When he died she came to live with Grandpa and took care of the girls and Grandpa at 7600 S. Broadway in St. Louis across the street from the park. Grandpa had a cigar store there. Grandpa died suddenly of consumption January 27, 1883. My dad, Henry X Buchmann had a barbershop and one of his patrons told him he knew of a nice girl Hammer in Carondelet...that is what 7600 South Broadway was called then. So Dad met Mom and that started the courting. In winter, he used to tell that when ice was on the streets often it was hard for the horses to pull the street car up the hill about 4500 South Broadway so he and others would get out and push the car...help the horses. Real love.

Now why Dad, Grandpa, was called German? Librarian read from World Encyclopedia and if I understood correctly she was a little confused by the switching back and forth. At the time he was born 1860 it was French territory. French Revolution in 1871 and Germany got control of the territory. He was in German army. After WWI Germany lost control and went back to France in the years 1944-45. It is now French territory. My High School classmates called me "Frenchy."

Hope this covers what you are wondering about at present. If I can help you, I'll try. While I was working I wanted to see the Rose Bowl parade and on my own I got name of a Motel Saga in Pasadena where the parade passed in front of the motel but I could not get a plane back in time for opening of school. How loyal. Now I wish I would have missed a day back in school. Came across the reply the Saga Motel sent me at that time. Memories.

Keep going and lots of love to everyone...
(signed)Aunt Marie

Marie E. Buchmann.

St. Louis Post-Dispatch Obituary

Marie Elizabeth Buchmann

A funeral Mass for Marie Elizabeth Buchmann, a retired teacher, will be celebrated at nine a.m. Wednesday at St. Mary Magdalen Church, 4294 Bancroft Avenue, St. Louis.

Burial will be in Mount Olive Cemetery. Miss Buchmann, 84, St. Louis, died Sunday, March 19, 1989 at Barnes Hospital. She suffered from Lou Gehrig's disease.

Miss Buchmann graduated in 1926 from the St. Louis Music Conservatory and got her bachelor's degree in 1932 from St. Louis University. She began her career as a private music and piano teacher and as a substitute teacher in the St. Louis public schools. She later taught kindergarten at St. Roch's School. She taught kindergarten at the Missouri School for the Blind from 1947 until 1974 when she retired.

She is survived by three nephews, Herbert Alois, Kenneth Henry and Carl Emile Buchmann and three nieces, Rose Marie Buchmann Roach, Emmy Lee Buchmann Williams and Lois Jeane Buchmann Kluga.

As I Remember Henry X and Drusilla

by Herbert Alois Buchmann, January 30, 2000

May 1896   Tornado damages some houses Ninth & Geyer where Henry X had his barber shop and resided upstairs from shop. This is what I was told by my grandmother, Silla. One of the babies (Florence, b. 6/12/1895) was put in the kitchen stove oven during the tornado for safe keeping. Of course there was no heat in the stove.

1923   Henry X, Drusilla, Florence and Marie moved to 18th and Shenandoah. By this time Henry X had sold the barber shops and retired. He worked part time in neighborhood barber shops.

1925-1926   Trip to Colorado in Hupmobile, Henry X, Silla, Floss and Marie. Since there were no motels at that time, they stayed with farm families and in rooming houses. They tell of one night the only place to sleep was in a place like a porch with hard bunks covered with straw. When Silla woke up and looked at the ceiling it was covered with mosquitoes.

The Hupmobile   I don't know what year it was, but it was a big square boxy thing. Two doors, a flat windshield with a visor that was an extension of the roof to keep the sun and rain off the windshield. There was a spotlight in the middle of the cracked windshield. I don't know how much light this spotlight made, probably not much. On the back was a box for tools and a spare wheel and the tire attached. Wheels were wooden spokes with some kind of tire. Solid or pneumatic I don't know?

1928-1935   My parents would visit Henry X and family on Friday nights. Henry X would play with Spotty, a small dog they had at that time. Grandfather would walk back and forth in the kitchen, from the refrigerator to the back door, about ten to fifteen feet, with his hands clasped behind his back, keeping out of Silla's way. The sink and stove were on the opposite side of the room which was Silla's area. Some of the visits included my father and me getting a haircut by Henry X, then Henry X had his hair cut by my father.

Meal to Remember   Silla would prepare a meal of potatoes, turnips and a pot roast with gravy. She liked to season the roast with red hot peppers which she left in the gravy. Once I thought the red stuff was a small tomato. I bit into it, swallowed some and that was all she wrote I upchucked the meal on the spot and never looked at a red pepper again.

Another Memory   Grandmother liked to bake bran muffins with raisins. Well, somehow she managed to slightly burn the muffins only on the bottom. Now have you ever tasted a burned raisin? I kept thinking Silla didn't like me very much.

On our Friday night visits, Henry X would have a bottle of his homemade wine on the table, now and then I would get a taste. Henry X also liked to smoke a hand rolled cigar. Silla didn't allow smoking in her house. He would have to go outside in nice weather or down the basement in the winter.

The house on 18th Street   The house on 18th street was heated by coal stoves. In the kitchen was a combination gas/coal cooking and heating stove and one heating stove in the middle bedroom where Floss and Henry X slept. I don't know how Silla and Marie's bedroom was heated. All I remember were the votive candles on the dresser. At night it sure was spooky! All in all there were four rooms in the unit. The living room was heated by a gas heater when necessary. During the Christmas Season they put up a forerunner of an articial tree and a manger scene set up with carbon filament bulbs.

1890-1920   During Henry X's career as a proprietor of barber shops, he had five or six shops up and down Broadway in the Soulard area, or 'French Town' as it was known then in St. Louis. The shops were manned by barbers he hired. Shave was fifteen cents and a haircut was twenty-five cents. Henry X found that one of his shops was coming up short in the till. Henry X filled in at this shop a couple of days and found that one barber would throw the quarter in such a way that it would bounce up just enough to catch in his shirt cuff. This story was told to me by my father.

1918-1922   Uncle Floss took over the barber trade when Henry X wanted to retire. Later as the barber shops were sold, he branched out into the music business, selling and tuning pianos. He also had a contract to tune pianos for the St. Louis Symphony orchestra.

Saturday visits Every now and then on a Saturday, Henry X would take me back to his workshop next to the garage. He would rummage around and come up with some sticks rolled up in newspaper. They were kite sticks and I can't imagine where he got them. I sure had fun making my own kites and flying them. Before we left the work shop, Henry X noticed a new rat hole in the dirt floor. He found a bucket of broken glass and put some of it in the rat hole.

Rage   Sometimes during the Big Depression when things were tough and the renters were late with paying, or couldn't pay at all, Henry X would go into a rage; off on a verbal tirade in German which I couldn't understand, but I think they were cuss words to the effect that "we can't eat bricks." Silla was hushing him since I was in the room.

1932   New car 1932 four door-six cylinder DeSoto. The family visited Uncle Floss in the hospital and later on at St. Joseph's in Eureka, Missouri.

1964-1965   My mother and father moved to the west coast, stayed six months, moved back to Washington, Missouri where they passed away later on.

The Buchmann brothers around 1904

Floss, Emile, Arthur

Uncle Floss

Uncle Floss was a shadow figure in our childhood. We knew he was definitely a "different" kind of uncle and Mother would tell us he acted the way he did "because a piano fell on him when he was young." This explanation was about as credible as the one about finding babies in the cabbage patch, but we believed it.

I remember one Sunday afternoon, possibly in 1937, when our family had gone to St. Louis to visit Henry X and Drusilla. Floss was seated at the kitchen table and he apparently addressed an ugly remark to my mother. Dad hustled the four of us and our younger cousin, Kenny, out the door and told our older cousin Herb to take us for a walk down to the river. I don't know what occurred in the hour we were being herded to the Mississippi River and back, but when we came up the sidewalk Mother and Dad had their coats on and were standing by the back door. We went straight home and Dad never again uttered the name of Uncle Floss.

I knew that Floss was admitted to the Danville Illinois Veteran's Home in 1940. We were told it was for treatment of his "problem," presumably caused by the piano. Since then our families always use the catch-line, "A piano probably fell on him when he was young" to explain all sorts of oddities.

Florence Andreas Buchmann was born in St. Louis on June 12, 1895. His brother Arthur was two and a half years old. Younger brother, Emile, would be born four years later, in 1899, and in 1905 "the girl" Marie arrived. There is no record of Floss's early life until he and brother Arthur are inducted into the U.S. Army in July of 1918. Floss was discharged seven months later as a Corporal, in February of 1919. His brother, Arthur, was discharged at the same time, so it likely that both men received regular honorable Army discharges.

My cousin Herb is five years older than I and he told me "the Florence story" as he remembers it from 1932:

> *What he did from 1919 to 1929-30 I don't know except cut hair and tune pianos. I heard he was an outstanding piano tuner for the symphony orchestra. He became violent and ran away from home with the car to the Boot Heel. My dad rescued the vehicle from the locals. Then the family sought medical help. Floss was admitted to the St. Louis Insane Asylum where over the years shock and hydrotherapy treatments were administered.*
>
> *I remember visiting Floss with the family and he used to swat the demons off his shoulders and talk to them. I guess I was about ten or eleven at the time, what an experience for a young mind. Treatment was terminated at the St. L.I.A. as nothing more could be done. He was then admitted to St. Joseph's Hill Infirmary in about '39-40, I'm not aware of any treatment there, except spiritual guidance. As the expenses started to take toll on the family resources, other avenues of care (warehousing) were explored. My father enlisted the help of a local ('45-'46) congressman in cutting the red tape for Floss to be admitted to the Veterans Hospital in Danville Ill. You know the rest of the story. EXCEPT WHERE ARE FLOSS' PAPERS?*

In a second note, Herb adds:

> *What I forgot to say yesterday is that by the time Floss was admitted to the V.A., the die was cast and whatever treatment was available did little good. In fact Floss was to be released when Aunt Marie retired, she never told the hospital of her retirement. She wanted to be free to travel and do as she damn well pleased. TRUE BUCHMANN STYLE. Also, I think she destroyed ALL of Floss's records on purpose now that I think about it, there's nothing in her papers that refers to him. So be it.*

With this information in hand, I contacted the Medical Center Archivist at the Danville Veteran's Hospital in 1998, requesting a medical history of my uncle. They sent me copies of his complete clinical record and the autopsy report. Floss was diagnosed with schizophrenia at the time of his admission to Danville. Diagnosis and treatment of mental illness was not very advanced in 1940 and it is difficult to determine what diagnosis a modern-day psychiatrist would offer. The clinical record reveals a chilling tale of treatment:

Excerpts from the Danville Veterans Hospital Records for
Florence (Floss) Buchmann
1.He was admitted to the Hospital in 1940 and the first ten years of his hospitalization was relatively uneventful.

2. His first treatments were ten years later. In 1950 electroconvulsive therapy was used four times for a trial.

3.In 1951, forty-four insulin shock therapies were used. The record states, "This does not appear to alter his psychotic behavior."[12]

4. From 1956 to 1966 Floss received minimal doses of Thorazine.

5. From 1966 to 1969 he received increasing doses of Thorazine and Mellaril and Navane. This regimen appeared to control his behavior and he was transferred to the Intermediate Medical Service in October of 1969.

6. Medication was discontinued for four months and then reordered and increased until February 1976. He received no anti-psychotic medication after that. The record does not provide a reason. On July 28, 1979 Floss awoke with a temperature of 104.9 degrees and was pronounced dead of bronchopneumonia at 8:05 p.m. that evening.

We know now the sad but true story of our Uncle Floss. But in our hearts we all still want to believe the story of our childhood, "because a piano fell on him when he was young."

---

[12] Shock therapy was the mental illness treatment of choice at this time. It is seldom administered now and RARELY to treat schizophrenia.

Florence (Floss) ANDREAS BUCHMANN

WORLD WAR I

In Tower Grove Park - DeSoto car - Henry X, Drus., Floss

Danville IL Veteran's Home

l-r Loss, Marie, Henry X

Floss, Henry X, Drusilla

Floss & Drusilla

Emile and Marie

Emile with family dog

Henry X and Arthur (far right) with neighborhood guys

50th wedding anniversary at Bevo Mill, October 29, 1939

Standing from left: *Art, Herb, Art's Marie, Emile, Henry X, Drusilla, Marie, Leota*
in front: *Carl, Rose Marie, Lois Jean, Emmy Lee, Kenneth*

not pictured: Uncle Floss who resided in Danville Veteran's Home in 1939

Emile at 'Solemn Communion'

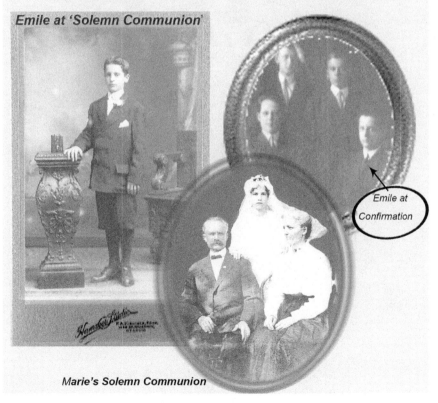

Emile at
Confirmation

Marie's Solemn Communion

Henry X & Drusilla with grandchildren
at the Bevo Mill in October 1939

front: Carl, Henry X, Drusilla, Kenny
Rear: Herb, Emmy, Rosie, Jeanie

Herb, Aunt Marie & Spotty on 18th Street in 1932

Ken & Herb

Marie, Ken and Herb Buchmann

Rob Roach and Barbara Lommen, with her parents Harry and
Tris Lommen, visited Rosenwiller in October 1998. Some
excerpts from Rob's letters and notes:

We spent one week in mid-October in the Haut Alsace region
in the small village of Balbron, about 25 km from Strasbourg. The area
is mostly vineyards and on our first day we were sight-seeing and came
upon workers who "just happened to have some extra tools laying
around," so we joined in and cut grapes for a couple of hours. Hard
work and we weren't even close to being as fast as the locals. Our
reward, however, was very sweet. The workers invited us to join them
for lunch at big picnic tables set up under a huge tree at the edge of the
vineyard. About thirty of us enjoyed a big pasta dish that the owners
of the vineyard and winery brought for everyone and of course, bread
and cheese. The meal started with a big glass of champagne, followed
by red and white wine in copious quantity (both were rough, but tasty).
The dessert, special that day because the owner's son was celebrating
his six-month birthday, was a delicious apple cake with coffee, more
cheese and some wicked strong brandy. We left after lunch, sleepy and
happy.

Driving through the hills from Balbron to Rosenwiller was very
beautiful and we caught sight of the church steeple long before we
could see the town. The valley and the surrounding hillsides are
covered with vineyards, which had turned a beautiful yellow. The smell
of crushed grapes pervades the air, that and the pungency of manure.
I can imagine that in less prosperous times, if farming or the vineyards
weren't producing well, it would have been difficult to make a living
here.

Barbara, as you know, speaks perfect German and French, plus
Dutch and English, and she adjusted to the Alsatian dialect, which is a
mixture of French and German, very easily. In the local dialect
"Buchmann" sounds a lot like BUSH-man. I learned very quickly that
to remark to an Alsatian that someone is a "good Frenchman" is
definitely NOT a compliment. Most of the people we met more easily
identify with being German than being French. To me, they seem to
have the best of two worlds in Alsace.

We had the copy of Mom's letter from the Mayor, Alfred
Engel, and had hoped to meet with him, but he was ill so we met with
his assistant who was very helpful. She told me that Mayor Engel had
Buchmann relatives. She gave us the addresses of several Richert and

Jost families who were still living in Rosenwiller, but said the last of the Buchmann families had died out several years before.

We went to visit Andre Richert. He was on his way to a meeting, but said his sister lived 'just up the road' and she would be interested in talking with us. We went, and after Barbara assured her we were NOT with Jehovah's Witnesses, she became very friendly and talkative. Neither she nor Andre had any written records, but she remembered family talk about the great grandmother who married 'a Buchmann.' Then she remembered that there was still one Buchmann (now Weiskopf) living in Rosenwiller, so off we went to see Madame Weiskopf, nee Buchmann. She appeared on the sidewalk, just as we were knocking on her door. She was very friendly and we talked about a half hour, but she didn't invite us in.

Madame Weiskopf (nee Buchmann) and Barbara

She thought she was related to Henry X through one of his younger brothers (he had nine younger siblings, so that could be a possibility). She got a little teary-eyed when she remembered hearing about her grandfather's brothers who had gone to the USA. She remembered family expectations that riches might come back to them someday from America. Her grandfather was named Xavier who could be a brother of Louis.[13]

A few days later we went up to Strasbourg hoping to find additional records. What we learned is that all of their parish and civil records have been copied and microfilmed by Mormon missionaries years ago and are probably the records Mom has accessed in Salt Lake City when she began the genealogy search. However, I'm thinking the LDS archives in Salt Lake cannot compare to the wine, atmosphere and culture in Alsace even for research purposes!

---

[13] The names, Xavier and Louis, were common in early Buchmann generations. It is difficult to be certain which Xavier or Louis she was referring to.

Barbara Lommen in Rosenwiller in 1998

Alsace-Lorraine: *Encyclopedia Brittanica 2007*

Area comprising the present French départements of Haut-Rhin, Bas-Rhin, and Moselle. Alsace-Lorraine was the name given to the 5,067 square miles (13,123 square km) of territory that was ceded by France to Germany in 1871 after the Franco-German War. This territory was retroceded to France in 1919 after World War I, was ceded again to Germany in 1940 during World War II, and was again retroceded to France in 1945.

Historically, the area was at the centre of Charlemagne's Frankish empire in the 9th century and later became part of the Germanies of the Holy Roman Empire, remaining a German territory under various sovereignties up to the Thirty Years' War. The Peace of Westphalia (1648) concluding that war gave control of Alsace-Lorraine to France.

Because of its ancient German associations and because of its large German-speaking population, Alsace-Lorraine was incorporated into the German Empire after France's defeat in the Franco-German War (1870–71). The loss of Alsace-Lorraine was a major cause of anti-German feeling in France in the period from 1871 to 1914. France also suffered economically from the loss of Alsace-Lorraine's valuable iron-ore deposits, iron- and steelmaking plants, and other industries to Germany.

Under German rule, Alsace-Lorraine was classified as a Reichsland (imperial state) and was denied effective self-government until 1902. Moreover, its population was initially enthusiastic over the new French republic, and German rule remained unpopular for some years among the inhabitants, who continued to protest the German annexation.

Thousands of residents who considered themselves French emigrated during this period. By 1905, however, many of Alsace-Lorraine's Roman Catholics had been alienated by the French republic's anticlerical policies, and so they shifted their aspirations toward an autonomous Alsace-Lorraine within the German Empire. Thereafter, especially with the grant of a constitution in 1911, some progress was made toward Germanization in the region. Alsace-Lorraine was returned to France in 1919 after World War I. The French government's attempts to rapidly assimilate Alsace-Lorraine met with problems, however, especially in France's plans to substitute state-run schools for the region's traditional church schools and in its attempts to suppress German newspapers (German being the written language of 75 percent of the inhabitants). As a consequence, Alsace-Lorraine developed a strong "home rule" movement in the 1920s and unsuccessfully sought autonomy within the French Republic.

Early in World War II, the collapse of France in 1940 was followed by the second German annexation of Alsace-Lorraine, which was again returned to France in 1945. Since then, many of the French prewar governmental policies that had clashed with the region's particularism have been modified, and the autonomist movement has largely disappeared. Linguistically, the German dialect known as Alsatian remains the lingua franca of the region, and both French and German are taught in the schools.

Part Two

Emile and Leota

From the Newspaper Index at Belleville Public Library:

5/15/1917 Leota **GROMBACH** appointed teacher at Union School.

8/28/1920 Emile Henry **BUCHMANN** Professor elected Instructor of Turners: Appointed Physical Culture instructor of Public Schools.

6/1/1921 Emile Henry **BUCHMANN** Instructor of Physical Culture department to give training to teachers.

6/9/1921 Emile Henry **BUCHMANN** re-appointed Director of Belleville Turners @ $1400 per year.

9/1/1922 Leota Emma **GROMBACH** appointed teacher at Jefferson School.

9/15/1922 Emile Henry **BUCHMANN** directs dancing classes at Turner's gymnasium. To be solo dancer in Fall pageant at Lincoln Theater.

7/2/1923 Emile Henry **BUCHMANN** attends Camp Brosius at Elkhart Lake Wisconsin for advanced physical training course.

6/2/1924 Leota Emma **GROMBACH** reappointed teacher at Jefferson School.

6/30/1924 Leota Emma **GROMBACH** weds Emile Henry **BUCHMANN**

7/2/1924 Emile Henry **BUCHMANN** resigns as physical education director of public schools.

4/29/1925 Emile Henry **BUCHMANN** elected delegate to National Convention of American Turner Association.

6/16/1926 Emile Henry **BUCHMANN** resigns as physical instructor at Turners.

7/1/1926 Emile Henry **BUCHMANN** Resigns as Physical Education Director of Belleville Turners to assume duties of Superintendent of physical education of public schools. Salary of $2100 per year.

Emile and Leota

At Home in Belleville for 25th Anniversary
June 30, 1949

Emile and Leota

The Stories:

My Autobiography

I, Leota Grombach, came into the world on a hot stormy Monday afternoon in June. Since 13 was the day, everyone thought that would be unlucky but that was not true. I have had a very happy life.

My parents and my two and a half year old brother were my constant caretakers until I was able to help myself. From all reports I had long black hair and big blue eyes when I was born. My legs got strong enough to hold me and I was running after my brother when I was only one year old. I grew fast because my teeth were strong and I could chew my food well and I liked milk and vegetables.

My next playmate that I remember was a pug dog named Punchy. I loved to pet her back and one evening when my mother and daddy wanted to keep me busy while they played cards, they told me that if I petted Punch for ten minutes she would lay money like chickens lay eggs. I did and lo and behold when I looked under her tail I found two nickels. To my sorrow that was the last time I ever found any money under her tail.

When I was almost ready to go to school there was a World's Fair in St. Louis. My, but that was a long ride on a streetcar. My family went there for the day and I do remember seeing a cow made out of butter. I also remember seeing Eskimos in their igloos.

When I went to first grade I was so proud to own a slate and a slate pencil tied to it with a red string. I learned to write my name and every time I picked up my pencil with my left hand my teacher slapped my hand with a ruler. I wrote with my right hand. I always liked school and was only happy when I made an 'A'.

When I was ten years old I knew I wanted to be a teacher. I am so glad that I was able to go to school and to college.

One time my Sunday School gave a picnic and several girls asked me to go with them and hide our lunch under a tree and eat whenever we wanted to. We didn't want to share. We were naughty, weren't we? Let me tell you what happened to us. While we were playing some pig came and ate our lunches and we had to go hungry all day. I learned a bitter lesson. I should have been kind and done what I had learned at Sunday School. I went every Sunday for five years without missing.

We had eight grades in the school I went to; there was no junior high. When I went to High School I took part in all of the activities, especially the dramatics. I went to parties and dances and always acted the way I was supposed to.

Notes on the Text:
This "My Autobiography" by my mother, Leota Grombach (Buchmann), turned up in a bundle of old papers one of the grandchildren had. Mother was born in 1898. This piece appears to have been written for one of the grandchildren when mother was in her 80s. I treasure it for it illustrates her "schoolteacher----a moral to be learned" self at its finest!

Leota continues in another letter to the grandchildren:
"Your grandmother is writing this to tell you about some of her life as she remembers it and to acquaint you with how things were in the olden days.

I was born June thirteenth 1898, in Belleville, Illinois. Things were different then, no TV, no radio, practically no automobiles or airplanes. People traveled by horse drawn carriages, streetcars or trains. There was no electricity, no telephone in our house until I was about ten years old. We had coal oil lamps-then gaslights and later electric lights. I did all of my schoolwork at the dining room or kitchen table by light of a coal oil lamp. There were no refrigerators, no running hot water, no electric toasters or other appliances. To take a bath in warm weather a washtub was filled with water drawn from a cistern. It contained rainwater, which was collected when it rained and the water was soft'.

We had ice boxes which were wood boxes in which chunks of ice were placed (usually ten cents worth) as requested from the iceman who drove his wagon drawn by a team of horses down the streets. We kids liked to follow the iceman and beg small pieces of ice that fell off when he chipped it with an ice pick.

I really think I had a happy childhood. Not having TV or radio was no deprivation since we knew nothing of such things. We relied on scooters, coaster wagons, roller skates, ice skates, sleds, kites and other homemade toys. We made our own baseballs by wrapping string around a small rubber ball and covered with pieces of glove that mother sewed to make a cover.

We had no money and occasionally got a few pennies to spend for 'penny candy.' Rarely got a nickel to buy an ice cream cone with two scoops of ice cream.

We made snowmen in winter and built forts of snow where we hid to throw snowballs at our enemies. Hockey was fun. Tin cans were used as pucks and small branches of trees (properly shaped) were used as hockey sticks. In spring we played ' kick the stick', red-light and mumbeldy peg which was played with a pocketknife. Points were scored when you flipped the knife and it stuck in ground. Kites were made of newspapers. Marbles was the best game. Each of us had a marble bag with a string drawn through top. It held the taws, bimpy[14] fancy shooters. A circle was scratched on the ground and each player put marbles in and the object of game was to see how many of your opponent's marbles you could shoot out.

We had our chores daily. Going to the store for foodstuffs daily, sweeping walks, and in winter keeping the wood box filled and ashes carried out. Kitchen chores were plentiful too. We had a coal burning heater in parlor and the kitchen stove. These kept

---

[14] Word appears to be "bimpy" but am not certain.

us warm when we were close. One time I got too close while taking a bath by the stove and blistered my rump.

I always wanted a piano but as daddy said, "Rich people have pianos and we're not rich," so I settled for elocution lessons at fifty cents per week. I loved it and did well with monologues and drama. My high school years were a breeze and I did well. Graduated in 1916 and knew I wanted to teach school. At age sixteen, I worked as a clerk from ten in the morning until eight at night for fifty cents a Saturday. Saved it all so that I could go to Normal for six weeks. Got my certificate in Nov 1916 - was in classroom in January 1917 and had job at forty dollars per month. I had never seen a country school but I managed and loved the experience. I was very happy, had many beaus, danced till dawn, partied and sang in group...."

She has some notes at the end; probably as a reminder for the next page, which was never written....

" wrap goose grease flannel cloth around neck mustard plaster,
Tonic: sulphur and molasses cleans blood, Asiphidity bag,
Rhubarb sauce good for liver (cleans pots too)
Sassafras tea"

The One-Room Country School

Mother always told us that from the time she was a little girl "I knew I wanted to teach school." She graduated from Belleville High School in June of 1916 and managed to save enough to attend "the Normal School" (now Illinois State University) for a six-week session that fall. By November of 1916, she had earned an elementary teaching certificate qualifying her to teach school in the state of Illinois. By January of 1917, six months shy of her nineteenth birthday, she had a job for forty dollars a month teaching in a one-room country school near Edgemont, Illinois. She loved to tell us the story of her first day. Mother had to stretch to reach five feet, and back in 1917 she would have been referred to as 'a slip of a girl.' She wanted to look professional and make a good impression, she'd tell us, and so she borrowed her mother Emma's "old-looking" shoes and wore her best dark shirtwaist, the fashionable hem just sweeping the floor. She took the streetcar to the end of the Edgemont line and then, lifting the skirt in one hand to keep the hem from dragging in the dirt, walked several miles along the country road to the schoolhouse.

Sixteen pupils, first through eighth grade, ages six through sixteen, were busy at their kneehole desks. Seated on spindly wooden chairs at the rear of the room were four men. Black-suit somber, arms akimbo, each of them nodded only slightly as she entered the schoolroom. She unfastened the pins from the stylish wide-brimmed hat she'd borrowed that morning from her friend Alma and put the hat carefully on a vacant desk at the front of the room.

"You are the new teacher candidate," were they asking me or telling me, she wondered? Nothing more was said. Unsmiling, arms folded, the four men sat. Sixteen youthful faces beamed up at her; four old faces looked down at her. She told us later, "I didn't know what to do or what I should say, so I did the only thing I could think of...I started to teach the children." And she taught the children all morning, shared their meager sack lunches at noon and taught the children all afternoon. An older boy knew when to ring the final afternoon dismissal bell and the kids finally raced for the  doors, freedom and home. Still the four men sat with arms crossed, faces blank.

Relating this to us years later, Mom would smile, clearly pleased with her eighteen year old self. "Well, I could see they were waiting for me to do something, so I just put my hat back on (well, it was Alma's hat really, you know), picked up my bag and walked to the door. 'Ahem' I thought I heard one of them clear his throat. I stopped walking and turned around and looked over my shoulder. And was I surprised! All four of them were grinning at me. 'You'll do,' they said in unison."

We all four loved this story... it intrigued us...especially the part where she doesn't talk to the four men when she enters the schoolroom for the first time. "Didn't you wonder who they were? Did you know they were the School Board? Weren't you afraid when they stayed the whole day to watch you?" we'd ask. We couldn't imagine her not interrogating the men, finding out their personal histories, the names of their family members, their most intimate secrets.

My mother was a woman who used to mortify us all as teenagers by talking, and giving advice, to strangers in the bus station, on the street, in the market. And everyone loved it, everyone that is but her teen aged children who were usually red with embarrassment. When we rode the bus to St. Louis, a thirty-minute trip, all four of us would get her to board first and help her get seated. It was best if we could find her a seat up front near the driver, facing forward. Then we would scurry to find a seat as far back as we could, distancing ourselves and hoping that nobody would guess we were with her or that she was our mother. She always thought she had four courteous children when in truth we were running for cover. When my own children were teenagers they too were utterly humiliated every time "the genetic flaw" surfaced and I would begin conversations with people I had never met. - -MOTHER - - -.

Mother taught in the one-room country school for a year or two and then was hired to teach fourth grade in the Belleville school system. One day, so the story goes, the principal brought a young man to her classroom. "This is Professor Buchmann, he's just been hired as Director of Physical Education for the Belleville School District and I'd like him to observe your teaching this afternoon," the principal told her.

"I thought he was handsome, but sort of stuck-up," she'd tell us with a smile. He'd tell us, "I knew I was going to marry her the minute I set eyes on her." We thought that was the best part of the whole story. And the WHOLE story is another story!

How Leota and Emile Met in 1920

Transcribed from a note written in 1982 by Leota to her grandchildren

I was teaching at the Jefferson School. Emile was Director of Physical Education for District #118. He was my boss then. Since the Music Director was there too we chatted in the hall and danced a bit during the recess period. It was the usual custom to come to the rooms to present new material, instead he came and said, "I'd like for you to conduct the class today." What could I say to the boss-man—surely not what I was thinking!

He planned coming to my class last (noon) so children could be dismissed and then he hung around on the pretense to show me new material, and told me that he enjoyed the short dance and would like to take me dancing at the 'Avalon Ballroom' the next Sunday! Sneaky! I accepted and since he commuted

weekly to St. Louis, I planned to meet him at the Street Car Terminal. When I told my mother she nearly had an attack; no daughter of hers was going to another city to meet a man. Did I tell you I was twenty-two years old by then? After much discussion she relented with the provision that I put a dollar bill in each shoe so in case he wasn't there I could come home and be safe.

HE WAS THERE!!! This is what went through his mind; will I know her? I only saw her twice; no coat or hat on! Well, he knew me and then we got on another streetcar and rode and rode. While dancing the first dance, he very sheepishly said, "You know I'd like to call you by your name, but I really don't know your name. You know me, but who are you? I can't call you Miss Jefferson." We had a good laugh and the rest of the story ends happily. Now at eighty-four it is a precious memory.

1935

1924   LEE **a
n**   PROF.   1949
        d

don't miss this

**Twenty-Five Years and Four Kids Ago
We Settled Down On Honeymoon Row.
Come Over July 3rd, 'tween Four and Eight
And Help Us Celebrate!**

**R. eply   S. oon   V. ery   P. romptly
By June 27, 1949**

Uh - Unh!   No Posies! . No Presents!   PLEASE!

1949

David W. interviews Grandma B. (1971)
(transcribed from David's tape recording)

David: (age 9)   And now for my Social Studies homework, I'm going to interview Mrs. Leota Buchmann. Where did you live at this time, Mrs. Buchmann?

Grandma: I lived in Belleville Illinois.

D: When you lived there, what was your income, during the Depression, during the 1930s?

G: During the 1930s, I lived on East "C" Street in Belleville and I had a family of four children and a husband who worked as a professional physical education teacher earning about $1200 a year. That was our only income.

D: And about how much a year would you spend on odds and ends and groceries and necessities like that?

G: To be frank, we spent all of it on the things we needed. There were no 'odds and ends' and frills. We bought what we needed and used what we bought.

D: OK. During those times when so many people were going broke and needed money, was there a lot of stealing and things like that?

G: Not that I recall. I think everybody stayed close to home. In the first place, the discipline in the home was of an entirely different nature. Boys and girls were so busy helping at home so that they could stay above board, as you might say, financially. Because they had to do the chores themselves, they had to do the errands. Many of the boys had to do odd jobs so they had no time to loiter or steal.

David: What did you do for entertainment - - -. things like that?

Grandma: Well there wasn't too much entertainment. We found our entertainment within ourselves in our homes. In the spring and summer the boys and girls in the neighborhood played games in their yards. Their daddies often played with them. They played football, they played 'kick-the-stick,' which you probably don't know. They played 'run sheep run' and everybody in the neighborhood joined. They had no need for money in those kinds of things.

D: Around where you lived were there a lot of richer, more wealthy children who acted vain or anything to yours?

G.:   No. No. No, there was nothing like that for everyone was in the same predicament. Everybody had less income and they had just about the same expenses. There was no difference of classes or 'you have more than I do.' Everybody knew that they did the best they could. Now, on entertainment, maybe once in a month or maybe two months, we would save and go to a show. Now at that time you could go to a show and see three features at the movies and see an act on the stage, and the father and mother paid twenty-five cents each and the children were admitted free. Then we got a hamburger for ten cents and came home. And that was a big day as far as we were concerned.

D: When you went to a movie, what kind of movie would the whole family go to at that time?

G: Well, they were all what you'd call good movies. There were no 'X or R-rated' movies at that time at all. We'd see cowboy pictures, those were favorites; we'd see Charlie Chaplin, we'd see W.C. Fields and probably some times on the stage we were lucky. We saw Ginger Rogers and saw Eddie Cantor and a few like that. All for the price of 25 cents.

D: When you went to the movies, would you pay for such things as popcorn, trifles, things like that?

Grandma: No. There were no things like that. No popcorn stands. We ate our dinner and we were taught and knew that we didn't dare ask for anything until Daddy said it was proper to have it. And once in awhile we'd get a treat like a hamburger and sometimes we'd just come home and eat. There were no frills or asking 'may we have this or that,' because the children knew they couldn't have it. We didn't have it.

David: Could you afford a pet, a dog or a cat?

G: We had a dog. I don't know if we could afford it or not. But the dog was not fed dog food, didn't know what it was to go to a vet. The dog ate what we ate, the scraps that were left and seemed to be quite satisfied.

D: Were there a lot of scraps left over at that time?

G: Not too many. I grant you that.

D: OK. Did your children take their lunch to school, the school that they went to?

G: Fortunately we lived close enough to the school to come home for our lunches. And our main meal was at noon because the daddy in the house worked from 3:30 on, so we ate at noon. But there was a ruling in the school that if you lived within twelve blocks of the school you were not allowed to bring your lunch. There was no lunch room. There was no supervision. If you brought your lunch, you just sat on the steps and ate it. Very few children carried their lunches.

D: If you did live out of twelve blocks, you could still go home?

G: If you wanted to, you could go home. But you were not allowed to bring lunch if you lived within that radius.

D: OK. did you own a house?

Grandma: Yes, we owned a house. We owned it long before the Depression. We bought the house in 1924 and we bought it and went into what you called 'Building and Loan.' You pay so much per month on the payment of the principal. And during the Depression we were fortunate enough to be able to keep those payments up. When you got your pay, that was the first thing you did. You took out the amount of money that was necessary to pay the house payment, let's say. And as long as you could do that, then you knew that your house was secure.

David: The people who would rent out houses, the landlords…if you knew anybody who did rent a house, would they take their prices up steeply every now and then?

G: No. No. They were glad they had the houses rented. They were glad they could get people to pay the rent.

D: What about clothing? Did you make your clothing, or did you buy it? Or did you just have hand-me-downs from other people?

G: There was a little bit of all. We bought some. The father of the house always was the first to be clothed. He had to be out in the public and he had to work, so his clothes budget was always taken out first. The wife usually made the things for the children, if she could. And always bought out of season. By that I mean, when the summer sales were on, you bought for next summer or when the fall sales were on, you bought for the following year. In other words, you watched the sales and bought out of season. And you sewed what you could and did with what you had and there were lots of hand-me-downs among groups of friends. They would hand down the clothes to the younger ones in the group and that way we were clothed conservatively well.

D: I notice lately most of the children, the kids around, will make fun of other children….guys if they're wearing 'high-water pants'. Did most of the boys in that time wear high-water pants? I mean pants that didn't fit too well.

G: I don't think so. Most of them wore long pants. I think sometimes they wore what they called 'knickerbockers'.

Grandma: I don't know if you children know what knickerbockers are, but it's the pants with a kind of a bloomer and it is fastened at the knee. And no, I don't think it would be allowed. I think the teacher was very strict about that and the parents were strict about it and I think the children had compassion for one another.

David: OK. What about food? Eggs and things like that? Where did you get your food, the kinds of things you needed every week?

G: Well, there were butcher shops, individuals, and there were grocery stores and baker shops. And now on the baker shops, you usually went to the shop on the second day after the bakery was sold fresh and you bought day-old bakery at half price. You got twice as much. We didn't know what fresh bakery was. The butcher shop, you were able to buy a nice roast for family dinner for fifty cents. The grocery store had the other necessities. There were some canned goods. But you had a garden usually. And all summer you canned the things and put them in your cellar or your basement, as you might say. And then in the winter you had those vegetables to prepare. You didn't know what frozen foods were and you knew very little about canned foods. You usually canned your own. And you baked and you did those things. You had no problem. The farmer came with his produce, fresh eggs, cream, cheese, some milk, and vegetables. And you bought from him.

D: OK. A lot of these stores that were around, the bakery and the butcher shops. Were they...did they go out of business; did some of them go out of business for necessity of food, sugar, things like this?

G: Yes, some did. But there were plenty of things. The only thing that wasn't plentiful was money. You could buy if you had the money.
D: OK. Thank you very much. You've helped us very much. This is my grandmother. My name is David Williams and this is my grandmother. So thank you very much for listening to us. And that will be all. Goodbye.

David Williams, Grandma and Andy Roach in 1963

What I remember about Grandma Buchmann

From Jill DeMichele (granddaughter)

I can hear her voice. The great grandchildren will be amazed. I was surprised they had a phone at all when she was ten. That would have been 1908. I can't imagine having to work so hard to take a bath. Grandma told me that the first time Grandpa came into her classroom, he said that he knew he was going to marry her. She met him in St. Louis for their first date. Grandma's parents weren't going to let her go on the train or bus. But they agreed if she promised that she would stay on the train and return home if she didn't see him at the St. Louis station. Well, Grandpa was there, and the rest is history.

From: Andrew Roach (grandson)

I don't remember Emile, but the memories of Grandma that I have are of her insisting that we don't hate anybody, of helping her put up the storm windows with Dad, getting out of the car and hustling up to the porch for one of her patented wet kisses, of course the afternoons of football after Thanksgiving. I wish I remembered more. The tape Dave Williams had of his interview with her from a class assignment brought back a lot by listening to her. I guess part of what is hard to describe are her mannerisms and speech pattern.

We Promise Her

"Promise me you kids will always stay close to one another"
As a deathbed request, this wasn't a hard one to honor.
Mom was eighty-six. Her mind was still sharp as a newly minted
penny, although congestive heart failure had caused her once-
shapely dancer's legs to swell with edema. She was hospitalized in
Belleville and my sister and I were able to visit two or three times
a week from our homes in Decatur and Springfield. Mom
expected to be released from her latest hospitalization and hoped
to return to the red brick bungalow on East "C" Street that had
been her home since the day in 1924 that Emile carried her
across the threshold as his new bride.

The house had been a wonderful family home. In those
days, one modern bathroom for a family of six was considered
sufficient. The three large bedrooms were upstairs, as was the
single bathroom. We could easily convert the large dining room
into a first floor bedroom for her, but there didn't seem to be a
practical way to add a bathroom downstairs. This, would present
a problem when (or if?) Mother would be physically able to
return home.

Every Friday afternoon that cold March in 1984, I'd leave
the university in Springfield early so that I could be in Belleville
to spend a few hours with Mom at the hospital before I drove on
to Edwardsville. We were all totally distraught. Mother was due
to be released in another week. She couldn't return to her home
because of the stairs; moving to either Decatur or Springfield
didn't seem to be an option. She dreaded going to an actual
nursing home, and the ones that were available in Belleville in

I remember leaving St. Elizabeth's Hospital one week, crying and praying through my tears. I took a wrong turn leaving the hospital and ended up turning east onto Illinois Street instead of heading west. I knew I could pick up Illinois Route #13 at the end of Illinois Street and continue west to Route #157 and Edwardsville, so I continued on south. I almost missed the turn that day. Workers were just finishing putting up a huge sign at the junction:

Four Fountains Residential Center
Now Open...Apartments Available
Move In Today!

I wheeled in and went to the Residential Renting Office to inquire. The place was lovely with two floors of apartments surrounding a two-storied atrium. However the apartments were available only to persons who needed no nursing care or assistance and the management required a signed medical statement attesting to that fact. The stated health and activity level requirements for apartment living were too stringent for Mother to meet.

But then, Mother wasn't filling out the questionnaire. I was. So I filled out an application with what I called 'a little compassionate deceit.' I knew that my sister and I could figure out some way that Mother could manage living by herself and it would be a wonderful place for her to enjoy the little time she might have left. I put down a deposit and picked out an apartment with a balcony view of downtown Belleville.

The next week we met with Mother's young doctor. He had been very frank with us as to mother's prognosis and reiterated his earlier opinion that she would not live out the year. I told him what I had done and he said, "There is no way she can manage living there by herself without some nursing care." We knew that. "But if we can figure out a way to have someone with her all the time, will you sign the admittance papers?" I pleaded. It took a little more talking and discussing, but he was a kind man and besides, Mother had been his father's fourth grade teacher at the Jefferson School. He signed the admission papers.

Mother was thrilled! No nostalgia or weeping over leaving the house she had lived in for sixty years. We picked out the furniture she could use in the new apartment and split up the rest among the family. We sold the house on "C" Street and took her home from the hospital to Four Fountains and her new luxury apartment. Our plan was that each of us would 'visit' a week at a time. With the four of us taking turns, and the grandchildren visiting when they could, it worked out perfectly. What is so wonderful to us now, looking back, is that each of us had the opportunity to enjoy private time with her that summer.

I remember one day when it was my visiting week, she decided her hair was too long and difficult to manage. So I brought along the family barber shears and I began to cut her hair. When I was a little girl, my sisters and I used to take turns brushing Mother's hair. As I combed her hair that day and began trimming it, it was almost as if we were transported back forty years to our family kitchen. "Daddy always liked my hair short," she said. I didn't know that.

The summer of 1984 was a precious one for Mother and for the rest of us. She left us that August, given the gift of a gentle and peaceful death.

"Promise me you kids will always stay close to one another" were her last words. We promised. And one year later her children and her grandchildren gathered in Phoenix, Arizona to enjoy our first Buchmann family reunion, keeping the deathbed promise we lovingly had made to her.

Nine of Leota's grandchildren
at the second family reunion in
Taos, NM, September 1992

front row; David, Jill, Julie
middle : Andy, Kim, Caron,
rear: Phil, Rob, Craig

August 1984, after Leota's Memorial Service

Pictured in the front row: David, Kim, Carl, Jill, Jeanie, Emmy, Chris, Rob
Center: Herb & Kathy, Aunt Marie, Rosie, Carolyn, Julie
Rear: Phil, Jimmy   (not pictured:Andy, the photographer)

Christmas in Belleville in 1959

Back row: l to r: Jim Williams, Carl Buchmann, John Kluga, Bob Roach
On ends of couch: Emmy Williams(holding Andy) Rosie Roach
Seated: Carolyn Buchmann, Leota, Emile,
                       Jeane Kluga (holding Rob)
Front row: Kim Roach, Jill Williams, Julie Williams

Leota's Surprise 75th Birthday Party (1973)

Front: David, Phillip, Caron, Craig
Center: Rob, Jill, Grandma
Rear: Kim, Julie, Andy

Paw-paw & Rob-1958

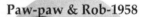

Kneeling: Rosie & Emmy
Center: David & Phil
Middle: Jill, Grandma, Julie, Andy
Rear: Kim & Rob

Leota's 85th
BIRTHDAY GALA

June 13. 1983

featuring

The BUCHMANN TWINS

and their SUPPORTING
cast

Players .... Emmy, Rosie
Jim, Jim
Kim, Phil, Andy
Music ..... Jim M.
Narrator ..... Andy
Limericist ... Jim W.
Script ..... The Twins
Editing .... Phil
Dresser .... Kim

Program

Scene I ... The Elocution
Scene II .... The Teacher
Scene III .... The Courtship
Scene IV .... The Honeymoon
Scene V ..... The Firstborn(s)
Scene VI .... The Costumer
Scene VII ... The War Years
Scene VIII ... The Group
Scene IX ... The Clubber

Grand Finale ....
The entire company

Scene I   The Elocution

Scene VI:
The Costumer

Scene II:
The Teacher

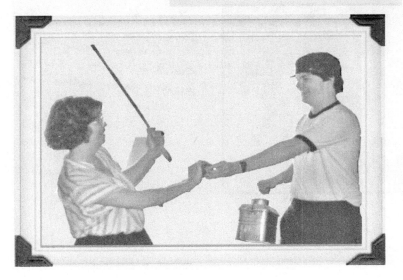

Grandma Buchmann with Kim and Phil Roach
Summer 1984

1970 - on back porch in Belleville

From left:
Leota, Caron (on lap)
Carolyn + Craig (back row,
Phil, Kim, Julie, Rosie
Emmy (hidden behind David)
David + Jill

June 1941

Part Three

Growing Up Belleville

An original oil painting of the cherry tree and round bench in the backyard at 420 East "C" street in Belleville by artist Jeane (Buchmann) Kluga

The twins and Jeanie pose on the bench in 1932

"All Passes—Art Alone Endures."

Buchmann's School of The Danse

Studios

New Turner Hall
Belleville

Metropolitan Bldg., Room 208
East St. Louis

Belleville, Ill., January 1929.

Dear Friends:—

This letter may be a surprise or just a bit of information. Regardless of how it may appear to you, I am anxious to introduce myself as the successor to Miss Helen Hirschfeld, who has so efficiently carried on the dancing art in East St. Louis for many years.

I am Mr. Emile H. Buchmann, director of Buchmann's School of the Danse. The inclosed circulars, which are old ones, will probably give you all the additional information. Do not pay any attention to class schedule or tuition prices in them.

All classes will remain the same, also the tuition fees. The only change will be the Thursday classes, which will be held on Saturday afternoons. Kindergarten at 1:30 P. M., and Intermediate at 2:30 P. M.

We are anxious to announce the re-opening of our tap and jigging class for adults on Mondays at 7:15 P. M. There will also be a class for beginners in Ballroom dancing; also an advanced class in which the Tango, Chicago, Hesitation Waltz, Dago Walk, Finale, and advanced Fox Trot steps will be taught. This class will start at 8:15 P. M. on Mondays. These three classes will start on Monday, February 4th. We urge you to be there and register so that definite arrangements can be made. Call Hirschfeld School of Dancing, Metropolitan Bldg., on Fridays between 4 and 6 P. M.; or Saturdays between 9 A. M. and 4 P. M., for information.

Strangers are always asked for recommendations. Therefore, we are ready to be recommended by those whom you would naturally ask.

To the Mothers of East St. Louis Children:

Mr. Emile H. Buchmann has taken over the Helen Hirschfeld School of Dancing

In turning over my school to Mr. Buchmann, I believe that I am placing the school in the hands of a conscientious and capable artist. A man who can develop in any child or person the natural grace and talent which may be present. Mr. Buchmann has already accomplished wonderful results with children and students of the dance. I have placed my school and classes in Mr. Buchmann's hands with the full confidence that he is one of the best artists in the community.

I earnestly recommend Mr. Buchmann to mothers of East St. Louis children and to students who wish to carry their training further under skillful professional guidance.

Sincerely,

Helen F. Hirschfeld

Dear Friends:—

Last summer during the months of June, July and August, my little daughter, Jean, was a pupil of Professor Emile Buchmann. At that time I had ample opportunity to watch and judge Professor Buchmann's methods and system, and I found them excellent. He was very successful with Jean during the time she was his pupil.

I am very sorry to see Miss Hirschfeld discontinue teaching; but since she is, there is no one whom I would rather see take over her classes than Professor Buchmann.

I have been retained as pianist, and hope that you will transfer your patronage from Miss Hirschfeld to Professor Buchmann, as he is well qualified to take her place.

Yours sincerely,

Virginia V. Geissert

It will be my endeavor to maintain and continue the high standard of teaching developed by Miss Hirschfeld. Your cooperation in making this change is solicited by remaining as faithful to this school as before. Let us work hand in hand and make this school the greatest success East St. Louis has ever had.

A class will be formed for any type of dancing if a sufficient number apply.

We urgently invite you to at least pay us a visit and become acquainted with our work.

Respectfully yours,

Emile H. Buchmann

Early History of Belleville

1801 - Settlements were made in the vicinity of Belleville. Many of the pioneers were of Pennsylvania Dutch descent.

1813 - Thomas Harrison built the first cotton gin in Belleville.

1814 - Frenchman George Blair founds Belleville. George donates an acre of his land for theTown Square and an additional 25 acres that adjoined the Square for the new County Seat. Belleville becomes the county seat of St. Clair County, replacing Cahokia. George names the city "Belleville" for "Beautiful City" in French.

1814 - Joseph Kerr opens the first store in Belleville.

1817 - James Tannehill opens a distillery, Belleville's first industry.

1818 - Illinois becomes a state.

1819 - Belleville is incorporated as a village. Population: 150.

1821 - The first state hanging takes place in Belleville near the site of the Henry Raab school. Timothy Bennett is sentenced to death for the murder of Alphonso C. Stewart on September 23.

1821 - Belleville Academy is established to provide young gentlemen with an opportunity for higher learning.

1822 - Whipping posts constructed in the public square. Used once. Later used as hitching posts.

1825 - William Fowler opens the first commercial coal mine.

1832 - Belleville's first brewery, and the first in the state of Illinois, was opened by Jacob Fleishbein in 1832.

1836 - Residents established the Belleville Public Library. Today it is the oldest Public Library in the State. The first books purchased were Sparks 'Life of Washington', a 12 Volume set. Today, the volumes are held in the Library vault.

1841 - Belleville's first Fire Department is organized with 2 stations and and a team of volunteers.

1842 - The Cathedral of St. Peter at 200 W. Harrison Street is founded.

1849 - Cholera epidemic hits Belleville. Town Trustees purchase land from Philip B. Fouke for $400.00 to found the Walnut Hill Cemetery as a municipal burial plot.

1850 - Belleville is incorporated as a city. Population: Estimated at 4,000. Theodore Krafft is the first Mayor.

1861 - The first national miners' union meeting in the country took place in Belleville when the American Miners' Association was formed.

1862 - Eckert's Country Store and Farm opens on Route 15. Today it is the largest Pick-Your-Own orchard in the Country.

1864 - Belleville Philharmonic Society is formed. Today it is the second oldest Philharmonic Orchestra in the Country.

1874 - Belleville's first street railway is operated.

1891 - Land is purchased for a City Hall and the structure is completed in 1892.

1904 - The Belleville Shoe Company is founded. They produce their first military footwear for the Great War in 1917. Today they are the largest suppliers of military footwear to the U.S. military.

1913 - The first automobile accident victim is buried in Walnut Hill Cemetery.

1917 - Scott Air Force Base opens for formal flying instruction. The base is named after Corporal Frank S. Scott. The Air Service Balloon and Airship School opens later in 1922.

1920 - The Belleville Jaycees are founded. Today they are the 4th oldest chapter in the World.

1921 - The Lincoln Theatre at 103 East Main opens as a vaudeville house. In 1927 the orchestra is replaced by a theatre organ.

1937 - The Veteran's Memorial Fountain was built by local Veterans of Foreign Wars as a memorial to American servicemen at a cost of $600.00 because of donated materials and labor.

1944 Buchmann Twins graduate from BTHS.

1949 - World's largest catsup bottle erected in nearby Collinsville IL.

Growing up Belleville

The Stories:

The Buchmann School of Stage Dancing

Leota and the Scott Field Sewing Room

Growing up Belleville

The Barber Scissors of Henry X

Family Hair

The Age of Innocence

Like Mother Used to Make....NOT

Leaving for College

Uncle Herb

Carl remembers

Jeanie remembers

Christmas Memories from Emmy

The Buchmann School of Stage Dancing

The motto of the Buchmann School of Stage Dancing was "All passes art alone endures." Throughout my childhood I pondered its meaning. Not until I was an adult did I realize that a comma after the phrase "All passes," clarifies the meaning precisely.

Dad owned and operated three dancing schools from 1926 until the late forties, after WWII. One school was in our hometown of Belleville Illinois. The largest was in adjacent East St. Louis, a fairly prosperous city at that time, and the third was in nearby Granite City Illinois. The earliest information we have as to his interest in dance is from a Belleville Daily Advocate newspaper index dated September 15, 1922, which states:

"Emile Henry Buchmann directs dancing classes at Turner's gymnasium. To be solo dancer in Fall Pageant at Lincoln Theater"

Emile would have been living in Belleville for at least two years by 1922. He was appointed Physical Culture Instructor of the Belleville Public Schools and Instructor at the Belleville Turnverein (Turners) in 1920, at the age of twenty-one. Where, and how, he learned to dance well enough to be featured as "solo dancer" in the fall pageant at the Lincoln Theater is unknown. We do know that he attended Butler University in Indianapolis to study medicine. Why he switched to physical education and dance is a mystery. Emile was at Butler during the 1918 Spanish influenza epidemic where he hovered between life and death for days on a cot in the school gymnasium. Harried volunteer nurses in homemade gauze masks cared for the hundreds of stricken students. He would tell this story sadly in his later years. I never knew if his sadness was for the many young college students who did not survive that terrible epidemic or for the fact that not once in all the weeks he lay stricken did his family in St. Louis ever write or inquire about his condition.

When he would tell this story, he would also tell us that he was a great disappointment to his mother who had expected him to become a Catholic priest. When he told her he was not going to give his life to the Church but instead wished to go to college, Drusilla, his mother, threw herself across the foot of her bed, swooning and crying, "You have killed me. You have killed me." The connection between these two stories I can only ponder.

Leota and Emile were married in June of 1924 and in July of 1926, Emile was appointed Superintendent of Physical Education for the Belleville Public School District at a salary of $2100 a year. That year he produced the first "Buchmann Dance Revue" on the stage of the local Lincoln Theater. Two years later in April of 1928, when my twin sister Emmy and I were fourteen months old, the '3rd Annual Buchmann Revue' featured:

The Buchmann Twins
World's youngest twin acrobats on the stage"

All seats for this dance revue were forty cents. Fortunately the dancing schools continued to grow and prosper and when, during the grim Depression years of the 1930s, the Belleville school system abolished the position of Superintendent of Physical Education Dad turned his full-time energies and ambition to the dancing schools. His timing was fortuitous. In 1932, Shirley Temple had burst upon the movie scene with her "Baby Burlesk" skits. By 1934 her movie hits, "Bright Eyes" and "Stand Up and Cheer" featuring the grand production number, 'Baby Take a Bow' were playing to standing room only crowds across the nation. The country was deep in the throes of depression blues and tiny Shirley Temple with her corkscrew curls, twinkling tapping toes and dimpled smile was the nation's darling. Every parent hoped his or her child would be discovered as the next Hollywood child star - - - but first the child would have to learn to tap dance! A half-hour class lesson was fifty cents. Private lessons were one dollar. Somehow, even in those deep Depression years, families managed to scrape up money for the luxury of 'tap and toe' dancing lessons for their offspring.

THE RECITAL or Annual Dance Revue was held each spring on the stage of the Lincoln Theater. Mother designed the costumes for each class of tiny dancers. She would order bolts of glimmering sateen, strands of marabou and sequins and yards and yards of net from the costume book of Dazian's 'fabric supply house of the stars.' From her collection of costume ideas she'd clipped from newspapers and movie magazines, she would select and adapt designs for the 'production numbers' that Dad had taught his dancers to perform. She would sketch (copy) the design, then draw a pattern on big sheets of newsprint. She'd allow about an inch seam, so that the pattern could be used for different sizes. She'd deliver the patterns, material, and basic sewing instructions to each class. Many of these women had never sewn before so Mom would have to help each of them master the basic construction of a leotard and show them how to gather the gauzy net to fashion a tutu. It was a source of hidden merriment in our house when the tiny dancers lined up for the first time in their homemade costumes at dress rehearsal. "Made from the same pattern!" my mother would hoot. Some of the leotards would be cut high at the crotch, some drooped, and some ended at the knees. An unlucky few wore thigh-length outfits. No matter, each mother was PROUD!

Again, I have no information how or when Leota learned costume design and pattern making. I suspect that Emile needed a costume designer for his stage shows and Mom stepped up and started doing it. When we three girls were all in high school and going to parties and dances, we all would travel to St. Louis on the bus and shop the department stores for formal gowns. Mother would have the outfits "charge-sent" which meant the packages would be delivered to our home in Illinois sans Missouri sales tax. She would meticulously copy each outfit, often in almost identical material as the original, then travel back to the St. Louis department store with the dresses carefully tissued and folded in their original wrappings, to return them for a full credit. None of us would consent to go with her on these "return" trips for we *knew* the salesclerks would know by looking at our guilty fourteen year old faces that we had never had an intention to BUY the clothes, our mother was just going to copy them. Like all teenagers, we were sure our Mother was the only home seamstress to do such a thing!

Miss Virginia played the piano for all the dancing classes. She could slow down the tempo or speed up to keep pace with uncertain or confused chorus lines. Her skill in emphasizing the BEAT of the music helped countless lip-counting tiny hoofers end up together, *almost* in step. By popular demand, Dad was the primary instructor although Miss Louise, a former pupil, helped with some of the beginner and ballroom classes.

The East St. Louis Studio was on Broadway and classes were held each Saturday. The four of us took turns helping each week. We'd catch the bus with Dad from the corner at the end of our block in Belleville and ride to the Studio in East St. Louis. Dad called us his "office manager for the day" and we were entrusted to answer the phone with "Buchmann School of Stage Dancing" and to keep the roll-call roster of classes. We were paid a dime for a full Saturday, but the treat of going to lunch at the White Castle hamburger stand with Dad and Miss Virginia and riding a half hour each way with him on the bus were the real payoffs.

The Big Band era of the late 1930s and early 40s found America swinging and swaying in ballrooms across the country. Ever sensitive to popular trends, the Buchmann School of Stage Dancing dropped its emphasis on "tap and toe" and offered ballroom dancing classes for teens and adults. Seventh graders were signed up, sweaty palms and all, to learn the fox trot, waltz and tango. My sisters and I were what Dad called "universal partners" which meant we were not supposed to dance with the most popular nor the best dancers in the class. We were assigned to seek out the worst dancers, the least-sought after partners and work with them in the corners of the ballroom hoping to bring them up to the level of the others in the class. Apparently, we weren't always too happy in this role as an entry from the diary I kept when I was fifteen attests:

April 15, 1942
Geeminy......this dancing school business sure isn't what
it's cracked up to be. Dad's got a bunch of asparagus
growers up at the studio and we're supposed to teach them
how to rumba when they hardly know how to count.

Nearby Scott Field, renamed Scott Air Force Base in 1948, is one of the oldest continuous-service Air Force installations in the country. In 1917 the original Scott Field consisted of just less than one square mile. Belleville was a very insular town of about 20,000 in the period between the Wars and there was very little fraternization or mingling between the townspeople and army personnel. The townspeople and the soldiers peacefully coexisted with an unspoken policy of benign indifference. The few "army brats" transported to the local schools were treated as outsiders and largely ignored.

However by 1942 Scott Field was a major Army base. Soldiers on leave poured into the little town of Belleville where there was little entertainment except that afforded at the local corner saloons and two movie theaters. Always alert to the knocking of golden opportunity, Emile met with the local base commander and got permission to hold a series of ballroom dance classes on the Army base. Dad promised to bring partners and to teach the latest dance steps to the soldiers. I remember the first Friday night the classes were to begin. Mother had been on the phone all week to her friends trying to round up twenty or thirty young women to fill the chartered bus Dad had hired to transport his promised "partners" to Scott Field.

"No daughter of mine is going out there to dance with those soldiers even if there is a war on," she heard over and over. Only five of us made the trip, Mom, Dad, my two sisters and I. Emmy and I were barely fourteen and nearly four and a half feet tall. Jeanie was a year younger and about the same size. Dad was undaunted. All of us were wonderful dancers, he told us over and over, and we were to visualize each of those soldiers as a potential Fred Astaire.

Waiting for the dancing professor and the promised dancing partners were over one hundred young soldiers. And into the huge army field house walked my dad and mother with their three underage scrawny daughters. I'm certain Dad gulped. I know Mom and the three of us did. But with barely a moment's hesitation he introduced us all, divided the group in half and lined the men along each side of the immense room. Dad took center stage and lined up half the group, the ones learning to 'lead,' showing them how to place their right hand 'gently' on the woman's back and exert just a SLIGHT bit of pressure to signal direction and step. The others, dancing backwards in the style of Ginger Rogers, were divided into four groups, each led by mother or one of us. Dad selected a record, cranked up the Victrola, and set the needle in the groove as my sisters and I exchanged a *"What is he thinking?"* look. And the music began. Somehow the soldiers got so caught up in counting the fox trot...and a ONE..and a TWO..and a THREE and a FOUR. . . and the waltz....ONE two, three....ONE two, three, and were so focused on not stumbling or stepping on one another's feet that the two hours flew by. Dad made it fun for them and for us.

The next Saturday morning our phone at home literally rang off the hook. The word was out that Professor Buchmann had taken his OWN wife and his teen-aged daughters out to Scott Field to be dancing partners for the SOLDIERS!

"If he takes his own girls," they'd say. Every unmarried woman, as well as their mothers, was calling to put their name on the list for the next week's excursion. The following Friday Dad filled two busses to go to the army base and, much to our delight, the three of us never had to help with the soldier classes again.

These dancing classes, despite the bizarre startup, turned out to be extremely popular. Dad soon moved the group to his studio in Belleville and ran three classes with one hundred fifty men in each class. Mother masterminded the logistics of getting

Uncle Sam's Nephews at Scott Field Given Chance to Learn How to Dance

Emile Buchmann, head of the Buchmann School of Dancing, has sent out an S O S for girls in East St. Louis, Belleville and other communities in this area to serve as dancing partners for 100 Scott Field soldiers who are learning how to dance — ballroom style. Above left, Buchmann teaches the LaConga with the aid of six Belleville girls.

From Belleville News-Democrat

one group out and the next group in. The men each participated in one-hour shifts and the women "partnered" all three groups.

The rules for participation were strict; no drinking, no pairing off or smooching or even meeting outside after class. Mom had enlisted some of her cronies as chaperones and I remember the classes had the reputation of being as strictly run as a church social. There was no U.S.O. in Belleville until several years later, so Dad's dancing classes were really the main recreation outlet for many young Air Force men and Belleville women. I remember Mom and Dad attended scores of weddings for couples who initially met at the "dancing classes for soldiers" that Professor Buchmann started in 1941.

Leota at the sewing machine in 1943

Leota worked tirelessly to start the Belleville Scott Field Soldiers Sewing room in 1943. Dad had started a series of dance classes for soldiers at Scott Field and of course Mother was his helper. Many of the young men (she calls them "boys" which is what they were) confided in her that they had to pay outrageous sums to a local tailor shop to have their insignias sewn on their uniforms or to have their pants hemmed. She enlisted the help of her bridge club and one of the most worthwhile volunteer services of the war was born: the Belleville/Scott Field Sewing Room. Emmy found a copy of this precious letter from Leota in which she gives instructions to her "ladies" in the Soldiers Sewing Room.

March 1943

Dear Friends and Volunteer Workers,

The committee wants to use this method of communicating with you for it is hard to get to see all of you personally. First, I want to thank you for the splendid job that you are doing. Alone, we could not do this splendid work but together we are doing a worthwhile job. You are all working tirelessly to help the boys and that is the purpose of the Sewing Room.

There are a few standards that the Belleville/Scott Field Activities has always maintained and we would appreciate your cooperation in maintaining them at all times. To avoid any misunderstanding and any hard feelings we would appreciate it if you would read these suggestions carefully and benefit by them and help anyone.

We sell insignias - 15 cents. In sewing on insignia please collect 10 cents before boy leaves so that there will be no errors if new work comes in before he comes back for his coat. Insignia are sewn 1/2 inch from shoulder seam. We do not sell chevrons. They are sewn 4 1/2 Inches from shoulder seam. We do not charge for our services, but we welcome a small donation. You know we are self-supporting and get no money from any fund. Last month we bought over $400 worth of thread. It is easy to tell a boy that there is no charge but if you want to contribute you may drop something in the box. Do not let him give you the money for he may only want to give a small sum and it may embarrass him.

At all times consider the boy first. Especially consider his feelings, remember he is just as much in need of kindness as he is in need of mending. In handling the soldier, speak friendly to him. Please do not speak short and snap him off. He gets orders snapped at him all day long and a change of tone and attitude will help him a lot. Let each soldier feel that you have a personal interest in his problem. When he enters the room greet him friendly and courteously. If any boys show any signs of disrespect handle it very tastefully, do not let him get too friendly and keep him in his place. We will not tolerate any suggestive language. The ears and eyes of the citizens of Belleville are glued on every move so help us stay above any possible criticism.

Let's always maintain harmony among each other. The Committee has been working together in harmony and we have our first quarrel to see. We love our work and when there is a job to do we all pitch in. We welcome help and suggestions from one another and do the things that mean most to the service man.

Volunteers, please welcome newcomers. We often ask folks to come in any day. If it happens you see someone new come in on the day that you are accustomed to working, do not make him or her feel they have walked into a "Frigidaire." Instead, teach them the "tricks of the trade" and make them feel they are one of us. How can we do a big job if we act other than "big"?

REMEMBER:
We are doing a swell job
We are doing it well
We are going to keep on
And make this room heaven for the soldiers and not a --**#---------

Well, you know what I mean.
Here's to 2000 chevrons next week
Yours sincerely,

Leota Buchmann
Belleville/Scott Field Activities Committee

Growing up Belleville

Growing up in the small Midwestern town of Belleville Illinois was wonderful. The population was under 20,000 when I was a kid, and that was counting all the soldiers' wives and families who settled in the town to be close to their servicemen at Scott Field. Belleville had some light industry, a Griesedieck brewery (we called it the 'beer-y'), a stove manufacturer and a couple of shoe factories, but it was considered a bedroom town for nearby St. Louis. For ten cents round trip, we could take a twenty to thirty minute ride down Main Street, past Signal Hill through East St. Louis and across the Mississippi bridge to downtown St. Louis. The local custom was that once a child turned twelve, he or she was considered old enough to ride the bus unaccompanied by an adult. As I rarely went anywhere without my twin sister, we rode together on our twelfth birthday.

The bus stop in St. Louis was at the downtown Farmer's Market in a big shed-type building. We had to walk through the Market to get to the department stores. I have no idea what in the world we shopped for; we certainly didn't have any money with us other than bus fare and lunch money. We always ate lunch at the Forum, which was the first automated food restaurant we had ever seen. I remember standing in wonderment, staring at the selections behind the little glass doors and finally making a choice, inserting my nickel and watching as the partition magically slid up, allowing me to (quickly) slide out the plate before it slammed down again. We were allowed to go to St. Louis about once a month. I know that I have never felt quite so grown up as I did on those trips.

Regionally, Belleville is considered a "German" or "kraut" town although it was founded by a Frenchman, George Blair (hence the French name 'Belle Ville,' beautiful city). My grandmother, and her parents before her, lived on Church Street, an older neighborhood of simple brick cottages known locally as "German street houses" since the front doors opened directly onto the street or, occasionally, the sidewalks. The great German migration to the Illinois area began in 1833 and by 1834 many had settled in the Belleville area. These early German settlers were intellectual and scholarly men; many of them graduates of fine German universities. As they settled the Belleville community, they founded cultural outlets similar to those left behind in their homeland. By 1836, residents established the Belleville Public Library, the oldest in the state, predating the Illinois State Library by three years. The Germans also organized choral and dramatic groups and literary societies. The Belleville Philharmonic musical society, founded by German settlers in 1864, is the second oldest philharmonic orchestra in the country.

As in many small German communities, the public schools were a source of great pride. My mother and both her parents were born in Belleville and told of their grade school education when many of their classes were held in German. German language classes were compulsory in the grade schools until shortly before WWI when anti-German sentiment escalated in the area.

But my story is set in the 1930s and 40s. There were two great grade-school holidays, Field Day and the School Picnic. A city proclamation on June 18, 1858 decreed "This is the Picknick Day of all the free schools" and this Holiday continues today, making it reportedly the nation's oldest such tradition. None of us could sleep the night before the School Picnic. First the Parade. Parades were a big part of our lives back then. We would dress up in our best party-dresses with hats made of some kind of construction paper or tarlatan. I imagine there was a certain degree of competition among the teachers as to which class had the most attractive head-wear. Hundreds of grade-schoolers would march down Main Street and around the Public Square

and fountain and then mill around until our parents claimed us for the ride out to the park. At the park, our families would stake out a shady spot, throw down a blanket and begin unpacking the picnic baskets. I'm sure this was a great time for visiting for them also, but for us kids it was a time to RUN FREE. We would tear around the park, running, chasing, hiding, tagging, and when we got tired, we'd just go back to where our families had thrown down their blankets.

Field Day was usually scheduled two weeks before the School Picnic. And of course there was a Field Day parade also, same route but this time we would all be clad in shorts and colored shirts. I think our school, Bunsen, wore red. For weeks every grade school would stage tryouts for the Field Day track and field events. Even though there were organized teams, every child had to compete in some event at their grade level. Emmy and I usually made the Bunsen School relay race team; we were small and could run like the wind. I remember spending many warm May evenings practicing sprints and passing the baton on the street in front of our house. Since every child had to participate in at least three events, we also learned to broad jump and high jump. It didn't matter how expert any of us was really, we were "on the team." Field Day had to be a masterpiece of organization, hundreds of kids jumping and running and yelling and cheering. At noon we'd eat our sack lunches under a tree with our class and then, after a short rest on the grass, resume our jumping and running and yelling and cheering. Looking back, I suspect it was a lot more fun for us kids than it was for our teachers.

BIG TURNOUT: People turned out in their finest to watch Belleville's school children and bands march around the Public Square in 1938. It was already a tradition.

1938 School parade- photo by Belleville News-Democrat

Marching bands were big in Belleville. My brother, Sonny, is musically gifted but the three of us are not. We do have rhythm, and we learned to read music through countless agonizing hours at the piano keyboard, but we all wanted to march in the parades, so we joined the bands. The first time I saw the Broadway musical, 'Music Man' I laughed out loud, for that is surely the method we used to learn our instruments.

The folks bought Sonny a set of drums. He is the only one of us who continued in music and he played with a couple of dance bands all through his high school years. Alan Dixon, our former Senator from Illinois, played trumpet in one of them and the boys held their practice sessions in Dixon's garage. Mother and Dad weren't willing to buy instruments for the three of us; we always thought it was because it would have been too expensive, but I believe now they knew that none of us had any talent. The Belleville High School band offered "loaners" so that determined which instrument we learned to play. I chose the oboe, Emmy had to take a clarinet and Jeanie got a French horn.

The oboe is a double-reed instrument with simple fingering, but complex tonguing. It is traditionally the instrument that tunes the orchestra, sounding a "clear bright true middle C." So here I was, tone deaf, trying to sound a "clear bright true middle C" and not having a clue how close I was blowing. I practiced hard and I learned the music and, since I was the only oboe in the high school orchestra, I was essential. When I was a sophomore, Jane Kurrus came to BTHS from Signal Hill and she played the oboe also. Her playing was as ragged as mine, but I had seniority, so I stayed first chair. We became firm friends. We knew how bad we were, but nobody else seemed to mind. The oboe is one instrument that sort of blends into the orchestral sound, so other than the crucial tuning with the "clear bright true middle C" and an occasional two-bar solo trill, our poor playing didn't really affect the over-all sound. The next year, a young oboist named Harvey Imber joined the band. Harvey was an excellent musician and on Challenge Day he quickly bumped both of us down to where we belonged. Challenge Day was always dreadful. Each "chair" was allowed to challenge the musician in the higher chair. Jane never challenged me, probably to save both of us the public humiliation of having to 'solo' in front of the entire orchestra. When I was notified that Harvey was challenging me for the first chair, I really wanted to feign illness, leave town, any excuse not to go to school that day. My dad would not allow that so I went to band practice and simply conceded my chair rather than play. I feigned grace, which was better than humiliation. Jane, however, was not so easily assuaged. "We've had these chairs for two years," she was now bumped down to third chair. "Remember, after all, he's only a freshman." We hatched a plan.

The band customarily played for high school assemblies. On the fateful day, the music selected featured a two bar oboe solo, by Harvey of course. We surreptitiously inked in two flats on the treble clef of his score, changing the key from C to B flat.

Yes, I am ashamed of my sixteen-year-old self, as is Jane. Possibly there may come a day when Jane and I are held accountable for our adolescent creative meanness and we shall be forced to 'fess up.' Until that time, we are content to let it remain one of those slightly wicked nostalgic stories of our high school days.

The twins in the high school band around 1942.

Carl and Jeanie in Junior High band.

From the *"Bellevinois"* 1943

Band

Dear Jean, Please don't forget to will me your horn. Jean Fick

DIRECTOR	Rosemary Edwards	Leroy Muskopf
Edwin Peters	Thomas Ervin	Arnold Mueller
	Bob Fietsam	Marian Nold
DRUM MAJORETTES	Orville Frishcorn	Lavon Paule
	Donald Gamble	James Pflasterer
Katherine Boyd	Robert Gardner	John Rothweiler
Edith Marsh	Marjorie Gemin	Helen Ross
Shirley Jean Peters	William Grommet	Verna Rauschkolb
Arline Ward	Dorothy Graves	Harold Rutter
Ethel Wegner	Helen Mae Grossart	Webster Schott
	Jean Grossman	Joyce Schleicher
DRUM MAJORS	Louis Grossman	Donald Sexton
Wayne Kissel	Robert Guest	Robert Shurtleff
Tom Wainwright	Paul Hass	Elizabeth Storck
	Paul Hassler	Virgil Stock
Doris Austin	Tom Harrison	Charlotte Straub
Jean Abshier	Joyce Heinemann	Lloyd Straub
Doris Bedwell	August Hoeflinger	David Thompson
Don Blanchard	Jean Iberg	Vanna Thorman
Phyllis Bond	Robert Jack	Jack Tebbenhoff
Ralph Brown	Donald Kern	James Thurgate
Ralph Budde	Kenneth Krause	Russell Viehman
Carl Buchmann	Betty Krummrich	Vernon Vogt
Emmy Lee Buchmann	Jane Kurrus	Opal Walthes
Rose Marie Buchmann	Walter Malzahn	Robert Wehrman
Lois Jean Buchmann	Jeanette Meckfessel	Edward Wirth
June Crockett	George Mercurio	Franklin Williams
Dorothy Davis	William Mertz	Norman Wright
Pat Dennis	Clarence Meyer	Robert Wright
Eugene Dill	Robert Mentzer	Harold Yung
Robert Dick		

The high school band plays for all of the home football games, the basket ball tournament, parades, patriotic rallies, concerts at Scott Field, Fairview Sanitorium, school assemblies and school music department programs. It sponsors a Military Ball annually which is one of the high lights of the social affairs on the campus.

Everyone appreciates the band.

[77]

The Barber Scissors of Henry X

We live, not by things, but by the meaning of things. It is needful to transmit the passwords from generation to generation.
Antoine de St.-Exupery, Generation to Generation

The fraying yellowed twine secures my thumb; my fingers seek their place. I pulled these ancient barber scissors from the bathroom cabinet on "C" Street the day of my father's funeral. My brother and sisters  were downstairs tending to Mom and the last of the many neighbors and friends who'd come to pay their last respects. I'd wandered upstairs, unwilling yet to let him go, touching his clothes, his books, wanting some final contact.

"Conjuror" is etched on the shank of these scissors that were brought to America, from the Alsatian town of Rosenwiller in 1884, by my grandfather, Henry X. In his My Memoirs, dictated to his daughter Marie in 1925, Henry X relates that at the age of sixteen:

> ". . . *my father put me to a little town about 7 miles from our home to learn the cabinet maker trade by Albert Keckmann, an expert in that line; after 2 years apprenticeship I was learned out and made my examination with honors to my master, as well as to my parents." That year I had to be ready at any time for a call in case I was needed during that year. After*

the year was expired I asked for permission to go to America, that was in 1884 in April. I got the permission but with the understanding that I work for the Fatherland while in America in case of war. German Army. I could not get any work as a cabinet maker in St. Louis and being I was the company barber in the Army, so I tried that trade and found a job at Fourth and Spruce Street for a weekly wage of one whole dollar after 3 weeks there I left and went to work for a Charles Feb, 2718 Chouteau Ave. There I had a little more, got $3.50, board and wash a week and room. In October 1884 I became the boss of the barbershop at 1012 Geyer Avenue."

I remember my Dad, Emile Henry, third child, third son, telling tales of sweeping up the Geyer Avenue barber shop after school and sometimes getting to rinse and shelve the men's moustache cups. The barbershops were sold before any of us were born. Henry X held to the "old country" belief that owning property was the surest way to prosperity so he used the proceeds from the sale of the three barber shops to buy a succession of four-family flats in south St. Louis.

There are four children in my family, born within two and a half years of one another. When we were all teen-agers we would joke that "four kids in two and a half years" was the reason my dad left the Catholic Church. We all thought this was hilarious; oddly enough, Dad did not find it amusing. My twin sister and I, Rose Marie and Emmy Lee, are the oldest, my sister, Lois Jean is almost exactly a year younger and my brother, Carl Emile, is eighteen months younger than she. Carl was called "Sonny" from the day he was born until years later when he joined the Marine Corps rising to the rank of full Colonel. He convinced us then that Marines are definitely never, not ever, called "Colonel Sonny."

Dad learned barbering from his father, Henry X. Dad would position the four of us on chairs around the kitchen table. We knew to sit quietly until our turn on the kitchen stool which served as the barber chair. One time it would be "oldest to

Emile learns the barber trade from Henry X

youngest" and the next round, "youngest to oldest." This rotation was important to my brother and me; we were, after all, the youngest and the oldest, but didn't mean much to the two in the middle. The joy of being first was that you were allowed to leave the scene of torture and didn't have to "sit still and be quiet" while awaiting your turn.

Dad would fasten the kitchen towel around my neck, and pick up his weapons, the trusty "Conjuror" scissors and a tortuous hard-rubber comb. Eyes were all we were allowed to move. One twitch or wiggle and WHAP with the hard rubber comb. "SIT STILL PLEASE" and we all four sat frozen still. I remember the itch of the cut hair on my neck and the misery when a shorn strand landed on my nose. I'd try to dislodge it by blowing "up and around" while Dad worked to even out my Dutch boy bob at the back. My sisters and brother would be squirming and giggling on their chairs anticipating his next WHAP to my head with the dreaded rubber comb.

I took those old barber shears home with me that sad day almost fifty years ago, along with wonderful memories of my grandfather Henry X and father Emile. When the frayed, yellow twine secures my thumb and my fingers find their places along its curved handle, I feel a wondrous connection to them both.

I remember my 'magic muscle memory' anticipation when I lined up my three oldest children for their first 'Buchmann style home-haircuts.' "I'm the third generation of hair cutters in this family," I tell them. "Youngest to oldest this time. SIT STILL PLEASE." I adjust the shears in my hand. - -Were Dad's and grandfather's thumbs as small as mine? I snip away. Just as I'd envisioned, the generational knowledge clicked in and the scissors snip, cut and trim perfectly, exactly as they were forged to do so long ago in that tiny village in far away France.

Family Hair

Ever since I gave up my Dutch-boy bob at age eight, my hair has been the bane of my existence, my 'cross-eyed bear.' Dad had gorgeous hair. I remember it as snow-white and wavy, but photos of him in his 30s and 40s show him with thick dark curls. He would tell us that as a young boy he hated his corkscrew curly hair. Hoping to straighten it, he would grease his head with Vaseline and sleep in a tight stocking cap.

Mother's hair was like thread, or soft wispy cloud tissue. It was thin and mousy-brown although, even at the age of eighty-six, she was proud that not one of the few hairs on her head was gray. As kids we learned to braid on those thin brown strands. She would sit patiently still while we each parted and combed and folded three long stringy plaits. When Mom discovered wigs at about age seventy, she was transformed. She never quite mastered the art of putting the wig on straight and the grandkids delighted in whispering, "Grandma, your hair's on crooked." She'd tip that wig a little more forward or sideways....no mirrors for her...and grin, delighted with herself.

When we girls were in eighth grade we would twist our hair into tight buns and secure them with long skinny soft leather strips that looked like shriveled up sausages. Later, in high school, softer styles were popular so we would use large pieces of cloth, rag rollers we called them, to achieve a soft wave. We all copied Hollywood hairstyles so when actresses with a front pompadour roll and long straight side hair appeared on the silver screen, we adapted our rag-rolling technique to achieve the same look. Some of my friends had hair long enough to straighten with a flatiron. Our mother would never have let us iron our hair, even if we could have grown enough hair to flatten across the ironing board. "You'll burn yourselves," I can hear her screech.

Pin curls came next. I learned to sleep with my head twisted on the pillow to dodge the stab of the hairpins, and later flat bobby pins. We washed our hair once a week at the most and I don't remember using any special soap or shampoo. Conditioners and crème rinses were still far in the future, although I do remember one of mother's friends recommending something called 'Tincture of green soap' and Mother buying a small bottle for the four of us to share.

Each afternoon, as soon as we got home from high school, we would pin up our hair. Mother and my brother knew they were to speak loudly, "Oh, hello Stan," to greet any of the numerous high school boys who might drop by after football practice. Hearing this, all three of us would leap up the stairs, "take our hair down" and saunter casually down to the kitchen. It's a tribute to this basic early warning system that not once, not ever, did any of the three of us get caught with our hair up in pin curls. Truthfully, in those simple days, we would have said, "hairs up." Not until I left for college did I learn the word was singular.

Marriage brought further complications to the hair maintenance routine. How to maintain the romance of the marriage bed with hair twisted into ringlets and secured flat on my head with bobby pins? Thus began the Saturday morning beauty parlor ritual. I had a standing appointment sandwiched between two of my best friends and our morning was three-quarters social event and one-quarter beauty care. We traded the names of new stylists as we did recipes and child-care tips. Our "hair-men" (that is what we called them) were as vital to our lives as our obstetricians. We'd follow them from one salon to another, knowing all the while that some of them were terrible snobs. I learned many years later that there was a hot rivalry between two well-known 'parlors' as to which "did" the most prestigious heads for any important social event. It's difficult now to imagine Springfield, Illinois as it was in the early 50s; provincial, politically conservative, self-contained, self-satisfied, smug. The banks were small and locally owned. We always wore hats and gloves when we went 'downtown' to shop at Bressmers, Barkers and Rolands. Franklin Life was relatively new in town, the telephone company had not established a downstate office, no Horace Mann, no medical school, no Lincoln Land, no Sangamon State or the University of Illinois at Springfield (UIS).

Those were the days of "big hair." I could have my hair done on Saturday morning, teased, sprayed and lacquered, and with much judicious picking at it with a chopstick like tool and some careful positioning on the pillow as I slept, I could keep it presentable until my return to the beauty parlor the next week. I truly don't think I shampooed my own hair between Labor Day and Memorial Day for twenty years.

Did the Women's Liberation Movement bring us hair liberation as well? Maybe it was simply serendipity but when my generation, trapped for years as slaves to our hairstyle, discovered that short cuts, the natural look and blow-dryers were in and teased salon-ed hair was out, we too shouted, "Free at last. Free at last."

The Age of Innocence

I had eleven best friends. Two of them were my sisters. In 1939, the local Lincoln Theater announced the premiere showing of "Gone With the Wind." The movie ran almost two and a half hours and, as it was reported in the local newspaper, Clark Gable as Rhett Butler used language "not fit to print in this family newspaper." We were wild to go. The party lines buzzed and, finally, most of our mothers agreed that we could attend the Saturday matinee showing of the film. In those days movies ran continuously, with only newsreels and cartoons separating a rerun of the main feature. We ALWAYS sat through movies at least twice, which would mean a five-hour session at the movies.

I can't remember if popcorn was a staple at theaters in those days. I don't think so. Even if it had been available, none of us would have been allowed to buy it. So our mothers packed us each a wax paper wrapped bologna sandwich and we were off to see "Gone With the Wind." We sat through it THREE times that afternoon and evening and I can still remember my quick intake of breath each time Clark said to Scarlet "Frankly my dear, I don't give a DAMN"- - - -how deliciously shocking that was!

By the time we were fourteen we had acquired some knowledge of the world. Basically, what we knew for sure was that if we "did it" our fathers would kill us. It was not until years later that we ever figured out what "it" was - - - and longer still before any of us ever actually "did it." After a formal dance when we were seniors, we had a sleep-over at Jane Kurrus's home in

Signal Hill. She had a big house with a huge dormitory loft in the attic. Our dates took us to Jane's house where we'd all change into blue jeans and gather in the kitchen for soda and snacks. Her Dad would bring coat racks from his funeral home so that we could hang up our ball gowns (that's what we called the tulle and taffeta creations our mothers had sewn). This particular evening Evie Schneider repeatedly asked each of us when we would be ready to go to upstairs to bed. With winks and nods and whispers of 'something important to tell us,' she finally convinced us that we needed to politely say goodnight to Jane's parents and retire.

It was after two a.m before the twelve of us finally straggled to the attic loft. "Who has the sex book?" Evie asked. The sex book was important to our little group for it was our only source of vital information. I can still quote the pertinent passage verbatim. After ten pages extolling the sanctity of the sexual act and marriage (no separation here, the sexual act and marriage were synonymous) the book graphically described the culmination as "two reeds waving together in the moonlight." That was what we knew. "Well," said Evie, whose older sister Marie had just become a bride, "it's not like that at all."

Then she told us what her sister had told her. "She did that? On her wedding night?" The shock of Rhett saying he didn't give a damn was nothing compared to this bombshell! How innocent we were. And how lovely it was. By four in the morning we had sworn a solemn pact:

> *"I solemnly swear that IF I ever do THAT on my wedding night, I will send a postcard with 'I DID IT' to every one of you, my special sisters."*

This past September (2005) our high school class held its Sixtieth Reunion. Seven of the surviving eleven of us met for lunch. We talked of our families, our children and grandchildren. We talked of many things, among them how innocent we'd been and how lovely that was and it was mentioned, in passing, that none of us remembered ever receiving (or addressing and mailing) the promised postcard.

Jeane   *Rosie*   *Emmy*

Like Mother Used to Make....NOT

Mom was a terrible cook. I'm not sure I knew this when I was a kid. My grandmother lived a few blocks from us and she did most of the cooking at our house when we kids were growing up. Every Thursday she would bake large pans of cloverleaf rolls. I can remember racing home from school those days in anticipation of the yeasty kitchen smell and the first taste of the rolls as they came out of the warm oven. Sometimes, in the summer, she would let us roll the dough into small even balls and put three together to form the cloverleaf. It always seemed magical to me when she would let us peek into the oven to watch the fat globs of dough puff up into the rolls. "Belleville Grandma" was Mother's mother and "St. Louis Grandma" was Dad's mother. We called them by those full names, for clarification I suppose, although as far as I recall they were never in the same place at any given time.

Belleville Grandma would tolerate no one in the kitchen while she cooked, and she cooked for us every day. She would use "every pot in the kitchen" according to my mother, and then trot back to her cozy clean apartment, leaving the cleaning up for mom and us kids. We rarely ate poultry for my father didn't like it. Back then, chickens didn't come on foam trays wrapped in plastic. The local farmers would cruise the neighborhoods with a truck full of live birds and my grandmother would select a choice one. She'd swing it around by the neck to kill it and then chop off its head with a hatchet. Sometimes the chicken would hop around after its head was off and we kids would madly chase it around the yard, imitating its wild hopping. My brother liked to help pluck the feathers after Grandma dipped the bird in a tub of scalding water, but we girls always scampered away, grossed out by the next scenario when she'd shove her hands up the chicken's back end, pulling out its guts.

My mother would go into the kitchen sporadically and say, "Now remember, mother, Emile does not like the gizzards to be in the gravy." Grandma would mutter, "He'll never notice, I'm chopping them real small this time." The fact that he always noticed and always picked them out didn't seem to make much of an impression on my grandmother. She continued to put the gizzards in the gravy; mother continued to tell her not to put the gizzards in the gravy and my father continued to pick the gizzards out of the gravy. I guess this was what one might call a family tradition.

Belleville Grandma did most of the cooking for our family while we kids were at home. She died in 1945 when all four of us were away at college, so none of us had any experience with my mother's cooking until we were adults. Thanksgiving was her big challenge and the operative words were "more is better." If any of us, grandkids included, ever casually mentioned that we liked a specific vegetable, it would earn a permanent spot on subsequent menus. Six or seven vegetable dishes were the norm. She cooked all fresh vegetables by the "cooking off" method. This had to be her own invention for I have never heard the term used before or since. Mother's interpretation of "cooking off" involved boiling the vegetables for an hour or so the night before the dinner (just until they lost all flavor and color) then she would store them in the refrigerator to be reheated for the next day's meal. All the vegetables tasted and looked the same; most of them were grayish-green and indistinguishable from one another.

Mother liked everyone to comment on every dish, so that if one of us would say, "this cranberry relish is particularly good," she would look around and say, "well, what about the mashed potatoes?" and after we'd all say we had never tasted mashed potatoes quite like those, she would pause, take another bite, and say, "well, you haven't said anything about the lima beans." We kids still use her line today; it simply is not acceptable in our families to praise just one element of a meal. Someone will always say, "Well what about the mashed potatoes?" and the rest of us will double up with glee, remembering our dear mother and her struggles in the kitchen.

The wonderful part of this story is that all of us, adult children and grandchildren alike, loved to go to Belleville for Thanksgiving. Mom would be peeking out the front window waiting for us to arrive and as soon as she'd spy our cars turn onto "C" street, she'd dash out on the front porch and stand there waving and literally jumping up and down with excitement. Who cared about rubbery turkey, greasy gravy, 'cooked-off' vegetables or tough pie crusts when mother was so thrilled to see us she was jumping up and down on the front porch before we managed to climb out of our car.

(HOWEVER, her Easter rabbit cookies were wonderful!!)

Grandma's Easter Rabbit Cookies

3 cups flour   Mix like dough
2 teaspoons baking powder
1 cup butter
Beat Well

3 eggs
1 1/4 cups sugar
Mix all
Roll to 1/4 inch.
Bake 325   8 minutes
ICING: 1 lb.powder sugar, 3 teaspoons butter,
juice of lemon
red-hots for eyes

Leaving for College

Like most German communities, Belleville took great pride in its outstanding school system. Emmy and I entered public kindergarten shortly before our fourth birthday. Apparently the state of Illinois had no age regulations for entry into first grade, so students were permitted to enter kindergarten whenever they wished. I've never been completely certain if that was an established policy or if it was simply an expedient 'Buchmann interpretation.' There remains a possibility that we were allowed to start school at such an early age either because:

1. We met some loose achievement standard (we did know our colors).
2. The kindergarten teacher and the first and second grade teachers were all my mother's first cousins.
3. When we were four years of age, Jeanie was only three and Sonny was eighteen months old, and mother needed HELP!

Just our luck, when we were ready to move up to first grade, the state of Illinois required that students be within a few months of their sixth birthdays. We were barely five after our first year of kindergarten so we were HELD BACK. A blot on our academic records for sure and one that subsequent generations find extremely amusing.

Back then, students were sorted into regular (entering in September) and midyear (entering in January) classes according to birth-dates. Our February third birthday put us in a midyear class, slated for high school graduation in January of 1945. Reviewing our high school transcripts in our junior year, we discovered that by adding a couple of extra classes during the remaining semesters, we could finish high school a semester early and go through graduation in June of 1944. Dad was ecstatic. He reasoned that if the two of us could graduate early, he would gain a six-month grace period before Jeanie, also a February child, graduated in January of 1946. He'd have a full year and a half of paying only two college tuitions, before he started paying for three of us.

Dad wanted us to go to Washington University in St. Louis, a topnotch institution that offered us both full tuition scholarships. In the 1940s, at least in the Buchmann household, the operative term was 'Father Knows Best' but in this instance Emmy and I dug in our heels. No way were we going to live at home in Belleville and ride the bus to St. Louis to go to college.

Going to college, we argued, meant going AWAY to college. "OK," said Dad in, for him, an astonishing compromise, "if you don't want to live at home and go to Washington University, then maybe you both can work for a year and save up enough money to help out with room and board charges somewhere else." Panic time. We both KNEW that if we stayed home and worked for a year, as practical a solution as that might be, the chances of us getting to college after that year were between slim and none.

Several weeks later, surely in answer to our frenzied prayers, Dad got a letter from a Dr. Brewer asking if he could visit us in Belleville to explore the possibility that we might both like to attend James Millikin University in Decatur. He told Dad that the university had received our high school test scores and that he wanted to meet us. I remember peeking through the front door curtain to watch portly Dr. Brewer trot up our concrete porch steps. We discounted his slightly threadbare brown suit and his rumpled, soiled white shirt. We saw him as our savior, our knight in shining armor. Dad introduced himself and the two of us to Dr. Brewer and we chatted in the front hallway for a few minutes. Then, surprising to me even now, Dr. Brewer said he would like to speak to Dad alone, and the two of us went into the kitchen for a nervous thirty minutes drinking sugared hot tea with Mother and Jeanie and Sonny.

When we thought we could not stand the suspense for another second, Dad and Dr. Brewer came out from behind closed doors, both grinning conspiratorially. "Congratulations eggs," Dad said. (Why did he always call us 'eggs'.... surely a term of endearment, but one I haven't come across anywhere else?) "Dr. Brewer has just made it possible for you both to go to Millikin this fall on full tuition and room and board scholarships. AND you both have part-time jobs at the campus library to earn your spending money." No wonder Dad was grinning. Dr. Brewer no longer looked like a knight in shining armor, he was now elevated to Saint status in our eyes. What a wonderful answer to all of our prayers.

We learned later that our high math scores were what brought the Millikin recruiter to our door. Interestingly, when we registered that fall, we both declared ourselves as mathematics majors. That's why Millikin wanted us in the first place, we were good at math. The freshman academic advisor looked at us and said, "But girls don't do math." This was 1944. So Emmy and I, conditioned to 'Father Knows Best,' said, "OK, maybe we should be English majors?" And we were.

In the summer of 1944, before we were to leave for Millikin, Mother sewed each of us a campus wardrobe. Her motto was "mix and match" so we each had a red wool skirt with a red bolero jacket and a black and white checked skirt with a more tailored and buttoned checked jacket. The jackets and skirts harmonized and, she reasoned, gave us four outfits for the price of two. She stitched several white blouses, my favorite had long sleeves and soft white ruching around the V-neckline and cuffs. She made us each a pleated yellow and tan plaid skirt and we actually *bought* yellow wool sweaters to complete that outfit. These were the days of war-time gas rationing and I remember that Dad conserved his A-coupon allotment all summer so that in September he could drive us to Union Station in St. Louis for the train ride to Millikin and Decatur. We were beside ourselves with excitement. We each had received a small maroon and tan suitcase as a high school graduation present. The suitcases were small by today's standards, but our new wardrobes and the other things we were taking to campus fit into them easily.

I remember the ride over to St. Louis. Mother and the other kids must have been in school (colleges started in late September in those days) and Dad and the two of us piled into his old Plymouth. I think I sat in the front seat and Emmy squeezed in the back with the two suitcases. We'd never been on a train before and here we were going to Union Station to take the train to begin our new lives. I'm sure we both babbled on and on, for I don't remember Dad talking very much if at all. Union Station was enormous, but Dad knew his way around.

He bought our tickets and walked with us to the train platform. We kissed and hugged him goodbye and started walking down the long ramp to the coach car. I looked back to wave one last time and was astonished to see tears streaming down his face. I'd never seen my Dad cry. Emmy and I were surprised and maybe a little embarrassed by his emotional response to our boarding the train. We couldn't understand why he was crying; we knew he was thrilled with our scholarships to Millikin. What was his problem? Not until I took my own firstborn to enroll at Kenyon College in Ohio, almost thirty years later, did I truly understand why our Dad was crying in Union Station that long ago September day.

June 1948 Millikin graduates

Uncle Herb

I have fond memories of my Uncle Herb, mother's older brother. In our family, each of us was fortunate to be the favorite of one or another of my parent's relatives. Sonny, the only son, the "King" as we all referred to him, was unabashedly Mother's darling. I shone in the eyes of Uncle Herb; Jeanie was the pet of "Belleville Grandma" (Mother's mother) and Emmy

was the favorite of Aunt Roma (Mother's younger sister). These special relationships were accepted as one's birthright and we all e n j o y e d t h e m immensely.

Herbert Augustus Grombach was born in Belleville in 1895. He was a prankster, a joker, Huckleberry Finn and Peter Pan rolled into one. He married in 1929, although his wife Sada played a very minor role in our lives as, I suspect, she did in Uncle Herb's. Herb and Sada had no children. His main joy in life was being with the four of us. And if he could torment or tease my mother at the same time, he considered himself a great success. He knew he could always get a rise out of her by lying prone on the floor with his arms across his chest and calling to us, " You kids want to see how I'll look when I'm laid out?" I can still hear my mother's disgusted, "Herb, really, won't you ever grow up."

Herb was in the first contingent of men drafted from Belleville in WWI according to articles in the Belleville Daily Advocate dated July 30 and September 18, 1917. The paper reports that the first local draftees, Herb among them, left on the L&N railroad for Camp Taylor, Kentucky early one Sunday morning in September. An article from the Daily Advocate of July 12, 1919 tells us that:

> *Herbert Grombach, Aloys Bertelsman and William Becker who were overseas with the American Expeditionary Forces have returned home.*

Little factual family lore survives about Herb's military service. Our favorite story, and one he told over and over was of how he single handedly got the German forces to surrender in World War I. He was in the trenches in France (that part was true) and he'd tell us how he found a huge hunk of Limburger cheese and stuffed it into the back pocket of his uniform pants. At this point in the story he'd get up and strut across the kitchen, his butt stuck out, so we could picture the chunk of cheese with its aroma permeating the German's front-line trenches and air space. "Those Krauts couldn't stand the Limburger cheese smell so they surrendered to me right then and there," he'd tell us. That part, of course, was not true! We all believed this story for years. He was our childhood hero.

We called him our 'drunken uncle' but I doubt that he was actually drunken. He was garrulous, high-spirited and never met a stranger. He liked to drink beer and hang out with his storytelling buddies at the local corner saloon. When he could come up with a convincing story for Mother, he'd take Emmy and me with him for the afternoon. He'd lift us up and we'd do a soft-shoe on the long wooden bar. I am certain Mother never knew her twins were tap dancing on a bar, Saloon Queens at the age of three.

I vividly remember waking up one Sunday morning to the unmistakable bleat of a goat. We raced downstairs and there, tied to the old cherry tree in the backyard was a baby billy goat with a big red bow and a tag that read "For Sonny" tied around its neck. Before we even started for the back door Mom was on the phone, **"Herb, you come over here RIGHT NOW and take that goat out of here!"** My brother was inconsolable and his plaintive cry, " A guy can't even have a goat around here" was a family catch line for years.

Uncle Herb was my favorite family correspondent. He moved to Tacoma Washington in 1940 and we wrote back and forth regularly. I would write him a long letter and, almost by return mail, I would get a one-page answer on lined notebook paper:

> *"Hello Honey. How are you?   I am fine.*
> *Liked your letter. Love, Herb."*

And then of course I owed him a return letter. We all joked that he had his responses ready to mail when he walked to the mailbox to pick up our letters. Herb was equally predictable on the telephone. He called from the Pacific Time Zone, so the two hour time difference usually meant a late Friday or Saturday night call after he'd been out carousing with his buddies. To make a long distance call in those days one would place the call with the operator and then deposit a specific amount for a three-minute call. The calls were predictable. He'd say, "Hi Honey, how are you?" I'd say, "Hi Herb, how are you?" he'd get in another sentence or two until the operator would cut in with "Your three minutes are up." And he'd say, "Bye Honey." As communications, those phone calls were about as informative as his letters. However I always knew that the contact, not the content, was the important link between Uncle Herb and me.

Herb died suddenly in 1955. He was a cattle rancher and was delivering a herd of cattle to Burlington Washington when he was stricken and taken to a physician's office where he died of an apparent heart attack. I adored my Uncle Herb and miss him to this day.

This 'Shimmy Poem' by my good friend and mentor, Jacqueline Jackson, appeared in the Springfield Illinois Times on May 1, 2008.

Uncle Herb would have loved it!

Shimmy poem #1
Presented by Jacqueline Jackson

*the letters to my dad at
college exhorted study
frugality morality on this
subject grama sent clippings
a madison pastor saying no
sin among those that over-
whelmed ancient civilizations
is not rampant now this she
underlined and a chicago
proprietor of the midwest's
largest public dancehall said
he would urge all dancehall
operators to ban the shimmy
woddle toddle drag-waltz
shuffle-step tango and cheek-
to-cheek dancing must become*

*sane again **my friend rosie
roach when three she and
her twin sister who now
lives in decatur used to tap
dance on bars didn't tell mom
they were quite a hit daddy
owned a dance studio** I bet
they knew the woddle the
toddle the cheek-to-cheek*

Carl remembers

When I was in Jr. High School, the craze among high school girls was to have a bleached stripe of some sort in their hair. I remember my sisters trying it out on my hair first. They would put bleach in my hair and then dry it by having me stick my head in the oven. It worked.

I remember going to St. Louis to visit grandparents. It was an old house in south part of town, near an open-air market (what we would now call a farmer's market) and a Budweiser plant. It wasn't really a house; it was what we now would call a condo. As many times as I was there, I have no memory of ever walking through the front door of the place. We always sat in the kitchen, which was very large, and there was a wood/coal stove in the kitchen. The furniture in the living room was all covered with plastic. I probably sat in that room two times in my life. I don't recall how often we went there, although it was too much no matter the number. We would go to the city to a movie and stage show, go to Roses Italian restaurant on Franklin Avenue for spaghetti dinner and dad would usually call his parents. I do remember several times when he couldn't get out of going over to the house, and we would have to eat again because Dad did not tell them that we had eaten. Drusilla was, in my mind, a worse cook than Leota.

As I reflect, I always thought Henry X was a little henpecked. When we would visit, Henry X and Dad would go down in the cellar to talk. I also believe it was an opportunity for Henry X to hit the wine a little. I was never included in those chats.

I remember being able to con one of my sisters to iron a shirt or trouser when I started to date and didn't have any pressed clothes to wear. This was not often, but Emile was pretty damn strict about who Leota could iron for. This seems to run in the family. He also had a strict rule about never hitting any of the girls. I do not believe I always followed that rule, but when I didn't, I paid the price. I was spanked with a razor strap that always hung on the bathroom closet door knob. I always thought that it was a very cruel reminder of who was in charge. I never really had any doubt about that anyway.

I remember mother suffering with my morning paper route as much as I did. This was especially true in the winter time. She would start trying to wake me up about 4:30 a.m. and would stay with me until I was dressed. That was no easy task, because the heat was always turned down at night and it got very cold in the house. When whining about that I can hear Emile say, "that's what the blankets are for." But Leota hung in there until I was dressed and had some food in my belly before the dog and I were released to go forth and earn some money. I used this money to buy my own bicycle, contrary to nasty rumors that have been around for many years.

The girls were not allowed to get a driver's license so they never drove the family car. I had to earn the right to drive the car with various and sundry chores, e.g., cutting grass, washing car, trimming bushes, scrubbing front porch, etc. The slightest deviation was grounds for "no car this weekend."

One of my friends lived on a farm on the edge of town (David Emgee). His parents were quite a bit older than ours. We would take a bus close to the edge of town, walk to the farm, and wait for his parents to go to bed, then push the car out of the garage and down a hill to start it and we had transportation for the night. To my knowledge he never got caught. The other thing we did at the farm was a little more daring and illegal. The only reason I am willing to relate this is that the statute of limitations has already run out. There were five of us in this "group." We would go out in a far pasture, when we knew for sure where Mr. Emgee was, take a smallish size cow, and transport it to the stockyards and sell it. We would than split the proceeds and used the $ for undisclosed expenses (read beer and dates). There must be some significance in the fact that Dave Emgee and I both became lawyers. Again, to my knowledge this remained undetected.   TTYL Carl

Jeanie remembers

After Carl's wedding in 1958, we took Em and the girls back to Philadelphia and while there, Mom baby-sat and Em, Jim, Dad and I took an overnight to New York City over the 4th of July. We did a tremendous amount of stuff in twenty-four hours, but the dinner in Greenwich Village stands out. When the bill came, Dad checked it and told the waiter he'd made a mistake. The waiter was a typical New York haughty waiter and told Dad he had not made a mistake (without even looking at the bill). Dad told him again, and again, and the waiter kept coming back with the same answer. Finally Dad sad, "You've <u>undercharged me</u>." (I think it was a lot.) The waiter of course was flustered, looked at the bill and corrected it and Dad finally paid.

The rest of us sat there in amazement and said, "Why?...you gave him several chances." Dad's simple answer was, "You are either honest or you're not." I think that remark typifies our Dad as much as anything does.

Christmas memories from Emmy (1997)

When I was a child we always celebrated Christmas on December 24th, Christmas Eve. Home was a small German community in southern Illinois, during the 1930s.

I was twenty-one before I realized the rest of the world opened their packages on Christmas morning! To this day there is a certain aura about the night before Christmas for me. As a young married, I struggled to maintain my Christmas Eve traditions, but my husband couldn't adjust so I had to change. I can still hear the bewilderment in his voice when he asked, "but what do you do on Christmas morning?" I would answer, "The parents sleep and the children play with their toys." It seemed so simple!

As children, we hung our stockings on December 6th, the feast day of St. Nicholas, hoping for oranges and candy and dreading the lump of coal left for bad children. After St. Nicholas Day, the parlor doors were covered with sheets and no amount of pleading or "being good" allowed us even a peek.

There are no words to describe the anticipation, the crescendo of excitement building to that one magic moment when all the lights were dimmed, the parlor doors opened and we saw our Christmas tree with the fat old-fashioned bulbs and garish tinsely star for the first time.

The family, Grandmother, Mother and Dad and the four children, lined up outside the parlor door as soon as it became dark. It was oldest to youngest one year and youngest to oldest the next. No one ever forgot whose turn it was and although several of us campaigned for the "middle ones first" it never happened.

The year that is etched in my memory as though it were yesterday is the year Dad created a snowstorm in the fireplace and put a snowsuit on baby Jesus. Long before the advent of Cutex cotton balls and plastic zip-lock bags, my father fashioned tiny snowflakes stringing little wisps of cotton on fragile cotton thread. Did we have scotch tape in the olden days? If not, I still don't know how he managed to hang his make-believe snow strings inside the fireplace opening. Somehow he managed, and then, wonder of wonders, he hid a six-inch oscillating fan behind the crèche to create a gentle snowfall. No matter the snow moved sideways instead of down. Dad was an illusionist, not a realist. For years, I believed it snowed that night in Jerusalem and I wasn't too certain that the snow fell straight down either!

Today's child, weaned on laser light shows and electronic razz-ma-tazz would certainly snicker at my Dad's snow scene. I also smile when I remember, but it is a smile of tenderness and love for the simple pleasures of long ago. I admit it sounds tacky; cotton balls, a six-inch fan and baby Jesus bundled in a snowsuit. But I still get a tug when I think of that magic moment over sixty years ago when the parlor doors opened and it was snowing in the fireplace in Belleville, Illinois.

3rd ANNUAL BUCHMANN REVUE
—With—
THE BUCHMANN TWINS
World's youngest twin acrobats on the stage
LINCOLN THEATRE
THURSDAY, APRIL 19th, 1928
Our Aim:—"Better Than Ev
All Seats 40 Cents

DANCERS — Emylee, Rosemarie and Lois Jean Buchman, daughters of Mr. and Mrs. Emile Buchman, Belleville.

May 1931

The Third Annual
Buchmann Revue
The Buchmann School of The Danse

"ALL PASSES—ART ALONE ENDURES"

Friday, April 27th, 1928
High School Auditorium, East St. Louis, Ill.

By request, Thursday, May 3rd, 1928
Lincoln Theatre, Belleville, Illinois

Entire Production Conceived and Staged by—
Emile H. Buchmann

Costumes—Leota K. Buchmann

Music—Eugene Domserick

We wish to thank all mothers and friends for their kind cooperation

Studios—Belleville, Signal Hill and East St. Louis

IN RECITAL—Rose Marie and Lois Jean Buchman, Stanford Waldman and Emmy Lee Buchman, Belleville.

APRIL 1932

147

Rose Marie   Emmy Lee.

Nov. 1927.

14 Mo. Old.

Jeanie does a handstand

April 1929.

We called him "The King"

Family vacation at the Great Salt Lake in Utah

Jeanie the acrobat

april 1932

Rear   *Herbert*
Center: *Jeanie & Twins*
Front: *Carl & Kenneth*

Camp Robinhood, Green Lake Wisconsin

Summer 1946

Emmy   *Jeane*   *Rosie*

Part Four

1001 Williams Boulevard

Rosie and Bob in Jamaica
November 1, 1978

The photo on the preceding cover page was taken
in ROACH, Missouri, September of 1951.

1001 Williams Boulevard

The Stories:

Home is Where the Heart Sings

Phil Enters First Grade

The Fire, 1966

The Talking Christmas Tree

Mary's Sequel

The Eavesdropping Game

"But There are Rainbows in the Hall"

Home is where the heart sings

Some spaces, some rooms, some houses seem to nourish my soul while others flatten and depress me. The first home we bought at 840 South Lincoln in Springfield is the only house I've lived in that I didn't like. We bought it from my husband's employer. I didn't like him. Their only daughter was a freshman at Millikin when I was a junior. I didn't like her either.

That family, today, would be classified as seriously dysfunctional. Back in the 1950s, we just called them unpleasant. Mr. G. was cold, calculating and cunning. His wife was sly, two-faced and controlling. Their poor daughter was promiscuous, alcoholic and out-of-control. I always felt that their interpersonal ugliness had embedded itself into the walls and woodwork of the house, seeping out when it could.

When my Dad came up to inspect the house with us before we bought it, I remember his saying, "Honey, this house just doesn't feel right to me. I can't see you being happy here somehow." I was uneasy also, but we were young and expecting our second child and believed we needed more room. Despite Dad's misgivings and my apprehension, we bought the house for $20,000, which was a lot of money in 1956. The house was sound structurally and the kitchen was wonderful. We redecorated and tried to make it comfortable, but the house always felt unfriendly, aloof, and almost sinister to me, as if merely tolerating our presence. In the five years we lived there we experienced a number of weather-related disasters. A tornado took off the second-story sleeping porch; lightning struck the black walnut tree in the back yard that landed on the roof over Kim's back bedroom, the brick chimney blew down in another storm. Still, it was our first house and we were happy, but for me, the house was just shelter. I never truly felt at home there.

My dad died in July of 1960. He was only sixty years old and none of us were ready to let him go. I grieved and grieved and imagined that my stupid disaster-prone house was somehow responsible for my emotional state. My husband traveled on business in those days and one Tuesday one of my friends called to see how I was getting along. "I know what would cheer you up," she said. "Let's go look at houses. I've found one that will be perfect for you."

Looking at houses was the farthest thing from my mind at that time. Bob and I had never discussed moving although it surely was not a secret that I did not like the house. Kim was eight years old, Rob and Andy were four and two. We liked the neighborhood and the schools and planned to remain in the house, at least until the kids finished grade school at Hay-Edwards.

Nevertheless, my friend, Betty Blythe, picked me up and we met the realtor at a large two-story frame home in Washington Park at the corner of Williams Boulevard and MacArthur. I remember walking through the front door into a cavernous front hall flanked by solid cherry pillars and waist-high wainscoting. "I'm home," my heart sang. "I'll buy it," my voice sang. "Shouldn't you have your husband look at the house with you?" the realtor gasped. "No problem, I know he'll love it," I answered.

And he did. And we did. And we lived there happily ever after.

The Fire, 1966

(I found this letter I'd written to Mother in her papers after her death in 1984; she'd kept it almost 20 years!)

Friday, October 7, 1966

Dear Mother and All,

I've wanted to write this all week, but haven't had a minute to sit down! I really don't know quite where to begin with my latest tale of woe...so I guess I'll begin at the beginning since the enclosed newspaper clipping is more or less explanatory as far as what the latest excitement was! First of all, and most importantly, WE ARE ALL SAFE. Everyone was outside except Phillip who was being fed in kitchen. The fire started in attic at 3 p.m. on a beautiful Sunday afternoon. So we were very fortunate that it was daylight and no one was upstairs asleep.

Bob and I had been in Champaign for his office football weekend since last Friday and stopped by Decatur to visit and have lunch on the way home Sunday afternoon. I'd told the sitter we'd be home around two. We got into Springfield about 2:15. Bob wanted to check his mail at the office so we stopped there first and I decided to call Linda, our babysitter, and tell her that we were in town and would be home soon. The phone rang and rang....and since it was such a beautiful afternoon I was about to hang up and conclude that everyone was outside in the park...but I let it ring a little longer and finally a little voice answered. I asked "Kim- Linda?" and the voice said, "Mrs. Roach, this is Bonnie Barber. Your house is on fire." Talk about a heart-stopping moment.

Bonnie told me the children were outside and safe and the fire engines were still there. You can picture what kind of speed records we set getting to our house from the Paper Company! For some reason, incomprehensible to me, Bob simply could not run a stop sign. He was so nervous and so was I. I kept screeching over and over, "GO THROUGH THE LIGHT, GO THROUGH THE LIGHT....THE POLICEMEN WILL HELP

US," and he kept saying, "I just can't, I just can't." It's funny now, but it wasn't then, believe me. Of course we both realized that if Bonnie had been able to get in the house to answer the phone, it couldn't be too bad and she had told me the children were safe. Still we were terrified. Driving up to our house with three fire trucks on the street and all the neighbors gathered around was something I will never forget.

To make a long and involved story short, the blaze was in the rear of the attic where all our winter clothes were stored. Everything was destroyed....suits, coats, sweaters, and jackets, everything for all of us. There was a huge pile of smoldering clothing on the ground when we pulled up. Except for the clothes we had taken on our weekend trip, everything was burned. Also all blankets, sleeping bags, furniture, and other stuff that we had stored in the attic.

A young salesman from the Paper Company, Keith Hocking, has been living with us for a month and he is the real hero of the fire. Keith has just gotten out of the Marine Corps and is staying with us until he can get situated. He's very helpful around the house, irons his own shirts and fixes breakfast for us all. The boys follow him around like he's their platoon leader. Keith is twenty-two, I think, and because our weekend babysitter is only twenty-three, I decided it wouldn't work for the two of them to stay together in the house while Bob and I were away. She is married to a Marine currently stationed on Okinawa and Keith is certainly not 'the catch of the century,' but I decided to be a little prudish so I told Keith he couldn't stay at the house while we were out of town. He went to a Motel, but had come by the house in the early afternoon to play catch with the boys and check that everything was OK. They'd all been out in front of the house, in the park, playing football with Caramel, when someone driving down MacArthur saw smoke coming from the attic window. He yelled to Keith who sent Rob next door to call the Fire Department. Then Keith ran into the kitchen where Linda had Phillip in his high chair. They couldn't get him out of the high chair fast enough, so Keith grabbed high chair and baby and hauled them both out to the front sidewalk.

Keith then tried to get up to the attic but was driven back by the thick smoke; he ran down, grabbed a wet towel for his face and crawled up the attic stairs so he could see which section the flames were in. He then went back down, turned off all the power, made a quick tour to be sure no one else was in the house

and ran out the front door just as the fire engines pulled up. According to many of the spectators and neighbors, the firemen were charging ahead with axes and were determined to chop a hole in the southwest corner of the roof. The blaze was in the northeast corner, so if they had chopped the hole, they would have created a great cross draft and we'd probably have lost the whole house. Keith stopped them and forced them to follow him upstairs with gas masks until they could see where the fire actually was. He told me later that he realized then that he hadn't seen Kim. The boys were all accounted for, but, as he said, "I thought maybe she was in a corner reading somewhere and she'd never look up until the house caved in on her." So he ran back into the house to look for her. Rob had tried to contact Grandma Roach after he called in the fire alarm. There was no answer at her house so he called the Country Club and said, "This is Robert Roach, Jr. My dad is gone, our house is burning down, somebody over there better find my grandmother in a hurry!". Then he put in calls to the garage where she gets her car fixed, and the gas station where she fills up her car. By this time he had half the southwest end of Springfield either looking for Detta or on their way to our house. Many of our friends arrived before we did.

We drove up to the sight of three big pumpers with three huge hoses shooting water into our house. Complete chaos. Kim had gone up to the corner drugstore with a friend and was just walking home down MacArthur. She was crying, Rob and Andy were both crying and scared and all three were mighty glad to see us drive up. When the firemen finally allowed us to enter the house, there was water cascading down all the first floor doorways. A hose had broken on the front stairway and was spraying water all over. The upstairs hall and Robby's room looked like Niagara Falls. The blazing area of the attic was directly over Robby's room, so all the water damage to the furniture, etc., was mostly there. It took ages to get everyone calmed down (including me). Quite an experience to stand on the street with our friends and neighbors and watch our clothes flying out the attic windows, landing in a sodden, charred heap in the side yard.

Detta took Andy and Phillip home with her. Kim went to Patty Morgan's and Robby went down to Noah Dixon's for the night. Keith and Bob and I stayed to inventory all the clothes that were still smoldering. The police chief told us we had better do it immediately for "the scavengers would be by that night" and we'd never be able to establish our loss. So we picked through burnt scraps. I scribbled notes, "green ball dress, Bob's tuxedo," and on and on. I filled ten notebook pages that night and am still adding items- - -nothing to salvage.

We arranged for Andy to move in with Muellers and Bob and Keith went back to the house to check the attic again. Sure enough, it was glowing red, so they called the Fire Department again (8 p.m.). This time the Fire Department pulled up without the ladder truck (yes, this was the same crew that had been there all afternoon). Keith and Bob were filling buckets in Rob's bathroom, running up the stairs with them when the firemen arrived through the FRONT door, axes in hand. Any areas they'd missed flooding the first time, they flooded this time. It's a total mess. As to damage, that's a wild guess. Monday we started pulling out all the wiring, took up all the attic flooring, removed old insulation and will begin replacing roof and burned timbers. We will need to re-insulate, new flooring, deodorize everything (didn't realize how BAD smoke smells) plus roof repair, siding….the list goes on and on.

Rob's room on the second floor is a complete disaster; all the plaster ceilings in the house are waterlogged and falling; the back stairway is destroyed and walls and ceilings throughout the house are cracking. They told us the first step is to remove all the wallpaper in order to let the plaster dry and then assess how much can be salvaged. The full second story will have to be re-plastered before it can be painted or papered. Most of the floors are waterlogged also, so after they dry out, will have to be refinished, cleaned and varnished. There's structural damage to the south side of the house (it is bowing out) so it will have to be pulled back to plumb with turnbuckles in the attic. Doesn't that sound awful! On the first floor, all paper comes off, hall floor has to be replaced, everything cleaned and restored. We sent the furniture to the cleaners who hopefully can remove the smoke smell and damage. Every closet in the house (do you remember how many closets I have)? will have to be emptied, scrubbed, sterilized and repainted. What we can salvage of the contents is questionable. Want to hear more?

The beautiful cherry woodwork on the first floor….all of it…is warping and will have to be dried, cleaned and repaired. I could go on and on, but we really don't have a clue yet as to what we are really in for. It's been almost a week now and it seems to me that we have made little progress. There are ten or twelve workmen at the house every day, so something is happening. Today and yesterday I met with architects, contractors, decorators, yardmen, trash haulers, a cast of thousands it seems. Em and Jim came over to bring me some clothes and see the damage first hand. I had called them Sunday evening after I calmed down a bit, and it was a good thing for our fire was featured on the Decatur evening news! The kids are still bunking out with our friends and having a great time from all reports. Bob and Keith and I eat at Detta's and then I stay there with Phillip at night. She is too deaf to hear him at night, she says, and of course Lydia leaves at five. Bob and Keith go back to the house each night to keep an eye on things. I go over to Williams Boulevard about eight in the morning, and stay until suppertime. Kim and Robby walk over after school and are a big help and comfort to me. I'm grateful for our good friends, Patty Morgan, the Muellers and the Dixons, who have welcomed them into their homes and hearts, but I miss them dreadfully. Andy is having such a good time staying with the Muellers, (no rules!), we may have trouble persuading him to return home.

Everything is a BIG MESS. I doubt that we will be able to move back in very soon. And I don't dare bring Phillip back into the house with all the plastering and smoke smell; I can barely stand to be there myself, although I must admit I am having fun acting as" foreman" to all these workers. I think (hope) Detta and Lydia can survive at least another ten days. (Phillip is absolutely the CLEANEST baby in town…I think she gives him three baths a day.) Emmy's offered to take the baby to Decatur and that may be the perfect solution. Don't worry….that sounds silly, I know…but please, don't worry. We are all fine, we are grateful it wasn't worse and no one was hurt. It appears that it is going to be a long-dragged out mess and most of what has to be done has to be done by either Bob or me. I'll keep you up to date as we go along. On the bright side, Kim is quite the celebrity among the ninth-graders….all new clothes. She's walking around grinning from ear-to-ear.

Love…*Rosie*

Note: We moved to the Leland Hotel in downtown Springfield for a few weeks. Eight-month old Phillip stayed with Aunt Emmy in Decatur Illinois. We rented a duplex for a few weeks and then rented an unfurnished house belonging to Patty Milligan's mother until the Williams Boulevard house was repaired and habitable (February 1967).

Phil enters Butler School

Education was, and is, a core value of our family. One of my father's mantras was "use your head." Sometimes it encouraged us, sometimes it discouraged us. The four of us were expected to work hard and achieve high honors in school, and for the most part we did. We all pretty much passed Dad's valuing of education on to our own children. For my four, the road was long and sometimes meandering, but ultimately successful. Nevertheless, the one education-related incident that stands out most in my memory (and has been the source of much family merriment) is neither the graduations nor the Honors Banquets. Instead, I alternately groan and grin when I remember the first week we sent Phillip, the baby of the family, to first grade.

When Phil turned six and was ready for 'real school,' his older brothers were fourteen and sixteen. This was in 1972 and the older boys were at City Day School and Springfield High School and caught up in what passed for the hippie lifestyle in Springfield Illinois. Their language and expressions were fairly raw, and for the most part their father and I considered it a phase they were going through and other than insisting on adherence to a reasonable code of politeness and consideration in public, we didn't censor their language at home. I was an administrator at Sangamon State (now University of Illinois at Springfield) then, so the conversations at home were mild compared to what I heard every day from the students and faculty at SSU.

However, we all realized that some changes were in order so that Phil would understand that the words he heard from his brothers were not words he was to use in first grade at Butler School. Every evening at the dinner table, Rob and Andy would go through the list of words they deemed inappropriate for the first grade at Butler School. And Phil would solemnly nod and say in all of his six-year old solemnity " OK. OK, I know I'm not s'posed to say crap, or sh**, or f***," and the boys would grin and keep encouraging him, glancing up to see if their father or I was going to object to their taunting game.

September rolled around and Phil went off to first grade. The first week went smoothly. But the following week, he came home in tears with a note from the principal that he had been in her office and I was to call her the next morning WITHOUT FAIL. I couldn't imagine what my sweet child Phillip could have done to merit a trip to the principal's office. He was just six years old and a perfect angel! "Phil, whatever did you do?" I asked. "Well," he said through his tears, " they showed a movie about how you're not s'posed to go anywhere in a car with some man you don't know. And after the movie my teacher asked if any of us kids knew what the movie was about and I raised my hand." "So far, so good," I thought. Phil's sobs intensified,"and I told her the movie was about not getting into a car with a goddamned stranger. Then my teacher said, 'Oh Phillip Roach we do not say goddamned stranger in first grade at Butler School.'..and then I said, but my brothers told me the words we do not say in first grade at Butler School and those words are crap and sh** and f***. My brothers didn't tell me nothin' about no goddamned stranger."

And it goes on unto the next generation:

Thirty-four years later, in 2006, six-year old Jack Lommen, (Rob's son, Phil's nephew) is in first grade in Denver Colorado. As Jack told me the story over the phone, he was having trouble remembering how to print lower-case "b" and "d". " I get them mixed up all the time so my dad (Rob) told me he had this dream that helped him remember which was which. You just have to remember that 'b' goes with 'ba-zoom' and 'd' goes with 'derriere', dad said." "And did you get them straight?" I asked. "Yes, yes I did, the next day in school. And that's when the trouble started," he added. He explained that his teacher congratulated him on his progress and asked how he remembered and he repeated the story his dad told him and his teacher said, "Jack, that story is not appropriate for the first grade in this school."

The Talking Christmas Tree

Kim and I took five year old Phillip downtown to Bressmer's department store so that he could see Springfield's first "Talking Christmas Tree." Kim, nineteen, was home for Christmas from Kenyon College, eager to spend time with her baby brother. Fourteen years separated them, and now, three hundred miles. Kim was sure he'd "never really know her" so her holiday was intentionally "Phil filled."

Phil was the center of attention at dinner that evening with his description of the wondrous sight he had seen that afternoon. "It talks to you...it knows my name...it really is alive you guys...I know you don't believe me but it really talked to me...it said, 'hello there Phillip,' it did it did." Older brothers, Rob, fifteen, and thirteen year old Andy egged him on, mocking and teasing until the tears welled up behind his trusting blue eyes. Big sister Kim came to his defense, "Hey, enough already. I saw the Talking Christmas Tree myself. I heard it talk to Phil. The tree talked and THAT is THAT...end of conversation... lay off...OK?" "Right," says Rob, "I say we just go out and get ourselves one of those mag-eee-c talking Christmas trees." Phil's face lit up like a summer morning sunrise. "Oh please, please, could we Mom, could we Dad...oh please, please, please, please."

Next afternoon Rob, Andy and their dad searched Springfield's tree lots for the biggest fullest specimen tree they could find. It was a cardinal rule at our house, as it had been at home when I was a kid, that a Christmas tree, in order to qualify as a 'real tree' had to touch the ceiling, even better if it was so tall that almost a foot had to be trimmed from the top. We had ten-foot ceilings in our house on Williams Boulevard so they had to find a BIG TREE.

After much discussion we decided to set up the tree in the dining room that ran the full width of the house, from east to west, a common feature of Southern homes built at the turn of the century as ours was. The room measured roughly fifteen by twenty feet so there was plenty of space for the tree and the large dining room table that would be expanded to seat sixteen for Christmas dinner. We'd adopted the custom of putting up our tree well before Christmas. When I was a kid we never saw the tree until eight o'clock on Christmas Eve and it was magic. My children only know Christmas trees decorated in mid-December. I was the only one in the house who missed the anticipation and suspense and thrill of seeing the lights and decorations for the first time on Christmas Eve.

Rob and Andy told Phil that his "Talking Tree" was a special variety and not exactly like the one he had seen at Bressmer's. Our tree could only "talk" at certain preset times. They printed up a daily 'talking' schedule and posted it on the refrigerator door. Of course Phil, being five years old, couldn't read but he knew what the schedule said. Our magic tree would talk after Rob and Andy got home from school and for one half hour after dinner and before Phil's bedtime. Furthermore, the tree wished to have advance notice when it was to talk, so they told him it would be best if Phil would ask either Rob or Andy to ask the tree each time if it wanted to talk. The next two weeks were wonderful. There is nothing like a five year old believing in magic to put a sparkle into the Holidays. One of the boys would corral Phil while the other crept behind the tree. Crouching low behind the lower branches, they were completely hidden from view. The boys had taped an 'x' on the carpet about four feet in front of the tree indicating where Phil was to sit cross-legged waiting for the tree to acknowledge his presence.

Phil's enchantment and belief never wavered. The Talking Tree knew everything that was happening in our house. Now, over thirty years later, he says he doesn't remember the questions he asked, but he does remember his older brothers leading him into the room and his sitting square on the taped "x" and, most of all he says, he remembers BELIEVING!

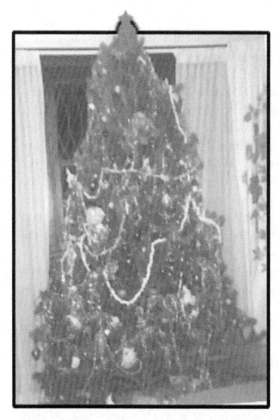

It was a special magical Christmas back then in 1971. Not surprisingly, the Tree quit talking after Christmas Day. Rob and Andy told Phil it had been a "special two-week Talking Tree." We left it up another week or two until the City Street Department announced their annual Christmas tree pickup. Magic or not, out it went to the curb for pickup. Gone but not forgotten.

Later the next week I was finishing dinner preparations in the kitchen and Phillip and the boys were watching TV in the library. I heard a hysterical screech and then a wail from Phil. "Oh No..Oh No....Mom...Mom...come quick...they're grinding up my Talking Christmas Tree...they're murdering it...make them stop...help .....help."

The City of Springfield had purchased a new chipper in concert with its inaugural tree pickup program and chose to air footage that evening of the chipper making short work of a pile of discarded evergreens. Among them, alas, was Phil's Talking Christmas Tree.

Mary's sequel

(NOTE: My beloved daughter-in-law, Mary Servatius Roach, delighted in the story of the Talking Christmas Tree and wrote this charming sequel in October 2000.)

"See, there's my star!" There was no mistaking Phil's tree. It was indeed the one being chewed up by the great big machine, flashing on the television screen. Phil had made his own star for the top of the talking Christmas tree. He'd asked Rob for help in drawing a star but found him busy on the telephone to Australia ordering a special sleeping bag capable of withstanding severely cold temperatures. Phil had looked around for Andy but he was at the office with their Dad helping with a big bulk mailing order that had to go out by the end of the week.

Finally, Phil found big sister Kim in the kitchen. Not yet trusting her artist's hand (that trust would come years later), Kim suggested they take a walk to the art supply store and buy a stencil. At home again, Phil cut out his stenciled star with the big scissors under Kim's careful supervision. He covered it with tin foil, adding red and silver hearts all along the edges. He had declared it his latest work of art. Whoever had dragged the tree out to the curb had not noticed that Phil's star was still attached. "Oh, Phil, we're so sorry about your star! We forgot to take it down! But next year, you can make a whole new one." Being a good-natured little boy, Phil seemed to accept the fate of his star but his heart still ached for the talking Christmas tree.

Phil's Mom tried to explain. "You know, Phil, every tree that dies provides seeds for the next trees that grow. You see how the machine is mulching up the tree. Then, they will take all the tree's needles and the bark and sprinkle them all over the forest floor. In a few years, your tree will have become many more Christmas trees." "Really? my tree will make lots of Christmas trees?" Phil opened his eyes wide. "Yes, that's right, sweetie. This way, there will always be enough Christmas trees for all the little boys and little girls, including you next year."

Phil stopped crying and wiped away his tears. He smiled and gave his Mom a hug. Just then, Andy and their Dad walked into the house. Phil ran to the door to greet them. "Hey, Dad, hey, Andy, guess what? My tree is going to be seeds so that other Christmas trees can grow for all the little boys and girls!"

CHRISTMAS PAST

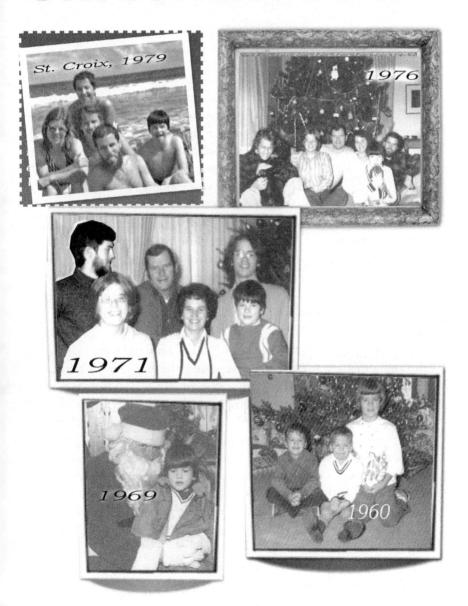

St. Croix, 1979

1976

1971

1969

1960

The Eavesdropping Game

Phil and I played an eavesdropping game. We were experts at tuning into private conversations going on around us. Our game has detailed rules and an elaborate point count system of scoring. Rule one requires that the player continues to carry on a rational conversation while eavesdropping. We give extra points for tracking two simultaneous conversations.

Our favorite eavesdropping site was Godfather's Pizza Parlor in Springfield. The tables are close together and there's a gentle underlying buzz of animated talk and clatter that camouflages and diverts attention from our listening. We went there last Tuesday evening. Ordered the large special with everything and chose a table halfway to the back corner of the room.

We polished off a pitcher of frosty cola and were halfway through our large pizza when we spotted our first mark, a middle aged couple shepherding an older woman. They seated themselves at the table to my right. Phil could see them, but patrons going back and forth to the counter blocked my peripheral vision. Still, I caught enough snatches of their conversation to stitch together a scenario. The older woman was celebrating her birthday and the younger couple was treating her to an outing at the pizza parlor. The tone of her voice when she said, "Oh, mother" clued me that the young woman must be the daughter-in-law. The man-son appeared solicitous toward both women. The impatient edge to his voice as he guided their menu selection led me to believe he was not accustomed to spending much time with his mother.

Skilled in stereo eavesdropping, Phil had tuned in to a young family nearby who were noisily dividing a cheese-sausage platter and a large pitcher of coke. "Gimme that piece." "Jody's got a bigger piece than me.....M-o-m." The uproar gave way to shoving kicking and snuffling as the family greedily gulped and chewed. The parents were indulging in their own version of kick and shove, physically to the kids and, oblivious to our attendant ears, verbally to one another. "I've told you, I <u>hate</u> to go out with these kids. We spend a fortune and they behave like pigs. I'm telling you, we're raising a bunch of spoiled ungrateful brats."

Phil's eyebrows shot up. He'd never heard parents call their kids 'brats', at least not in public. It was becoming enticingly obvious that some more interesting action would be forthcoming from this family table. I nodded, signaling that the family group was his and I would concentrate on the birthday bunch. They had received their order and Grandma was acting as hostess, passing out carefully cut equal slices, whining all the while. "Well, I know it is my birthday. Lord knows I'm reminded every time I look in the mirror how old and fat I am. I know you are <u>so</u> busy and just don't have time to call me or come to see me. I should be grateful that I have a birthday once a year and that my only son remembers me." Her voice trailed off. I could sense the tension in the trio. The errant son responded, "Now mother, you know that I think of you all the time. You know I have to work hard to keep you in that expensive nursing home you hate so much. But surely Margie visits you every week?" (Sure, I thought, put it off on old Margie, whose mother is this anyhow?) I couldn't see Margie, but from the tone of her response and the attentive shift in Phil's posture, I knew a murderous glance accompanied her icy rejoinder, ""Mother, you know how much we both care about you."

The clatter of a heavy tray and scraping of two chairs signaled completion of our listening perimeter as an attractive young couple settled down at the third table. I met Phil's glance with a wink and the challenge was laid. Could we possibly track three simultaneous conversations while chewing and swallowing and carrying on our own conversation? The family argument had escalated. The kids were totally out of control and were completely ignored as the parent couple slugged it out in a sordid recanting of every misdeed throughout their marriage. Good grief! It was their wedding anniversary...they were celebrating their anniversary!

By now, the birthday trio had deteriorated to a sullen and perfunctory exchange of "please pass the red pepper" "I'd like another small slice if you don't mind." A look of dismay shot across Phil's face. "Grandma's crying," he mouthed silently. The poor dear. It's her birthday and she's supposed to be having fun. Our newly seated third marks, the young couple, chewed in total silence. Neither Phil nor I had overheard anything but their food order. Were they courting? married? professional colleagues? friends meeting for a late beer? Phil got up to refill our pitcher of coke, a quick reconnaissance mission, hoping to discover the reason for the couple's grim silence. He returned to the table, sliding into his seat with a disgusted, "You simply are not going to believe this...that young couple behind us... They are glaring at one another.....THEY ARE NOT SPEAKING TO ONE ANOTHER! Mother, do you realize you and I are the only people at these four tables who are having fun."

We exchanged a sad and wistful glance and decided that our eavesdropping game wasn't quite as much fun that particular evening as we thought it would be.

"But There Are Rainbows in the Hall" (1981)

The realtor will be here to show the house at noon tomorrow. Another realtor, another prospective buyer. I wonder as I forlornly plump the pillows on the sofa for what seems to be the hundredth time, what will be wrong this time? Will it be the wallpaper in the front bedroom? The scuffed plaster where the boys parked their ten-speeds to keep them safe? Or will it be the front hall...the hall that opens its arms to hug me when I walk in the door...will the front hall look gloomy and cavernous to this new looker? I try to keep my expectations in check. I try not to count on a buyer, but a tiny flicker of hope begins. Will this one, this eighty-fifth one, be THE ONE? Please, God please let them like it. Please God let them buy it.

My husband died suddenly at Thanksgiving just over two years ago. The children and I were devastated. We took refuge in this house, our house that for twenty years overflowed with love and laughter and rocked with all the joy, craziness and sorrows of four lively children forging their ways to independence. My husband and I had always dreamed, almost secretly plotted, of the wonderful times we would have when the two of us were left to rattle around alone in the big house. Now suddenly the two of us living here were my young teen-aged son and me. Wrong dream. Wrong two.

Still, it's the house that holds us together. The house gives me a reason to struggle out of bed those mornings when I want to pull the blankets over my head and ignore the fact that my life is changed for all time. I love every crooked molding, every tricycle crack in the plaster. It is a magnificent home, built in the grand manner with high ceilings, hand-carved cherry woodwork, double pantries, leaded glass windows, and window seats and nooks and crannies designed to cosset rainy-day readers.

The house sits in a neighborhood of elegant large homes with expansive well cared for gardens and lawns. Washington Park is a Frisbee-throw out the front door. The first year after Bob's death passed mercifully. Looking back, I remember little but constant pain and tears. I tried desperately to fashion some kind of stability for myself, to find some way to insulate myself from the ever-present pain of losing my love. Some things worked; most didn't. The children and I, the five survivors, huddled together, each of us grieving openly in our own way, sharing and sustaining one another.

"Keep the house, Mom. Please keep the house." My heart agrees with them. Whatever the reasons behind their request, how can I bear to give up this dusty palace? On every bright sunny afternoon, precisely at three o'clock, the sun's rays light the leaded glass windows and flood the front entry hall with rainbows. For a few scant minutes every day prisms of light flicker from ceiling to floor. Our tiny, solemn-faced precious daughter would sit fascinated, with her dolls all in a row, to watch her 'light show.' Chubby little boys, in their time, chased the rainbows with jam-smeared fingers. "Gotcha this time. Mommy, Mommy, I grabbed the red." And how many times had those rainbow lights cheered me. There are low periods in the life of every family and we'd had our share of troubles. But somehow, we always told one another, "Things have to work out for folks who live with rainbows in their hall."

"Sell the house. It's too big for you and Phillip. Sell it. Sell it." My friends are right. My head agrees with them. It is too big. To have the exterior painted will be a staggering expense. The upkeep increases as the years pile on. Old homes are like old folks. They need plenty of attention, plenty of loving and plenty of indulgent tolerance.

I couldn't sell the house. Not just yet. Not before the Holidays. The first Christmas (we date our lives now from the day he died) we ran. Less than a month after the memorial service we couldn't face the "joys of Christmas past." Not in that house where he was up at dawn with the jolly "Ho Ho Ho" of a man born to play Santa Claus. A dear friend mercifully lent us a condo in Florida to hide in. And the next year we escaped to the sun and sand of St. Croix in the Virgin Islands. Even in that tropical paradise, our second Christmas without him was sad. What no one tells you about grieving is that after you steel yourself to get through the first year alone, all that is left to do is to buck up and steel yourself to get through the next year alone.

The second year I picked up more pieces and tried to patchwork a life for myself, working hard at the single-parent role. The following November found me running again. "We'll go back to Florida this Christmas," I tell the kids. But instead of agreement from the children, I see them sag. "Gee Mom," says Phil, age fourteen, "We haven't had a real Christmas since....well, you know since Daddy...and pretty soon I'll be too old to even be a kid." The other three, the "big kids" quickly took up their younger brother's plea. All away at college, they wanted to be "home" for this Christmas.

I told them I couldn't bear it. How could I unpack the wooden ornaments and angels we'd collected together during a lifetime of vacation curio shopping? How could I get through the motions of Christmas morning? How could I hold back the memories and the sadness to let the Christmas joy shine through? "I have an idea," said my take-charge oldest son. "Let's have a big Christmas party, a big one like you and Dad used to give." I gasp, "Oh, Rob, no, my God no...not a party, not at Christmas. I can't, I just can't do it." I felt what he was asking was impossible for me.

"Now wait a minute. Listen. We'll all five give it together. And we'll invite our own friends and all of your friends and Dad's friends who love us. All the people like Emmy and Jim and Uncle Teck and Uncle Rich[15] who watched us grow up and have really stuck with us this past two years. And we'll show them, they'll know, that we're doing OK, that we're going to be just

---

[15] Jim Teckenbrock & Rich Plain, childhood friends of Bob's.

fine." The excitement in his voice, even over the long-distance wire, was catching. I begin to think, "I can do this." Perhaps I can even unroll the six foot long "REJOICE" felt banner that we had hung in our dining room every joyful Holiday season, except for the last two when the joy was gone.

The telephone lines buzzed as the three at college synchronized their lists of "who do we care about and who cares about us." I was fascinated to discover which of our friends the children held dear; who mattered to them and who they perceived had supported and sustained us throughout our long mourning.

"THE PARTY" as it will always be known, was a smash! One hundred fifty friends, teenagers and octogenarians, filled the house with love and laughter. Each of them knew what we were trying to do. Some, may have thought we were trying too hard to make happiness appear where it had been absent so long. But it worked. The house did its magic. "REJOICE" was the message of the bright felt banner, of Phillip's one hundred carefully lit luminarias lining the front walk and of the two gigantic 'to the ceiling' Christmas trees. We did rejoice. "This is the way this house was meant to be, just the way it used to be. Happy. Alive. It's magic," said my sister with tears of joy that night.

"We did it. We did it. We made the house happy again," we beamed to one another. Grinning through our tears we acknowledged that we were almost whole again, almost ready to move along. January and the glow still lingers. Now I can sell the house. Now someone else deserves the opportunity to love it and enjoy it. "Yes, yes," say the kids, "we can let go now. It's OK now. The magic came back for a little while and we can take it along with us wherever we go. Let the house go, Mother. It is time to let it go." This time my head and my heart agree. I will put the house up for sale.

We paint. We scrub. We scour. We clean. We wallpaper. Phillip and I waterproof the basement, which for twenty years has been "slightly damp." We patch the roof, manicure the lawns, spray and shine everything in sight. The dogs, Carillon and Cleopatra, are banished. People troop through. For four "Open House Sundays" cars line the boulevard and parkway. "We love it," "What a magnificent home," "Look at the storage space," "What fun to live here." "I'll bring back my mother to see it, my father to see it, my uncle to see it, my carpenter, my banker."

Couple after couple are dazzled by the charm, the fireplaces, the large rooms and the beautiful park setting. Surely it will sell quickly. Some return four, five, six times. I try not to let my hopes rise. I try not to fall into the trap of looking for "a good sign." Is a third visit a good sign? "It's too big. It's too expensive. Too old. Too many bathrooms. Too much traffic. Not enough children in the neighborhood." Stop. STOP. Don't tell me. Please stop telling me why you are not going to buy my house.

> This is the wrong ending. A "happily ever after" section should be inserted here. The paragraph would begin, "Her lovely house is sold. She moves to a cozy little bungalow and starts her life anew." But that isn't happening. Our beloved home still wears its "For Sale" sign. It's been six months now. No offers. This is impossible. I cannot believe that no one wants to buy this house that I love.

> *"The realtor will be here to show your house at noon tomorrow." I wonder... will these be the people who will see the rainbows in the hall?*

–30–

OPEN HOUSE
Sunday, July 12, 1981
2-4 pm

1001 WILLIAMS BOULEVARD

ENJOY THE BEST OF BOTH WORLDS! The CONVENIENCE and EASE of CITY LIVING in
the beautiful environment of WASHINGTON PARK.
    This classic colonial home is within easy WALKING DISTANCE of the State
Complex, the new Revenue Center and downtown Springfield. Shops, theaters and
restaurants are located nearby. Lovely Washington Park is at the front door with
tennis courts, jogging paths, the Rose Garden, floral shows and Rees Memorial
Carillon for leisure enjoyment. The secluded brick sideyard patio furnishes
privacy, while the large front porch which may be screened in (screens in basement)
lets you enjoy the changing Springfield scene.
    The home was built in the early 1900s by Dr. Don Deal, purchased by the
widow of Lt. Governor John G. Oglesby in the 40s and occupied since 1960 by the
present owners. The spacious high-ceilinged rooms, designed for gracious entertain-
ing of an earlier year, adapt beautifully to comfortable family living.

    STORAGE: Butler's pantry; cherry corner cupboard in dining room; eight large
             closets; built-in drawers in two closets, built-ins in dressing room/
             bath. Floored and finished attic.
    BOOKS : Floor to ceiling bookshelves in library; built-ins in living room and
             two bedrooms.
    WOODWORK:Original cherry and oak woodwork and paneling.
    UTILITIES: Circuit -breaker panels in basement and upstairs hall. Hot-water
             radiators furnish economical radiant heating. Air-condition units in
             kitchen,living-room, dining-room, two bedrooms. Third unit in attic.
             Ceiling fan in library.

Phil and Michelle Roach at 1001 Williams
January 20, 2007

Part Five

Indulgences

Indulgency:

"an inability to resist the gratification of one's whims and desires."

Part Five will be of interest only to those persons directly descended from, or closely related to, the author. As often happens when one is chronicling the history of a family, the choice between 'what goes in' and 'what is left out' is very difficult. As I compiled the first four parts of this book, I realized there was a lot of information, e.g.,the Roach family history and some updates to the Buchmann chronicle, that might be of interest to my own children and grandchildren (dare I hope for great-grandchildren?) who might in future generations take up this story. Part Five, "Indulgences," is that material.

Indulgences

The Stories:

Robert Corwine Roach (a.k.a. Jack Miller)

My Story

Et Cetera

On a wintry day in Chicago in 1927 (either January twentieth, twenty-first or twenty-second, the records conflict) a healthy baby boy was born

to Charles Miller and his wife, Marie (Logan) Miller. The young parents named their son Jack Miller. Dr. Cunningham was the attending physician at the birth which took place at Washington Park Hospital, East 60th Street and South Vernon Avenue on Chicago's South Side, near the University of Chicago.

Photos courtesy of the Chicago Historical Society digital photo collection.

We know that Charles and Marie cared for infant Jack at their Chicago home, 2247 West Monroe, Ward 28, Precinct #2, until February 12th at which time he was admitted to the nursery of The Cradle Society in Evanston Illinois. He was adopted by Corwine Ewing Roach and

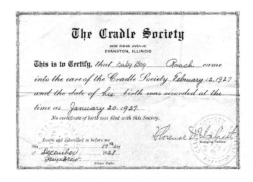

Henrietta (Day) Roach of Springfield Illinois who named him Robert Corwine Roach (adoption decree dated June 1927).

STATE OF ILLINOIS)
)SS.   IN THE COUNTY COURT OF SAID COUNTY.
COUNTY OF COOK)

IN THE MATTER OF THE   )
)
ADOPTION OF BABY   )
)
BOY MILLER.   )

We, Charles Miller, and Marie Miller, husband and wife, of Chicago, Illinois, being of legal age, and the parents of a male child, who was born at the Washington Park Hospital, on the 20th day of January, 1927, in Chicago, Cook County, Illinois, do hereby relinquish all the right, and interest, of every kind, nature and description, which we now have, or may have, in and to said minor child, and we do hereby enter our appearance in said case, and waive issuance and service of summons, and consent to an immediate hearing, and to the entry of the decree for adoption, as prayed for in the petition for adoption, and waive all right to appeal or writ of error. We do hereby consent to the adoption of the said child, by the petitioners, Corwine E. Roach, and Henrietta D. Roach.

We hereby consent to the appointment of a Guardian ad Litem for said Baby Boy Miller, and hereby confirm all acts as Guardian ad Litem for the purpose of adoption.

WITNESSES:

Bernice S. Dick   *Chas. Miller*

Edith M. Dick   *Marie Miller*

STATE OF ILLINOIS)
)SS.
COUNTY OF COOK)

On this 23 day of March, 1927, personally appeared before me, Charles Miller, and Marie Miller, the persons who signed the foregoing instrument, and acknowledged that the said instrument was their free and voluntary act, and was executed and delivered for the use and purpose therein set forth.

Edith M. Dick
                     NOTARY PUBLIC.

PETITION FOR ADOPTION OF CHILD   CO. C. FORM NO. 41—3-C-4-1920

State of Illinois $\Big\}$ s.s.   In the County Court,
SANGAMON COUNTY $\Big\}$

June   **Term, A. D. 192** 7

To the Hon. Ormal B. Irwin   Judge of said Court:

Your petitioners, Corwine E. Roach and Henrietta D. Roach   of

Springfield   in said County, would respectfully show unto your Honor: That they are residents

of said County, and are desirous of adopting a child so as to render it capable of inheriting their estate. That the

name of said child is Baby Boy Miller   that it

was of the age of five months on the 20th   day of June, A.D. 1927

last, and is a male child.

And further, that your petitioners desire the name of said child changed to that of Robert Corwine

Roach   Your petitioners would further show that the parents

of said child are still living and resides at Chicago, Ill.

and consents to the adoption of said child by your petitioners, as will appear from written consent filed herewith.

And further, that your petitioners are pecuniarily able to support, maintain, educate and care for said child.

and that it would, therefore, be to the interest of said child to become the adopted child of your petitioners. Your
petitioners would further show, that the parents of said child have entered their
appearance herein, waived service of summons and have consented
to an immediate hearing and to the entry of the decree for adoption as
prayed in this petition as will appear by copy of such notice filed here-
Your petitioners would, therefore, pray this Honorable Court to make an order declaring said child to be the with

adopted child of your petitioners and capable of inheriting their estate, and that the name of said child to be changed

to that of Robert Corwine Roach   as provided by the Act of the

General Assembly of the State of Illinois, Approved February 27, A. D. 1874.

Your petitioners further consent that the order of adoption herein, may be set aside at any time, if it is satis-

factorily shown to this court, that your petitioners mistreat, abuse or neglect said child in any manner.

Corwine E. Roach
Henrietta D. Roach

State of Illinois $\Big\}$ s.s.:   Corwine E. Roach
SANGAMON COUNTY $\Big\}$ and Henrietta D. Roach

the above named petitioners, being duly sworn, depose and say that the facts contained in the above petition by

them subscribed, are true according to the best of their knowledge, information and belief.

Subscribed and sworn to before me, this 28th   *Corwine E. Roach*

day of June   A. D. 192 7

Oscar A. Decker   *Henrietta D. Roach*

County Clerk.

STATE OF ILLINOIS
NOTICE OF A BIRTH REGISTRATION

CHILD'S BIRTH NUMBER

ROBERT   CORWINE   ROACH   , a male 112-27-3151
First   Middle   Last   This is the Official
child, was born at CHICAGO   on 1 - 22 - 27   Number under which the
                         Month Day Year   Birth Record is Filed

in the County of COOK , Illinois.   Officially registered in JAN. , 1927 and the

original certificate is now on permanent file with the Illinois Department of Public Health at Springfield.

Notice to: Mrs. CORWINE E. ROACH
            R.R. #3
            SPRINGFIELD, ILLINOIS

Lelia E. Stevenson
Governor

Roland R. Cross, M.D.
Director of Public Health

Bob made sporadic efforts to get information about his birth parents, but he was unsuccessful. After his death in 1978, I contacted the Cradle Society on behalf of the children and received the following reply:

The Cradle Society

2049 RIDGE AVENUE • EVANSTON, ILLINOIS 60204 • 312—475-5800

February 9, 1979

Mrs. Rose Marie Roach
1001 Williams Boulevard
Springfield, Illinois 62704

Dear Mrs. Roach: .

Your husband's sudden death must have been a very difficult thing for you and your children. You have our sympathy.

In Illinois - adoption records are impounded but the information you have requested is in our files and we are happy to share it with you.

As you probably know, records in 1927 contained little information - not in detail as they are today. But what we have, should be of interest.

Robert Roach was born on January 20, 1927 but not admitted to the Cradle Nursery until February 12, 1927 which means that his birth parents might have made an effort to keep him.. The mother had had good care in one of the best hospitals at that time and the doctor's report showed the tests on the parents negative - the baby on admission to the nursery was in good condition and continued to develop well. We do not have a birth weight but on February 13, 1927, he weighed 6 pounds, 14 ounces and continued to gain as we observed him until he was signed out on March 21, 1927 to his adoptive parents.

Robert Roach's natural mother was 25, of German origin. She had had a college education and possibly majored in music because her "musical" abilities were mentioned.

The natural father was 27, of Scotch origin. There was a description of him - "medium tall, blue eyes, dark brown hair."

As a married couple, they were described as not only "nice looking" but "fine young people." We do not have their reason to give their baby in adoption.

We have reason to believe they were in good health as we are sure that the doctor who cared for the family would have told us about health problems.

How we wish we had more to tell you. The year 1927 was not good for records either at the Cradle or any other agency. Please write if you have further questions. Our warm wishes.

Sincerely,

(Mrs.) Ruth McGee
Social Worker

The Buchmann Family

January 28, 1998

Ms. Rose Marie Roach
One Ginger Lake Drive West
Glen Carbon, IL 62034

Dear Ms. Roach:

I am writing in response to your letter regarding the records for your late husband, Robert. I appreciate your patience in waiting for this response!

I have reviewed the information that we have about his adoption. From what you had sent me, it appears that we only have two additional pieces of identifying information. One is the name of a doctor; the other is an address which I can only presume is the address of the birth parents at the time. In order for me to release this information to you, I would need a court order from a judge in Sangamon county specifically for the release of the Cradle record including identifying information.

The "record" of which I speak is six lines handwritten. When I read it, I believe there may be a different interpretation to a couple pieces of information shared with you by Mrs. McGee. One is that that birth mother is noted to have been "musical", and I believe that next to this entry is written "organ" and "bells". One idea may be to contact churches to see if they had an organist with her name around the time of the adoption.

The second piece is a short phrase after the birth father's name which I read to say "last year med", meaning to me that he may have been in medical school. Again these are only my interpretations, the handwriting is very old and it is difficult to make out the abbreviations.

I had a couple ideas about Washington Park Hospital. First, the area is near to the University of Chicago, so that hospital may have their records. Second, the Chicago Historical Society could probably tell you what happened to Washington Park Hospital. Finding their records might be a different story as often hospital records are not kept very long.

One additional piece of information that may be interesting but probably not helpful in your search is that your husband was known as "Beau" while he was in the Cradle nursery. While this may be a name given to him by his parents, it is more likely that the nurses here gave him that name.

I hope at least some of this information is helpful to you. If I can be of any further assistance please don't hesitate to contact me. My direct number is (847) 733-3217.

Sincerely,

Maureen Garton, LCSW
Director, Post Adoption Services

Detta and Corwine brought five month old Jack, now known as Robert Corwine Roach, home to Springfield in March of 1927. Much to everyone's surprise, on December fifteenth of 1927, his mother gave birth to his younger sister, Mary Leigh Roach. Mary Leigh was henceforth much favored over her adopted older brother by their mother. And that was the way it was.

Corwine Ewing Roach:
from Encyclopedia of American Biography,
The American Historical Company, Inc. NY 1954 pp. 281-283

Corwine E. Roach's career as an industrialist began early in life, for he was only twenty-seven years old when he founded the Capital City Paper Company at Springfield, Illinois, and he headed this organization until his retirement in 1948. He served his country as a captain in the US Army in WWI and became a leader among his industrial colleagues, having been president of both the Illinois Paper Merchants Association and the National Paper Trades Association.

A native of Virginia, Illinois, Corwine E. Roach was born on June 20, 1995, son of Samuel and Isabelle (Corwine) Roach. He was named for a maternal ancestor, Sir George Corwine, who was knighted by the King of England in the sixteenth century.

Mr. Roach graduated from James Millikin University in 1911 where he was a founding member of the Sigma Alpha Epsilon chapter. He was one of the organizers of the Springfield Kiwanis Club and served as president of that group. He was also a past governor of the Illinois-Iowa District of Kiwanis International and was lieutenant governor of his division and an International Trustee of the worldwide organization.

Mr. Roach was a member of the Sangamo Club, Illini Country Club, the American Legion, past exalted ruler of the Protective Order of the Elks, a member of St. Paul's Lodge No. 500, Ancient Free and Accepted Masons, the Springfield Consistory of the Scottish Rite, Ansar Temple, Knights Templar Commandery, the Royal Order of Jesters and a recipient of the highest Masonic honor, the 33d Degree of the Knights Templar.

Corwine & Bob
1950 Millikin Graduation

In 1950, the honorary degree of Doctor of Business Administration was conferred on Mr. Roach by Millikin University on the occasion of the same commencement at which his son, Robert, was graduated.

Drum Major at Springfield High School
1942

1962 in Washington DC

History of the Corwine Seal Ring

The seal is the coat of arms of the family in England where the name is spelled Curwen. Curwen Hall is near Workington, Cumberland county and was built in 1152.

George Corwin (or Curwin) from whom the ring has been handed down, was born in England on December 10, 1610. He came from Northampton England and settled at Salem Massachusetts in 1638; died Jan.3, 1685; married Elizabeth Herbert, daughter of John Herbert, mayor of Northampton, England.

Their oldest son, John (b. July 28, 1638; d. July 12, 1683) married Margaret Winthrop, daughter of Governor John Winthrop, Connecticut. John was the father of George Corwin. George Corwin received the ring from his grandfather.

George was born Feb. 26, 1665, died April 12, 1696. Married Lydia Gedney and had one child, Bartholomew, born June 21, 1693; died May 9, 1747. Married Esther Burt of England. Their oldest son, George, next to receive the ring, was born July 12, 1718 and died in 1780 or '83?. Married Abigail Hixon. Their son, Richard, was father of George who received the ring from his grandfather. Richard was born Dec. 1748, died Nov. 19, 1813. Richard married Sarah Snyder, lived at Maysville Kentucky.

George was born in New Jersey, Aug.6, 1780 and died at Portsmouth Ohio in May of 1852. Married Elizabeth Wilson in Ohio, May 5, 1800. She died in May 1850. They had no children. Just before his death he gave the ring to George Day Corwine at Sharonville (now Omega) Ohio, as the youngest George Corwine of nearest kin. George Day Corwine is the son of Amnon Bedan Corwine, who was the son of Amos Corwine, brother to George Corwine who presented the ring to Amos's grandson, George Day Corwine, who resided at Lincoln Illinois (**1931**).

NOTE: 1968
At the death of George Day Corwine, the ring was given for safekeeping to Corwine Ewing Roach who was the grandson of Amnon B.Corwine. Corwine Roach eventually passed the ring to the youngest direct descendant named George Corwine. Corwine Roach had a son and one grandson who carry the Corwine name as a middle name.

Robert Corwine Roach, great-great grandson of Amnon B. Corwine,
*at the village of Corwen in Wales **1994***

Henrietta (Day) Roach:

from Encyclopedia of American Biography,
The American Historical Company, Inc. NY 1954 page 282

Miss Henrietta Day, daughter of George Edward and Leigh (Gross) Day, was married to Corwine E. Roach on June 2, 1923. George Edward Day was the son of George and Henrietta (Shank) Day who came to Illinois from Pennsylvania and settled in Springfield in 1837. Mr. Day founded the prominent Springfield paint store known as George Edward Day Sons. Leigh (Gross) Day was the author of two children's books which attained nationwide popularity: *In Shadow Town* and *Border Land and Beyond.* For her subjects, Leigh Day took Springfield children (most often her daughters Henrietta and Leigh and sons George Edward and Eugene Gross) and illustrated her book with their photographs which she took, developed and printed.

lincoln library   Springfield's Public Library

March 17, 2007

Dr. Rose Marie Roach
1 Ginger Lake Drive W.
Glen Carbon, IL 62034

Dear Dr. Roach:

I want to thank you for the recent donation of materials to the Sangamon Valley Collection at Lincoln Library. Phyllis Brissenden brought the items to me this past Wednesday afternoon and I was very pleased to receive them. The Leigh Gross Day photograph album is very nice and will complement other books of hers that are already in the collection. The materials on the Yates Mansion and McHenry and Butler families are also items that will be useful to us. Coincidentally, I recently purchased some materials from the Prairie Archives bookstore that included a wedding gift registry book for Henrietta Day and Corwin Roach from 1923. So I was delighted to get more materials about them. Thank you again for the wonderful additions to our library.

Sincerely,

Curtis Mann
Springfield City Historian

326 S. Seventh Street · Springfield, IL 62701 · (217) 753-4900 · FAX (217) 753-5329 · Nancy Huntley, Director

Culver Military Academy 1942

1945 at Pearl Harbor
with Jim Teckenbrock

Bob and his younger sister, Mary Leigh, had a privileged and happy childhood. Their parents were prominent in Springfield social, civic and business circles and entertained frequently and lavishly. Corwine and Detta also traveled extensively on business and pleasure, leaving the children in the expert care of a succession of live-in housekeepers. Bob and

Mary Leigh were sent to boarding schools at the age of fourteen, he to Culver Military School and then Lake Forest Academy and Mary Leigh to Pine Manor in Washington, DC and Cranbrook Academy. Bob enlisted in the US Navy during his last semester at Lake Forest and was granted a high school diploma 'in absentia' that June.

After basic training at Great Lakes Naval Air Station, he was stationed at Pearl Harbor until his discharge in 1946. Bob enrolled at Millikin University that fall, along with four of his best friends from Springfield. They had been stationed together at Pearl Harbor, thanks to a friendly recruiting officer at Great Lakes who was a friend of Corwine's. They mustered out together, went to college together and all pledged Sigma Alpha Epsilon fraternity at Millikin, which just happened to be the chapter that Corwine had founded.

Bob majored in Business, preparing to eventually head Capital City Paper Company. We found this assessment of his college career in his papers after his death:

The best thing I got out of Millikin was the girl who will soon be my wife. I met her my sophomore year, and after six months of fighting competition, she accepted my pin and we've been sailing along ever since. We're being married this June, and from there on out is another chapter in this autobiography... .

RC Koach

Thanksgiving at Detta's

Detta's Placecards for Thanksgiving

Xmas 1966

Xmas 1977

Sangamon State University JOURNAL

Published by the Office of University Relations ● Sangamon State University ● Springfield, Illinois 62708

VOLUME 7, NUMBER 10

NOVEMBER 29, 1978

Roach soccer scholarship established

A scholarship to help a soccer player attend Sangamon State has been established in memory of Robert C. Roach, Sr., who died suddenly on Nov. 21. He was the husband of Dr. Rose Marie Roach, SSU associate dean of students.

Roach, who was 51, was an avid booster of soccer at SSU; and the scholarship is named the Robert Roach Memorial Prairie Stars Scholarship.

Many gifts in lieu of flowers and other memorial contributions have been received and continue to come in. Such gifts, with checks made out in the name of the scholarship, may be sent to University Relations, A-5.

Sollie awarded scholarship

Sangamon State's Associate Dean of Student Services Rose Marie Roach made the presentation of the first Robert Roach Memorial Prairie Stars Scholarship Award to Steve Sollie, who discusses members of the 1980 Prairie Stars with Dr. Roach as they peruse the SSU soccer guide. The scholarship honors her late husband who passed away in November, 1978.

A lovely tribute from Rob's friend, Tom Bundy from a letter I wrote to Rob:

"Jim and I went up to Springfield for Tom Bundy's wedding celebration. Tom made a point of coming over to me and said, 'I've been wanting to tell you something for a long time, but I'm afraid I will cry.' I hugged him and he went on, 'these words just keep resounding in my head.' Then he went on to relate that when he and Andy went to the St. Louis airport to pick you up after Daddy died, apparently you told him that Dad used to say, 'It's always better to burn out than to rust out.' And Tom said he has always tried to live his life like that. By that time, as you might well imagine, we were both in tears! "

Hope to talk to you soon...Love...MOM

Bob's Memorial Tree (left) at the Rees Carillon in Springfield's Washington Park

My Story

This "Story of Ten Generations" begins with *My Memoirs* written in 1925 by Henry X; next Aunt Marie's *Memories from Aunt Marie* written in 1989 when she was eighty-four years old and Leota's *My Autobiography*, written in 1982 when she also was eighty-four. Leota shared her childhood memories and gave (unsolicited) advice to her eleven grandchildren about living the good life. These stories have became precious to me and sparked my desire to organize them in book form. As I worked with the family stories, I realized, much to my amazement, that I had become the matriarch of this branch of the Buchmann family and I began to consider not waiting until I turned eighty four to fill in some of the blanks of my own story. When an old high-school boyfriend of Emmy's reestablished contact with the two of us in 2002, he requested that we send him:

"a brief vignette of your life from 1944 to 2002"

That was the impetus I needed, and I replied:

"Can I condense almost sixty years of living into one brief email message...the temptation is too great to resist! As you surely know from your correspondence with Emmy, we left BTHS and Belleville in the fall of 1944; two small town girls with one suitcase apiece boarded the train at St. Louis Union Station bound for Millikin University. We graduated a year early from BTHS (1944 instead of 1945) for we were eager to get on with our lives which turned out to be one of the worst decisions we ever made. Not until we arrived at Millikin did we realize that most of the males of college age were in the armed services. There were three men on campus, not in our class, but in the University. One was blind, one had one arm and the other one was sixteen years old. Incidentally, the sixteen year old, Leroy, turned out to be one of the scientific geniuses on the team that unraveled the secrets of DNA.

Our four years at Millikin were glorious. We pledged Pi Beta Phi. We had a short and somewhat undistinguished career as Millikin cheerleaders. Our sorority sisters made us try out and much to our chagrin, we were selected. We looked cute in our matching outfits, but we were lousy cheerleaders. We majored in English, through no fault of our own, and both of us did a little bit of writing and were on the staff of the college newspaper. I don't remember that we did much studying. The veterans from World War II returned to campus in 1946 and the fun began in earnest. We spent our last two years partying as I recall. We graduated in 1948 and Emmy and Jim Williams were married in October of that year. I stayed in Decatur and wrote advertising copy for a department store until my fiancé, Bob Roach, graduated in 1950. We were married in June of that year and moved to Springfield IL where he went into his father's business, the Capital City Paper Company (known to us as CCPC) and I embraced the 50s lifestyle of raising children and being very involved in the community. I loved that life.

Bob and I had four children. Kim, our only daughter born in 1952, Robert, Jr. in 1956, Andrew in 1958 and Phillip in 1966. I was active in many community organizations which was expected of young married women then. I was the first woman member of the Springfield Chamber of Commerce and the first woman to be invited to join the Springfield Kiwanis Club. I served as president of the Springfield Junior League, Springfield Art Association, Springfield Mental Health Association and Child and Family Services and served on the boards of a number of other community organizations. I discovered (*imagine*) that I really liked to 'be in charge,' solve problems and generally run things.

Springfield Illinois had the dubious distinction of being one of a handful of state capitols that did not have a four year university so in 1970, due partly through the efforts of a Citizen's Committee which Bob chaired, the state legislature granted a charter to a new senior university (junior, senior and graduate students) to be named Sangamon State University. I enrolled in a psychology master's program and can remember my first class. I felt SO OLD having been out of school for twenty-two years! I took a philosophy course expecting Socrates and Plato. Instead they were talking about Teilhard de Chardin and others I had never heard of! Lots of scrambling on my part, but the genie was out of the bottle and I was hooked. I finished a master's degree program in psychology and the University offered me a staff position as counselor and advisor to returning women students. Part of my attraction to the university was that they believed having someone on staff who had "good connections" to the Springfield community would ease the 'town-gown' tension. Springfield, in the 70s, was a fairly conventional, provincial, stuffy town. There was a certain amount of added prestige to having a university in town, but the influx of 'radicals', freethinkers and liberal professors engendered a certain amount of unease among the natives.

I had not anticipated working at all. None of my friends did and Bob and I were too impractical to think about things like saving for upcoming college tuitions. But the opportunity was too wonderful to pass up. I became the Assistant Dean for Student Life at Sangamon State University in the fall of 1972. Our daughter was in college, the two older boys in high school and Phillip, the baby, was starting first grade. I found the University environment exciting and addictive but it required a major adjustment for the entire family. I marched, along with my university friends, in support of various women's issues, notably the Equal Rights Amendment, which of course the Illinois legislature didn't pass, thus blocking its ratification. Throughout these years, and, perhaps, due to my involvement in various causes and crusades, I developed a strong sense of social justice and began to work towards incorporating principles of equality, justice, compassion and fairness into my daily life.

In July of 1978 I finished my Ph.D. in Higher Education Administration and in November of 1978 Bob died suddenly of a massive heart attack. We were both fifty one years old so you can imagine the shock and heartbreak of that time. The three older children were all still in college and Phil was only twelve years old so, as the old saying goes, I found out what tough really meant. I had pushed myself to finish the Ph.D. in record time and I realize now that it must have been ordained, for there is no way that I could have finished my dissertation, worked full time and kept the family together after Bob died. And without that advanced degree, I could never have moved up in the university administrative hierarchy as I did. Sangamon State University was folded into the University of Illinois system and is now known as the University of Illinois at Springfield. When I retired in 1993 I was the Associate Vice-chancellor for Student Services. If someone had told me in 1972 that I would end up being at the University for twenty-two years I would have hooted! I worked hard but those were wonderful years to be on a university campus. As you may imagine, the 60s causes and changes came a little late to central Illinois so I lived through the highs and lows of all the "movements" and became, as I am known to my sister Emmy and brother Carl, the "flaming liberal" of the family!

In 1981 I remarried. A mutual friend introduced Jim Miller and me and although I wasn't really expecting to enter into a new relationship our marriage has enriched both of our lives in ways we could never have imagined. He is a civil engineer and at the time we were married (November 1981) he lived in Edwardsville IL and was VP of the Granite City construction company founded by his late wife's father. I was not ready to give up my position at the University nor was I ready to give up the nurturing environment of Springfield. I had lived there since 1950, Phil was fifteen and in high school and, frankly, I just didn't want to move away. I've always been fairly skilled in drafting compromises (I grew up as a twin, after all) so we agreed that I would continue with my life in Springfield, keep my house there, and we would take turns commuting on weekends, a mere hour and a half drive on the interstate. It was a pretty radical arrangement for that era and one that gave many of my friends fits; however in truth some of them were secretly envious when I pointed out that I didn't do his laundry, we each had our own kitchen and did things our way (he had become a gourmet cook in his three years as a widower) and that when we were together we just had fun. In retrospect, I believe I enjoyed the twelve years of our commuter marriage more than Jim did.

I promised Jim that when Phil graduated from high school I would retire and move to Edwardsville. When that day came, my job was still too much fun and, in fairness, it seemed that Phil's college education was really my responsibility, not Jim's. So we extended our agreement until Phil graduated from college. That day came also and still I was dragging my feet. To be honest, I think I was simply afraid to move away from Springfield and my wonderful support system of friends and colleagues and go to a new town and then, I envisioned, have Jim die suddenly as Bob had. Irrational reasoning I know.....

After Phil got out of college, I amended the agreement and promised I'd retire and move south when our dog, Cleo, died. (Jim was not a dog lover and I felt as if I were doing him a favor!) But one day in early 1993, I realized I wanted to retire, sell my house and get on with the last quarter of my life - - - and the dog did die. I retired the end of April 1993; went to Russia with a group of my university friends, came back, sold my house and moved to Edwardsville/Glen Carbon that Thanksgiving.

I really enjoy this small town. There is a state university here, Southern Illinois University-Edwardsville, and we are close enough to St. Louis, Springfield and Chicago that I have the opportunity of indulging a lifelong passion for live theater. As kids, Dad dragged us to the St. Louis 'Fabulous Fox Theater' every Sunday afternoon to see live vaudeville and all four of us are theater junkies. I've made many good friends (all of them at least ten to fifteen years younger than I am). I became a Master Gardener in Springfield, so I have a fantastic garden down here and really enjoy 'digging in the dirt.'

I play only enough golf to justify owning clubs, read a lot, and am a 'badged visitor' at the federal prison in Greenville IL. I write grants and do research for a local historical restoration project, serve on several local community boards, play with my computer, and travel whenever and wherever I can."

Epilogue 2008:

I have been blessed with the love of two good men, four exceptional children, two spectacular grandsons and two wonderful stepsons and their families. I am profoundly grateful for the many blessings of my life, my parents and siblings and all the special souls who have crossed my path and enriched my life along the way.

HERALD AND REVIEW
PHOTO
Date Taken ___March 17, 1947___
Photographer _____
Ordered by _____ For Mon R
Subject __SAE Circus Dance__

NAMES

Robert Roach, Springfield
Rosie Buchmann, PiBeta Phi,
    Bellvile, Ill

Patsy McCottery, PiBetaPhi,
    Indianapolis, Ind.
Clement H.Wright Jr.,
    Chappaqua, N.Y.

MILLIKIN'S TWINS GET THEIR DIPLOMAS

Springfield Beaux Arts Ball 1969

The Board of Directors
of
The Springfield Art Association
requests the pleasure of your company
at the Madrigal Ball
for Dinner and Coronation of
Queen Kimberly Ellen Roach
Saturday, the twenty-fourth of November
Nineteen hundred and seventy-three
at quarter after six o'clock
Holiday Inn East

Junior League of Springfield

Pouring tea for Governor Otto Kerner from Mary Todd Lincoln's tea service in 1965.

1968 Governor's Delegation to NY World's Fair

Summer 1978 with Jeanie in California

My first cash crop!

Jamaica 1978

Sangamon State years

A 'fantasy' international tour with my friends Jackie
Jackson and Anna May Smith

1979 in Michigan with old friends

Dr. Burton Fryxell- our JMU muse

"Make Mom Happy--
Home for Christmas 1989"

back row: Phil, Andy, Jim Miller
middle: Rob, Kim, Rosie
rear view: Miss Cleo

"In a world that seems so uncertain, in lives that seem sometimes to ricochet from challenge to upheaval and back again, a dog can be counted on in a way that's true of little else."
Good Dog Stay, Anna Quindlen 2007

KiKi 1958

Caramel 1962

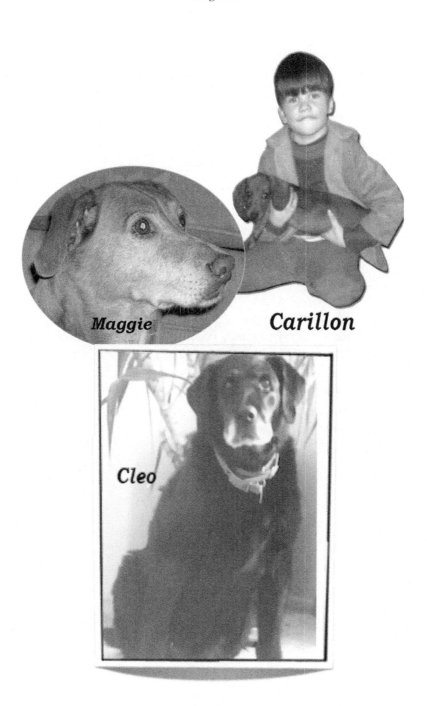

Maggie

Carillon

Cleo

Emile had a wry sense of humor which wasn't always appreciated by the rest of us. The story here is that he complained (good-naturedly of course) that after he had married off his third daughter in less than two years, he wouldn't be able to afford anything but a barrel to wear to work .

He and mother had this photo doctored, long before the days of Photoshop. Notice it is Leota's hand on his arm. They substituted this picture for the actual 'father-of-the-bride' wedding photo in my album and brought it to Springfield when Bob and I returned from our Canadian wedding trip. It is a lot funnier to me today than it was in June of 1950!

Family Weddings

It took me 50 years to finally admit Emile's idea was REALLY funny!

October 9, 1948

Jane Kurrus   Jeanie   Emmy   Rosie   Virginia Williams

June 17, 1950

Mary Leigh Roach   Jeanie   Rosie   Emmy   Jane Kurrus   Ann Daigh

Jeane & John Kluga
September 2, 1954

Carolyn Craig & Carl Buchmann
June 22, 1958

*Julie Williams
& John Doxsie*

*August 29,
1975*

Jill Williams & Dan DeMichele
January 2, 1982

Kim Roach and
David Poteet
June 9, 1990

Rob Roach & Barbara Lommen
July 7, 1991

Andy Roach & Mary Servatius
October 9, 1999

Nikki Ezelle & David Williams
July 22, 1995

Michelle Buick and Phil Roach June 12, 2004

Arthur Buchmann and family

October 30, 1948
Herb & Cathy Buchmann

Ken & Cathy Buchmann
October 20, 1988

4th of July   1986

Glen Carbon 1994

Xmas party- 2000

Bandolier Canyon 1991

Kauia 2008

"My sister and I, you will recollect, were twins, and you know how subtle are the links which bind two souls which are so closely allied." Sir Arthur Conan Doyle

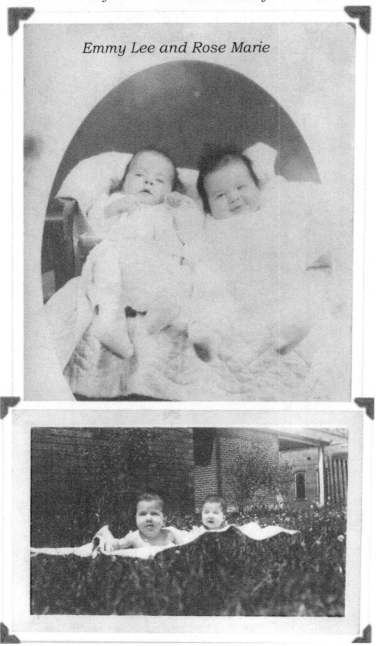

Emmy Lee and Rose Marie

February 3, 2007 in Puerto Vallarta

*If the twins are 80
and I am half of the 'twins'
Does that mean I am 40?*

*If the twins are 80
and I am half of the 'twins'
Does that mean I am 40?*

♫♫♥♫♫

1998 Talent(?) Show

at the

Poteet Theater

♪☺♪☺♪☺♪☺♪☺♪☺♪☺♪☺♪☺♪☺♪☺♪☺♪☺♪

1. "About"   – Jim
2. "The Dollar Bow Tie" *Please have dollar bill ready!* – Phil
3. "Magic Fingers"   – Jim
4. "A Sensitive & Heart Felt Ballad"   – Andy
5. "East meets West"   – David
6. "Beer Cap Boogie"   – Andy
7. "A Student Speaks"   – Kim

I N T E R M I S S I O N

You are NOT allowed to leave the theater!

Finalé

➡ The Red Hot Mama s and Papa s   – Jim & ❀Mom❀

- Applause -

Please no flash photography, the players might hurt you!

♪☺♪☺♪☺♪☺♪☺♪☺♪☺♪☺♪☺♪☺♪☺♪☺♪☺♪

The End

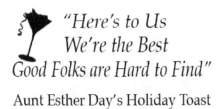

"Here's to Us
We're the Best
Good Folks are Hard to Find"

Aunt Esther Day's Holiday Toast

The family. We were a strange little band of characters trudging through life sharing diseases and toothpaste, coveting one another's desserts, hiding shampoo, borrowing money, locking each other out of our rooms, inflicting pain and kissing to heal it in the same instant, loving, laughing, defending, and trying to figure out the common thread that bound us all together.

~Erma Bombeck

Part Six

Family Trees

The BUCHMANN family lived in Rosenwiller, bas du
Rhin, Alsace-Lorraine France. The earliest recorded
ancestor of this line is Phillippe Buchmann born in
Rosenwiller in 1743.

Henry Xavier BUCHMANN, born in 1859 in Rosenwiller,
emigrated on the ship Waesland from Strasbourg
to New York, docking in New York harbor on April 29, 1885. He traveled to Belleville Illinois to stay temporarily with his ninety year old 'grand-uncle'. After one week, he went to St. Louis Missouri to stay with his mother's cousin. Henry died in St. Louis Missouri in 1948 at the age of 88.

Genealogy of the
Buchmann Family 1743-2007

First Generation

---

1. Phillipe BUCHMANN. Born in 1743 in Rosenwiller. Phillipe died in Rosenwiller on 23 May 1821; he was 78. Religion: Roman Catholic.

Phillipe married Anne Marie BECKERT, daughter of , in Rosenwiller. Born in Rosenwiller.

They had one child:

    2   i.   Phillippe (1788-1858)

Second Generation

---

2. Phillippe BUCHMANN. Born in 1788 in Rosenwiller. Phillippe died in Rosenwiller on 23 Mar 1858; he was 70.

On 9 May 1805 when Phillippe was 17, he married Julienne HUCK, daughter of Bernard HUCK & Gertrude SCHEIDT, in Rosenwiller. Born in 1787 in Rosenwiller.

They had the following children:

    3   i.   Xavier (1812-1858)

    4   ii.   Sophie

    5   iii.   Caroline (1821-)

Third Generation

---

3. Xavier BUCHMANN. Born on 16 Dec 1812 in Rosenwiller. Xavier died on 21 Jan 1858; he was 45.

He did not marry Brigitte RUDOLFF, daughter of Denis RUDOLFF & Gertrude BRONNER. Born on 24 Jan 1812 in Rosenwiller. Brigitte died in Rosenwiller on 11 Sep 1835; she was 23.

They had one child:

     6   i.   Louis (1834-)

On 22 Jan 1840 when Xavier was 27, he second married Julienne DEMARCK, in Rosenwiller.

4. Sophie BUCHMANN.

5. Caroline BUCHMANN. Born on 1 Apr 1821 in Rosenwiller.

Fourth Generation

---

6. Louis BUCHMANN. Born on 23 Aug 1834 in Rosenwiller, Bas du Rhin, Alsace-Lorraine, France. Occupation: Farmer. Religion: Roman Catholic.

On 12 May 1861 when Louis was 26, he married Marie Anne RICHERT, daughter of Francois Joseph RICHERT & Scholastique STEYER, in Rosenwiller,Bas Rhin,France. Born on 16 Nov 1834 in Rosenwiller, Bas du Rhin, Alsace-Lorraine, France.They had the following children:

7	i.	Henry Xavier Thomas Louis (1859-1948)
8	ii.	Edouard Xavier (1861-1919)
9	iii.	Marie Brigitte (1863-)
10	iv.	Elisabeth (1864-)
11	v.	Charles (1866-1869)
12	vi.	Marie Louise (1868-)
13	vii.	Charles (1869-)
14	viii.	Marie Madeleine (1871-1947)
15	ix.	Unknown
16	x.	Unknown

Fifth Generation

7.Henry Xavier Thomas Louis BUCHMANN Born on 18 Dec 1859 in Rosenwiller, Bas du Rhin, Alsace-Lorraine, France. Henry Xavier Thomas Louis died in St. Louis, MO, on 19 Feb 1948; he was 88. Buried on 21 Feb 1948 in Mt. Olive, Mo. Occupation: Cabinet Maker In France (Barber In German Army). Religion: Roman Catholic.

On 29 Oct 1889 when Henry Xavier Thomas Louis was 29, he married Drusilla Maria HAMMER, daughter of Michael X. HAMMER & Rosina SCHIRER, in St. Boniface,St.Louis,Missouri. Born on 26 Apr 1870 in Cincinnati, OH. Drusilla Maria died in St. Louis, MO, on 8 Dec 1958; she was 88.

They had the following children:

17	i.	Arthur Michael (1892-1967)
18	ii.	Florence Andrew (1895-1979)
19	iii.	EMILE HENRY (1899-1960)
20	iv.	Marie Elizabeth (1905-1989)

8. Edouard Xavier BUCHMANN. Born on 17 Oct 1861 in Rosenwiller. Edouard Xavier died in Amarillo, Potter County, TX,USA, in 1919; he was 57.

Edouard Xavier married Mary Louise DOEMKER. Born on 7 Feb 1872. Mary Louise died in La Mesa, San Diego County, CA, on 4 Jun 1946; she was 74.

They had the following children:

21	i.	Louie (1900-)
22	ii.	Josephine Bernadine Marie (1906-2000)
23	iii.	Edward (1910-1996)
24	iv.	Jerome L. (1913-1995)

9. Marie Brigitte BUCHMANN. Born on 9 Sep 1863 in Rosenwiller.

10. Elisabeth BUCHMANN. Born on 12 Nov 1864 in Rosenwiller.

11. Charles BUCHMANN. Born on 2 Nov 1866 in Rosenwiller. Charles died in Rosenwiller in 1869; he was 2.

The Buchmann Family

Fifth Generation

12. Marie Louise BUCHMANN. Born on 20 Oct 1868 in Rosenwiller.

13. Charles BUCHMANN. Born on 10 Aug 1869 in Rosenwiller.

14. Marie Madeleine BUCHMANN. Born on 30 Jul 1871 in Rosenwiller. Marie Madeleine died in Paris France, on 30 Jul 1947; she was 76.

Marie Madeleine married VOILLE.

15. Unknown BUCHMANN.

16. Unknown BUCHMANN.

Sixth Generation

17. Arthur Michael BUCHMANN. Born on 28 Dec 1892 in St. Louis, MO. Arthur Michael died in Franklin, Missouri, on 15 Mar 1967; he was 74. Buried on 18 Mar 1967 in Mt. Olive/St.Louis MO.

On 26 Jun 1921 when Arthur Michael was 28, he married Marie Catherine RECK, daughter of Alois RECK & Ann Josephine NEKVINDA, in St. Wenceslaus/St.Louis MO. Born on 23 Mar 1901 in Vienna Austria. Marie Catherine died in Washington MO, on 17 Dec 1975; she was 74.

They had the following children:

| 25 | i. | Herbert Alois (1922-) |
| 26 | ii. | Kenneth Henry (1929- |

18. Florence Andrew BUCHMANN. Born on 12 Jun 1895 in St. Louis, MO. Florence Andrew died in Veteran's Home, Danville, Illinois, on 28 Jul 1979; he was 84. Buried on 30 Jul 1979 in Mt.Olive Cemetery /St.LouisMO.

Sixth Generation

19. EMILE HENRY BUCHMANN. Born on 21 Aug 1899 in St. Louis, MO.
EMILE HENRY died in San Francisco, CA, on 30 Jul 1960; he was 60. Buried on 2
Aug 1960 in Walnut Hill Cemetery/Belleville, IL. Occupation: Physical Education/
Dance/Youth Counselor. Education: Butler University. Religion: Christian Science.

On 30 Jun 1924 when EMILE HENRY was 25, he married LEOTA EMMA
GROMBACH, daughter of Henry GROMBACH & Emma NEUTZLING, in
Belleville,IL. Born on 13 Jun 1898 in Belleville, IL. LEOTA EMMA died in
Belleville, IL, on 23 Aug 1984; she was 86.

They had the following children:

27	i.	Rose Marie (1927-)
28	ii.	Emmy Lee (1927-)
29	iii.	Lois Jean (1928-)
30	iv.	Carl Emile (1929-)

20. Marie Elizabeth BUCHMANN. Born on 25 Jan 1905 in St. Louis, MO. Marie
Elizabeth died in St. Louis, MO, on 19 Mar 1989; she was 84. Buried on 22 Mar
1989 in Mt. Olive, St. Louis, MO. Occupation: Teacher. Education: St.Louis
University St.Louis MO. Religion: Catholic.

21. Louie BUCHMANN. Born in 1900

22. Josephine Bernadine Marie BUCHMANN. Born on 17 Apr 1906 in Marion,
Williamson County IL. Josephine Bernadine Marie died in Springfield, Lane
County, Oregon, on 16 May 2000; she was 94. Buried in St. Mary's Catholic
Cemetery, Sacramento CA. Religion: Ordained As Nun.St. Rose Catholic Church
Sacramento CA.

On 1 Jun 1921 when Josephine Bernadine Marie was 15, she married Anthony
George STAYNOR, in Springfield IL. Born on 3 Aug 1899. Anthony George died in
Sacramento CA, in Jul 1962; he was 62.

They had one child:

| 31 | i. | Florence |

Sixth Generation

---

23. Edward BUCHMANN. Born on 14 Sep 1910. Edward died in Long Beach CA, on 5 Mar 1996; he was 85.

24. Jerome L. BUCHMANN. Born on 30 Sep 1913. Jerome L. died in Oceanside California, on 19 Apr 1995; he was 81.

Seventh Generation

---

25. Herbert Alois BUCHMANN. Born on 27 Oct 1922 in St. Louis MO. Occupation: Bank Officer. Education: Washington U. St.Louis. Religion: Catholic.

On 30 Oct 1948 when Herbert Alois was 26, he married Catherine Marie HARMS, in St. Louis MO. Born on 9 Mar 1932 in St. Louis MO.

They had the following children:

32	i.	Herbert Alois II (1949-)
33	ii.	Gregory Michael (1951-)
34	iii.	Barth David (1955-)
35	iv.	Cynthia Marie (1962-)

26. Kenneth Henry BUCHMANN. Born on 31 Dec 1929 in St Louis MO. Occupation: Veterinarian. Education: U.of Missouri/Columbia. Religion: Catholic.

In 1956 when Kenneth Henry was 26, he first married Ann PERKINS. Born on 2 Aug 1936 in St Louis MO.They had the following children:

36	i.	Diane Karen (1958-)
37	ii.	Eric William (1959-)
38	iii.	Brian Thomas (1961-)
39	iv.	Elaine Marie (1962-)
40	v.	David Andrew (1964-)
41	vi.	Neal Howard (1966-)
42	vii.	Kenneth Edward (1967-)

In Oct 1987 when Kenneth Henry was 57, he second married Cathy Jean KLOPPE.

Seventh Generation

27. Rose Marie BUCHMANN. Born on 3 Feb 1927 in Belleville, IL. Occupation: University Administrator. Education: Millikin, SSU, UIS, Illinois State.

On 17 Jun 1950 when Rose Marie was 23, she first married Robert Corwine ROACH, son of Charles MILLER & Marie LOGAN, in Belleville,IL. Born on 21 Jan 1927 in Chicago, IL. Robert Corwine died in Springfield, IL, on 21 Nov 1978; he was 51.

They had the following children:

43	i.	Kimberly Ellen (1952-)
44	ii.	Robert Corwine, Jr. (1956-)
45	iii.	Andrew Thomas (1958-)
46	iv.	Phillip Matthew (1966-)

On 7 Nov 1981 when Rose Marie was 54, she second married Fred James MILLER Jr., son of Fred James MILLER & Lillian COOKE, in Springfield,Illinois. Born on 11 Sep 1926 in Thomas, OK. Jim had two sons, Dale and Alan, by his first marriage.

Seventh Generation

---

29. Emmy Lee BUCHMANN. Born on 3 Feb 1927.On 9 Oct 1948 when Emmy Lee was 21, she married James Edward WILLIAMS, in St.Paul's Evangelical /Belleville IL. Born on 31 Jan 1923 in Decatur Illinois. They had the following children:

47	i.	Jill Diane (1951-)
48	ii.	Julia Moore (1954-)
49	iii.	James David (1961-)

29. Lois Jean BUCHMANN. Born on 25 Feb 1928 in Belleville IL.

On 2 Sep 1954 when Lois Jean was 26, she married John KLUGA, in Los Angeles CA. Born on 18 Dec 1924. They had the following children:

| 50 | i. | Jon Christopher (1961-) |
| 51 | ii. | Kyra Lee (1963-) |

30. Carl Emile BUCHMANN. Born on 15 Sep 1929 in Belleville, IL.

On 22 Jun 1958 when Carl Emile was 28, he married Mary Carolyn CRAIG, daughter of Hugh MacGregor CRAIG & Mary Helen HAMILTON, in Linton,Indiana. Born on 5 Aug 1935 in Syracuse, NY.

They had the following children:

| 52 | i. | Craig Eric (1962-) |
| 53 | ii. | Caron Susanne (1965-) |

31.   **Florence STAYNOR.**

Eighth Generation

---

32. Herbert Alois BUCHMANN II. Born on 22 Jul 1949.

On 27 Sep 1975 when Herbert Alois II was 26, he first married Marno McPHERSEN, in Ottawa Kansas. Born on 2 Dec 1951 in Kansas.

They had the following children:

54	i.	Brett Alois (1978-)
55	ii.	Arikka Alexandria (1985-)

On 5 Oct 1994 when Herbert Alois II was 45, he second married Katherine Ann GOSNEY, in Oletha Kanss. Born on 24 May 1952.

Herbert Alois II third married Sally PARKER.

33. Gregory Michael BUCHMANN. Born on 26 Mar 1951.

On 24 May 1969 when Gregory Michael was 18, he married Sherryl Denise ROSEMANN, in St Louis MO. Born on 17 Mar 1952 in St Louis MO.

They had the following children:

56	i.	Heather Renee (1969-)
57	ii.	Norma June (1974-)
58	iii.	Kyra Anne (1977-)

34. Barth David BUCHMANN. Born on 4 Jul 1955 in St. Louis MO.

On 11 Jun 1977 when Barth David was 21, he married Joann Elizabeth KUNDERER, in St. Francis Of Assissi/Oakville MO. Born on 7 Jul 1957 in St Louis MO.

They had the following children:

59	i.	Alesia Marie (1978-)
60	ii.	Tiffany Marie (1981-)

Eighth Generation

---

35. Cynthia Marie BUCHMANN. Born on 18 Sep 1962 in St. Louis MO.

On 22 Dec 1982 when Cynthia Marie was 20, she married Donald Patrick MURABITO, in Oakville MO. Born on 11 Dec 1960 in St Louis MO.

They had the following children:

| 61 | i. | Drusilla Marie (1991-) |
| 62 | ii. | Madeline Marie (1994-) |

36. Diane Karen BUCHMANN. Born on 5 Nov 1958 in Washington MO.

Diane Karen married Nelson KENNER.

37. Eric William BUCHMANN. Born on 6 Nov 1959 in St.Louis MO

On 26 Jul 1998 when Eric William was 38, he married Amy GUMMINGER. Born on 13 Nov 1971.

They had the following children:

63	i.	Alayna Nadine (2000-)
64	ii.	Claire Marie (2001-)
65	iii.	Jonah David (2004-)

38. Brian Thomas BUCHMANN. Born on 27 Apr 1961 in Washington MO.Brian Thomas married Anita BREZ. Born on 3 Dec 1963.

They had the following children:

66	i.	Emily Allison (1987-)
67	ii.	Abby Elizabeth (1991-)
68	iii.	Maggie Elise (1993-)

39. Elaine Marie BUCHMANN. Born on 20 Oct 1962 in Holstein MO.

On 17 Aug 1985 when Elaine Marie was 22, she married Kurt Alan WHITE, son of Leroy WHITE & Janice, in Treloar MO. Born on 29 Mar 1963.They had the following children:

| 69 | i. | Jeffrey Alan (1986-) |
| 70 | ii. | Lynn Marie (1988-) |

40. David Andrew BUCHMANN. Born on 19 Jun 1964 in Washington MO.

David Andrew married Teresa SISSUM. Born on 27 Jul 1960.

Eighth Generation

---

41. Neal Howard BUCHMANN. Born on 28 Feb 1966 in Washington MO.

Neal Howard married Amy SCHANTZ. Born on 21 Apr 1966.

They had one child:

    71   i.   Jack William (2002-)

42. Kenneth Edward BUCHMANN. Born on 5 Jul 1967 in Washington MO.

43. Kimberly Ellen ROACH. Born on 11 Jun 1952 in Springfield, IL. Occupation: Literacy Educator. Education: Kenyon College/U.of Illinois/U. Of Wisconsin/ Auburn University, SIUE.

On 9 Jun 1990 when Kimberly Ellen was 37, she married David POTEET, in Madison Wisconsin. Born on 17 Mar 1945.

He had one child, Thomas Poteet, from a previous marriage.

44. Robert Corwine,. ROACH, Jr.

Born on 14 May 1956 in Springfield IL. Occupation: Research Physiologist.

Education: Evergreen College, U. Of Washington, Cornell, U. Of New Mexico. On 7 Jul 1991 when Robert Corwine, Jr. was 35, he married Barbara Katrin LOMMEN, daughter of Harry LOMMEN & Gertrudis, in Wanssum,Limburg,Netherlands. Born on 20 Jun 1964 in Wanssum, Limburg, Netherlands.They had the following children:

    72   i.   Jack Henry (1999-)

    73   ii.   Charles Emile (2002-)

Eighth Generation

---

45. Andrew Thomas ROACH. Born on 12 Jul 1958 in Springfield, IL. Occupation: Oceanographer, Mathematician. Education: U.of Chicago/U.of Illinois/ U.of Washington.

On 9 Oct 1999 when Andrew Thomas was 41, he married Mary SERVATIUS, daughter of Don SERVATIUS & Betty, in Chicago IL. Born on 22 Feb 1961 in Chicago IL. Mary died in Chicago IL, on 17 Oct 2001; she was 40.

46. Phillip Matthew ROACH. Born on 15 Feb 1966 in Springfield, IL. Occupation: Computers. Education: Lincoln College.

On 12 Jun 2004 when Phillip Matthew was 38, he married Michelle Grace BUICK, in Phoenix AZ.

Born 14 Apr 1968. She had one child, Thomas Jon Lindstrom from a previous marriage.

Eighth Generation

_____

47. Jill Diane Williams. Born on 8 Sep 1951 in Decatur, IL.

On 2 Jan 1982 when Jill Diane was 30, she married Daniel DeMichele, in Decatur,IL. Born on 19 Aug 1948.

They had the following children:

74	i.	Daniel (1985-)
75	ii.	Thomas Daniel (1988-)
76	iii.	Joseph Daniel (1991-)

48. Julia Moore WILLIAMS. Born on 3 Mar 1954 in Decatur, IL.

On 29 Aug 1975 when Julia Moore was 21, she married John Robert DOXSIE, son of Louie Edward DOXSIE & Beryl Leah, in Decatur,IL. Born on 31 Jan 1953.

They had the following children:

77 i.Jill Suzanne (1983-)

78 ii.Jeffrey Thomas (1987-)

Eighth Generation

---

49. James David WILLIAMS. Born on 14 Aug 1961 in Decatur, IL.

On 22 Jul 1995 when James David was 33, he married Kammie Nicole EZELLE, daughter of Travis Kirk EZELLE & Donna Gail DUPELECHAIN, in Los Angeles,California. Born on 8 Nov 1968 in Lake Charles, Louisiana.

They had the following children:

79	i.Parker James (1998-)
80	ii.Carter Davidson (2000-)
81	iii.Windsor Nichole (2002-)

50. Jon Christopher KLUGA. Born on 27 Jul 1961 in San Francisco CA.

Jon Christopher married Amber Overlin. Born on 25 Apr 1961. She had two children, Charlie and Annie, from a previous marriage.

They had one child:

82i.   Catherine Jeane (2000-)

51 Kyra Lee KLUGA. Born on 24 Apr 1963 in California.

Eighth Generation

---

52. Craig Eric BUCHMANN. Born on 13 May 1962 in Camp Lejeune, NC.

On 11 Feb 1989 when Craig Eric was 26, he married Jana Dee RUSSELL, in Baytown,TX. Born on 18 Nov 1964 in Baytown, TX.

They had the following children:

83   i. Bryce (1991-)
84   ii. Connor (1993-)
85   iii. Andrea (1996-)

53. Caron Susann BUCHMANN. Born on 25 Aug 1965 in Camp Lejeune, NC.

On 5 May 1998 when Caron Susann was 32, she married James BROOKS, in Las Vegas NEV.

They had the following children:

86   *i*Sawyer Carl (2000-)
87   *ii.*Camryn   (2002-)

Ninth Generation

---

54. Brett Alois BUCHMANN. Born on 3 Jul 1978 in Shawnee Kansas.

55. Arikka Alexandria BUCHMANN. Born on 16 Dec 1985 in Shawnee Kansas.

56. Heather Renee BUCHMANN. Born on 2 Nov 1969 in St. Louis MO.

On 17 Aug 1995 when Heather Renee was 25, she married Patrick Lynn RILEY, in Lake Tahoe Nevada. Born on 21 Nov 1960 in France.

They had one child:

| 88 | i. | Stuart Michael (1997-) |

57. Norma June BUCHMANN. Born on 21 Dec 1974.

On 15 May 1999 when Norma June was 24, she married Rodney LEWIS, in Jefferson County MO.

She had the following children:

89	i.	Gregory Michael (II) (1992-)
90	ii.	Kayla Christine (1995-)
91	iii.	Karissa Madeline (1996-1996)
92	iv.	Madeline Christine (1997-)

58. Kyra Anne BUCHMANN. Born on 8 Jul 1977 in St Louis MO.

59. Alesia Marie BUCHMANN. Born on 17 Dec 1978 in St Louis MO.

60. Tiffany Marie BUCHMANN. Born on 16 May 1981 in St.Louis MO.

61. Drusilla Marie MURABITO. Born on 1 Aug 1991 in St. Louis MO.

62. Madeline Marie MURABITO. Born on 15 Apr 1994 in St Louis MO.

63. Alayna Nadine BUCHMANN. Born on 11 May 2000.

64. Claire Marie BUCHMANN. Born on 22 Apr 2001.

65. Jonah David BUCHMANN. Born on 15 Oct 2004 in North Kansas City

66. Emily Allison BUCHMANN. Born on 14 Oct 1987 in Washington MO.

67. Abby Elizabeth BUCHMANN. Born on 5 Jul 1991 in Washington MO.

68. Maggie Elise BUCHMANN. Born on 3 Apr 1993 in Washington MO.

69. Jeffrey Alan WHITE. Born on 18 Mar 1986 in Washington MO.

70. Lynn Marie WHITE. Born on 11 Mar 1988 in Washington MO.

Ninth Generation

---

71. Jack William BUCHMANN. Born on 27 Sep 2002.

72. Jack Henry Roach LOMMEN. Born on 25 May 1999 in Santa Fe NM

73. Charles Emile Roach LOMMEN. Born on 29 Aug 2002 in Santa Fe NM

74. Daniel DeMichele. Born on 14 Jul 1985 in Phoenix, AZ.

75. Thomas Daniel DeMichele. Born on 31 Aug 1988 in Phoenix, AZ.

76. Joseph Daniel DeMichele. Born on 5 Feb 1991 in Phoenix, AZ.

77. Jill Suzanne DOXSIE. Born on 6 Jun 1983 in Decatur, IL.

78. Jeffrey Thomas DOXSIE. Born on 23 Nov 1987 in Decatur, IL.

79. Parker James WILLIAMS. Born on 2 Feb 1998.

80. Carter Davidson WILLIAMS. Born on 27 Jan 2000.

81. Windsor Nichole WILLIAMS. Born on 21 Nov 2002 in Chatsworth CA.

82. Catherine Jeane KLUGA. Born on 1 Aug 2000 in San Jose CA.

83. Bryce BUCHMANN. Born on 1 Nov 1991 in Japan.

84. Connor BUCHMANN. Born on 11 Jul 1993 in San Diego, California.

85. Andrea BUCHMANN. Born on 6 Jun 1996 in San Diego, California.

86. Sawyer Carl BROOKS. Born on 18 Jul 2000 in Daytona Beach FL.

87. Camryn BROOKS. Born on 5 Mar 2002 in Daytona Beach FL.

Tenth Generation

---

88. Stuart Michael RILEY. Born on 1 Jun 1997 in St Louis MO.

89. Gregory Michael (II) BUCHMANN. Born on 19 Jul 1992 in St Louis MO.

90. Kayla Christine Czapala. Born on 21 Apr 1995 in St Louis MO.

91. Karissa Madeline Czapala. Born on 16 Jun 1996 in St Louis MO. Karissa Madeline died in St Louis MO, on 30 Oct 1996; she was <1. Buried on 1 Nov 1996 in St Louis MO.

92. Madeline Christine Czapala. Born on 22 Oct 1997 in St Louis MO.

Buchmann Surname Index

BUCHMANN

EMILE HENRY	19
Emily Allison	66
Emmy Lee	28
Eric William	37
Florence Andrew	18
Gregory Michael	33
Gregory Michael (II)	89
Heather Renee	56
Henry Xavier Thomas Louis	7
Herbert Alois	25
Herbert Alois II	32
Jack William	71
Jerome L	24
Jonah David	65
Josephine Bernardine Marie	22
Kenneth Edward	42
Kenneth Henry	26
Kyra Anne	58
Lois Jean	29
Louie	21
Louis	6
Maggie Elise	68
Marie Brigitte	9
Marie Elizabeth	20
Marie Louise	12
Marie Madeleine	14
Neal Howard	41
Norma June	57
Phillipe	1
Phillippe	2
Rose Marie	27
Sophie	4
Tiffany Marie	60
Unknown	15
Unknown	16
Xavier	3

BUICK
Michelle Grace	spouse of 46

COOKE
Lillian	parent of spouse of 27

CRAIG
    Hugh MacGregor   parent of spouse of 30
    Mary Carolyn   spouse of 30

CZAPALA
    Karissa Madeline   91
    Kayla Christine   90
    Madeline Christine   92

DEMARCK
    Julienne   spouse of 3

DeMichele
    Daniel   spouse of 47
    Daniel   74
    Joseph Daniel   76
    Thomas Daniel   75

DOEMKER
    Mary Louise   spouse of 8

DOXSIE
    Jeffrey Thomas   78
    Jill Suzanne   77
    John Robert   spouse of 48
    Louie Edward   parent of spouse of 48

DUPELECHAIN
    Donna Gail   parent of spouse of 49

EZELLE
    Kammie Nicole   spouse of 49
    Travis Kirk   parent of spouse of 49

GOSNEY
    Katherine Ann   spouse of 32

GROMBACH
    Henry   parent of spouse of 19
    LEOTA EMMA   spouse of 19

GUMMINGER
    Amy   spouse of 37

HAMILTON
    Mary Helen   parent of spouse of 30

HAMMER
    Drusilla Maria   spouse of 7
    Michael X.   parent of spouse of 7

HARMS
    Catherine Marie   spouse of 25

HUCK
    Bernard   parent of spouse of 2
    Julienne   spouse of 2

KENNER
Nelson   spouse of 36
KLOPPE
Cathy Jean   spouse of 26
KLUGA
Catherine Jeane   82
John   spouse of 29
Jon Christopher   50
Kyra Lee   51
KUNDERER
Joann Elizabeth   spouse of 34
LEWIS
Rodney   spouse of 57
LOGAN
Marie   parent of spouse of 27
LOMMEN
Barbara Katrin   spouse of 44
Harry   parent of spouse of 44
McPHERSEN
Marno   spouse of 32
MILLER
Charles   parent of spouse of 27
Fred James Jr.   spouse of 27
Fred James   parent of spouse of 27
MURABITO
Donald Patrick   spouse of 35
Drusilla Marie   61
MURABITO   Madeline Marie   62
NEKVINDA
Ann Josephine   parent of spouse of 17
NEUTZLING
Emma   parent of spouse of 19
OVERLIN
Amber   spouse of 50
PARKER
Sally   spouse of 32
PERKINS
Ann   spouse of 26
POTEET
David   spouse of 43
RECK
Alois   parent of spouse of 17
Marie Catherine   spouse of 17
RICHERT
Francois Joseph   parent of spouse of 6
Marie Anne   spouse of 6

RILEY
    Patrick Lynn   spouse of 56
    Stuart Michael   88
ROACH
    Andrew Thomas   45
    Kimberly Ellen   43
    Phillip Matthew   46
    Robert Corwine   spouse of 27
    Robert Corwine, Jr.   44
Roach LOMMEN
    Charles Emile   73
    Jack Henry   72
ROSEMANN
    Sherryl Denise   spouse of 33
RUDOLFF
    Brigitte   spouse of 3
    Denis   parent of spouse of 3
RUSSELL
    Jana Dee   spouse of 52
SCHANTZ
    Amy   spouse of 41
SCHEIDT
    Gertrude   parent of spouse of 2
SCHIRER
    Rosina   parent of spouse of 7

SERVATIUS
    Don   parent of spouse of 45
    Mary   spouse of 45
SISSUM
    Teresa   spouse of 40
STAYNOR
    Anthony George   spouse of 22
    Florence   31
STEYER
    Scholastique   parent of spouse of 6
VOILLE
    UNNAMED   spouse of 14
WHITE
    Jeffrey Alan   69
    Kurt Alan   spouse of 39
    Leroy   parent of spouse of 39
    Lynn Marie   70

WILLIAMS

Carter Davidson	80
James David	49
James Edward	spouse of 28
Jill Diane	47
Julia Moore	48
Parker James	79
Windsor Nichole	81

BLOOD RELATIVES OF HENRY X BUCHMANN

Surname	First Name	Birth Date	Birth Place
Father -			
BUCHMANN	Louis	23 Aug 1834	Rosenwiller
Mother -			
RICHERT	Marie Anne	16 Nov 1834	Rosenwiller,
Brother -			
BUCHMANN	Charles	2 Nov 1866	Rosenwiller
BUCHMANN	Charles	10 Aug 1869	Rosenwiller
BUCHMANN	Edouard Xavier	17 Oct 1861	Rosenwiller
Sibling -			
BUCHMANN	Unknown		
BUCHMANN	Unknown		
Sister -			
BUCHMANN	Elisabeth	12 Nov 1864	Rosenwiller
BUCHMANN	Marie Brigitte	9 Sep 1863	Rosenwiller
BUCHMANN	Marie Louise	20 Oct 1868	Rosenwiller
BUCHMANN	Marie Madeleine	30 Jul 1871	Rosenwiller
Grandfather -			
BUCHMANN	Xavier	16 Dec 1812	Rosenwiller
RICHERT	Francois Joseph	26 Apr 1801	Rosenwiller
Grandmother -			
RUDOLFF	Brigitte	24 Jan 1812	Rosenwiller
STEYER	Scholastique	13 Apr 1803	Rosenwiller
G Grandfather -			
BUCHMANN	Phillippe	1788	Rosenwiller
RICHERT	Charles	7 Feb 1774	Obernai
RUDOLFF	Denis	10 Oct 1776	Rosenwiller
STEYER	Francois Joseph	20 Mar 1754	Rosenwiller
G Grandmother -			
BRONNER	Gertrude	18 Mar 1772	Rosenwiller
FREY	Madeline	17 Jul 1779	Rosenwiller
HUCK	Julienne	1787	Rosenwiller
MEYER	Odile	17 Dec 1767	Rosenwiller

Surname	First Name	Birth Date	Birth Place

GG Grandfather -

BRONNER	Jean Georges	1734	
BUCHMANN	Phillipe	1743	Rosenwiller
FREY	Mathieu	1743	Rosenwiller
HUCK	Bernard	1743	Rosenwiller
MEYER	Jean	1743	Rosenwiller
RUDOLFF	Louis	1749	Rosenwiller
STEYER	Jean	1722	Rosenwiller

GG Grandmother -

BECKERT	Anne Marie		Rosenwiller
FUGER	Odile	1739	Rosenwiller
JOST	Odile		Rosenwiller
RECKEL	Marie Anne		Rosenwiller '
SCHEIDT	Gertrude	1743	Rosenwiller
WANTZ	Barbe	1740	
WOLF	Gertrude		Rosenwiller

GGG Grandfather -

BRONNER	Joseph		
FREY	Joannese		
FUGER	Francisci		Rosenwiller
HUCK	Mathieu	1722	Rosenwiller
SCHEIDT	Nicolas		Rosenwiller
WANTZ	Mathieu		

GGG Grandmother -

BRUNISIN	Maria		Rosenwiller
GRAUSS	Anne Marie	1720	Rosenwiller
MEYER	Anna Maria	1719	Rosenwiller
MUNSCHEN	Ursula		
WANTZ	Margarethe		
WERNER	Anne Marie		Rosenwiller

BLOOD RELATIVES OF HENRY X BUCHMANN

Surname	First Name	Birth Date	Birth Place

GGGG Grandfather -

GRAUSS	Andrea		Rosenwiller
HUCK	Jacobi		Rosenwiller
MEYER	Andreas	1694	Rosenwiller

GGGG Grandmother -

FUGERIN	Catherina		
HUCK	Maria		
	Rosenwiller		
MEYER	Catherina		
	Rosenwiller		

5G Grandfather -

FUGERIN	Joannis		

5G Grandmother -

GRONOLININ	Catherine		
SINNORINN	Anna		

Uncle -

RICHERT	Aloise	13 May 1837	
RICHERT	Charles	30 Sep 1829	
RICHERT	Joseph	19 Sep 1839	

Aunt -

RICHERT	Caroline	20 Feb 1832	Rosenwiller

Grandaunt -

BUCHMANN	Caroline1	Apr 1821	Rosenwiller
BUCHMANN	Sophie		
RICHERT	Madelein	25 Jul 1819	Rosenwiller
RICHERT	Marie An	7 Feb 1817	Rosenwiller

GG Granduncle -

HUCK	Jean Adam	25 Dec 1745	Rosenwiller

GGG Granduncle -

HUCK	Jacobi	4 Nov 1725	Rosenwiller

Surname	**First Name**	**Birth Date**	**Birth Place**
Son -			
BUCHMANN	Arthur Michael	28 Dec 1892	St. Louis, MO
BUCHMANN	EMILE HENRY	21 Aug 1899	St. Louis, MO
BUCHMANN	Florence Andrew	12 Jun 1895	St. Louis, MO
Daughter -			
BUCHMANN	Marie Elizabeth	25 Jan 1905	St. Louis, MO
Grandson -			
BUCHMANN	Carl Emile	15 Sep 1929	Belleville, IL
BUCHMANN	Herbert Alois	27 Oct 1922	St. Louis MO
BUCHMANN	Kenneth Henry	31 Dec 1929	St Louis MO
Granddaughter -			
BUCHMANN	Emmy Lee	3 Feb 1927	
BUCHMANN	Lois Jean	25 Feb 1928	Belleville IL
BUCHMANN	Rose Marie	3 Feb 1927	Belleville, IL
G Grandson -			
BUCHMANN	Barth David	4 Jul 1955	St. Louis MO
BUCHMANN	Brian Thomas	27 Apr 1961	Washington MO
BUCHMANN	Craig Eric	13 May 1962	CampLejeune,NC
BUCHMANN	David Andrew	19 Jun 1964	Washington MO
BUCHMANN	Eric William	6 Nov 1959	St.Louis MO
BUCHMANN	Gregory Michael	26 Mar 1951	
BUCHMANN	Herbert Alois II	22 Jul 1949	
BUCHMANN	Kenneth Edward	5 Jul 1967	Washington MO
BUCHMANN	Neal Howard	28 Feb 1966	Washington MO
KLUGA	Jon Christopher	27 Jul 1961	San Francisco CA
ROACH	Andrew Thomas	12 Jul 1958	Springfield, IL
ROACH	Phillip Matthew	15 Feb 1966	Springfield, IL
ROACH	Robert Corwine, Jr.	14 May 1956	Springfield IL
WILLIAMS	James David	14 Aug 1961	Decatur, Il

BLOOD RELATIVES OF HENRY X BUCHMANN

Surname	First Name	Birth Date	Birth Place
G Granddaughter: -			
BUCHMANN	Caron Susann	25 Aug 1965	Camp Lejeune,NC
BUCHMANN	Cynthia Marie	18 Sep 1962	St. Louis MO
BUCHMANN	Diane Karen	5 Nov 1958	Washington MO
BUCHMANN	Elaine Marie	20 Oct 1962	Holstein MO
KLUGA	Kyra Lee	24 Apr 1963	California
ROACH	Kimberly Ellen	11 Jun 1952	Springfield, IL
WILLIAMS	Jill Diane	8 Sep 1951	Decatur, IL
WILLIAMS	Julia Moore	3 Mar 1954	Decatur, IL
GG Grandson -			
BROOKS	Sawyer Carl	18 Jul 2000	Daytona Beach FL
BUCHMANN	Brett Alois	3 Jul 1978	Shawnee KS
BUCHMANN	Bryce	1 Nov 1991	Japan
BUCHMANN	Connor	11 Jul 1993	San Diego CA
BUCHMANN	Jack William	27 Sep 2002	
BUCHMANN	Jonah David	15 Oct 2004	North Kansas
DeMichele	Daniel	14 Jul 1985	Phoenix, AZ
DeMichele	Joseph Daniel	5 Feb 1991	Phoenix, AZ
DeMichele	Thomas Daniel	31 Aug 1988	Phoenix, AZ
DOXSIE	Jeffrey Thomas	23 Nov 1987	Decatur, IL
ROACH-LOMMEN	Charles Emile	29 Aug 2002	Santa Fe NM
ROACH-LOMMEN	Jack Henry	25 May 1999	Santa Fe NM
WHITE	Jeffrey Alan	18 Mar 1986	Washington MO
WILLIAMS	Carter Davidson	27 Jan 2000	California
WILLIAMS	Parker James	2 Feb 1998	California

Surname	First Name	Birth Date	Birth Place

GG Granddaughter -

Surname	First Name	Birth Date	Birth Place
BROOKS	Camryn	5 Mar 2002	Daytona Fla.
BUCHMANN	Abby Elizabeth	5 Jul 1991	Washington MO
BUCHMANN	Alayna Nadine	11 May 2000	
BUCHMANN	Alesia Marie	17 Dec 1978	St Louis MO
BUCHMANN	Andrea	6 Jun 1996	San Diego, CA
BUCHMANN	Arikka Alexandria	16 Dec 1985	Shawnee KS
BUCHMANN	Claire Marie	22 Apr 2001	
BUCHMANN	Emily Allison	14 Oct 1987	Washington MO
BUCHMANN	Heather Renee	2 Nov 1969	St. Louis MO
BUCHMANN	Kyra Anne	8 Jul 1977	St Louis MO
BUCHMANN	Maggie Elise	3 Apr 1993	Washington MO
BUCHMANN	Norma June	21 Dec 1974	
BUCHMANN	Tiffany Marie	16 May 1981	St.Louis MO
DOXSIE	Jill Suzanne	6 Jun 1983	Decatur, IL
KLUGA	Catherine Jeane	1 Aug 2000	San Jose CA
MURABITO	Druscilla Marie	1 Aug 1991	St. Louis MO
MURABITO	Madeline Marie	15 Apr 1994	St Louis MO
WHITE	Lynn Marie	11 Mar 1988	Washington MO
WILLIAMS	Windsor Nichole	21 Nov 2002	Chatsworth CA

GGG Grandson -

Surname	First Name	Birth Date	Birth Place
BUCHMANN	Gregory Michael (II)	19 Jul 1992	St Louis MO
RILEY	Stuart Michael	1 Jun 1997	St Louis MO

GGG Granddaughter -

Surname	First Name	Birth Date	Birth Place
Czapala	Karissa Madeline	16 Jun 1996	St Louis MO
Czapala	Kayla Christine	21 Apr 1995	St Louis MO
Czapala	Madeline Christine	22 Oct 1997	St Louis MO

BLOOD RELATIVES OF HENRY X BUCHMANN

Surname	First Name	Birth Date	Birth Place
Nephew -			
BUCHMANN	Edward	14 Sep 1910	
BUCHMANN	Jerome L.	30 Sep 1913	
BUCHMANN	Louie	1900	
Niece -			
BUCHMANN	Josephine Bernadine	17 Apr 1906	Marion, IL
Grandniece -			
STAYNOR	Florence		

"Some relationship, huh, kid?"

Genealogy of the Hammer Family

1680 to Emile and Leota

The Hammer Sisters and Tante Eva

Tante Eva (Mary Eva Hammer Severin) is seated in front

Behind her, left to right are Margaret (Aunt Maggie), Drusilla and Josephine (Aunt Sis)

Michael Hammer's Cigar Manufacturing Co.

at 7701 South Broadway in St. Louis, Missouri (abt. 1883)

Michael is at the right with arms folded. The other men are unidentified, but one or more of his brothers could be among them. Drusilla and Margaret are in the upper left window and Tante Eva and Josephine in the upper right.

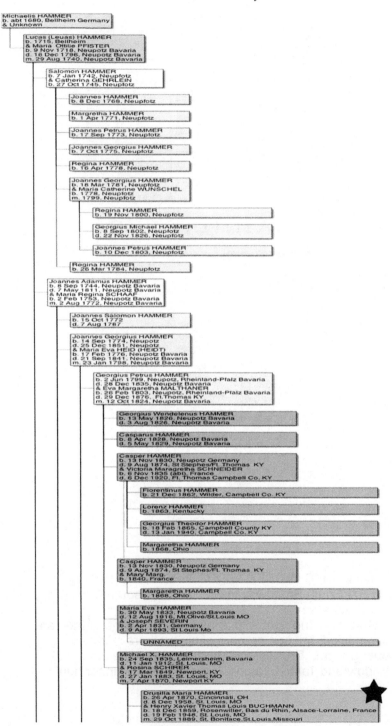

Michaelis HAMMER
b. abt 1680, Bellheim Germany
& Unknown

Lucas (Leuas) HAMMER
b. 1715, Bellheim
& Maria Ottilie PFISTER
b. 9 Nov 1718, Neupotz Bavaria
d. 16 Dec 1796, Neupotz Bavaria
m. 29 Aug 1740, Neupotz Bavaria

Salomon HAMMER
b. 7 Jan 1742, Neupfotz
& Catherina GEHRLEIN
b. 27 Oct 1745, Neupfotz

Joannes HAMMER
b. 8 Dec 1768, Neupfotz

Margretha HAMMER
b. 1 Apr 1771, Neupfotz

Joannes Petrus HAMMER
b. 17 Sep 1773, Neupfotz

Joannes Georgius HAMMER
b. 7 Oct 1775, Neupfotz

Regina HAMMER
b. 16 Apr 1778, Neupfotz

Joannes Georgius HAMMER
b. 18 Mar 1781, Neupfotz
& Maria Catherine WUNSCHEL
b. 1778, Neupfotz
m. 1799, Neupfotz

Regina HAMMER
b. 19 Nov 1800, Neupfotz

Georgius Michael HAMMER
b. 8 Sep 1802, Neupfotz
d. 22 Nov 1826, Neupfotz

Joannes Petrus HAMMER
b. 10 Dec 1803, Neupfotz

Regina HAMMER
b. 26 Mar 1784, Neupfotz

Joannes Adamus HAMMER
b. 8 Sep 1744, Neupotz Bavaria
d. 7 May 1811, Neupotz Bavaria
& Maria Regina SCHAAF
b. 2 Feb 1753, Neupotz Bavaria
m. 2 Aug 1772, Neupotz Bavaria

Joannes Salomon HAMMER
b. 15 Oct 1772
d. 7 Aug 1787

Joannes Georgius HAMMER
b. 14 Sep 1774, Neupotz
d. 25 Dec 1851, Neupotz
& Maria Eva HEID (HEIDT)
b. 17 Feb 1776, Neupotz Bavaria
d. 21 Sep 1841, Neupotz Bavaria
m. 23 Jan 1798, Neupotz Bavaria

Georgius Petrus HAMMER
b. 2 Jun 1799, Neupotz, Rheinland-Pfalz Bavaria
d. 28 Dec 1835, Neupotz Bavaria
& Eva Margaretha MALTHANER
b. 26 Feb 1803, Neupotz, Rheinland-Pfalz Bavaria
d. 29 Dec 1876, Ft.Thomas KY
m. 12 Oct 1824, Neupotz Bavaria

Georgius Wendelenus HAMMER
b. 13 May 1826, Neupotz Bavaria
d. 3 Aug 1826, Neupotz Bavaria

Casparus HAMMER
b. 8 Apr 1828, Neupotz Bavaria
d. 5 May 1829, Neupotz Bavaria

Casper HAMMER
b. 13 Nov 1830, Neupotz Germany
d. 9 Aug 1874, St Stephes/Ft. Thomas KY
& Victoria Maragretha SCHNEIDER
b. 6 Nov 1835 (abt), France
d. 6 Dec 1920, Ft. Thomas Campbell Co. KY

Florentinus HAMMER
b. 21 Dec 1862, Wilder, Campbell Co. KY

Lorenz HAMMER
b. 1863, Kentucky

Georgius Theodor HAMMER
b. 18 Feb 1865, Campbell County KY
d. 13 Jan 1940, Campbell Co. KY

Margaretha HAMMER
b. 1868, Ohio

Casper HAMMER
b. 13 Nov 1830, Neupotz Germany
d. 9 Aug 1874, St Stephes/Ft. Thomas KY
& Mary Marg
b. 1840, France

Margaretha HAMMER
b. 1868, Ohio

Maria Eva HAMMER
b. 30 May 1833, Neupotz Bavaria
d. 12 Aug 1916, Mt Olive/St.Louis MO
& Joseph SEVERIN
b. 2 Apr 1831, Germany
d. 9 Apr 1893, St Louis Mo

UNNAMED

Michael X. HAMMER
b. 24 Sep 1835, Leimersheim, Bavaria
d. 11 Jan 1912, St. Louis, MO
& Rosina SCHIRER
b. 17 Mar 1849, Newport, KY
d. 27 Jan 1883, St. Louis, MO
m. 7 Apr 1870, Newport KY

Drusilla Maria HAMMER
b. 26 Apr 1870, Cincinnati, OH
d. 8 Dec 1958, St. Louis, MO
& Henry Xavier Thomas Louis BUCHMANN
b. 18 Dec 1859, Rosenwiller, Bas du Rhin, Alsace-Lorraine, France
d. 19 Feb 1948, St. Louis, MO
m. 29 Oct 1889, St. Boniface,St.Louis,Missouri

First Generation

---

1. Michaelis HAMMER. Born abt 1680 in Bellheim Germany.

Michaelis married (spouse unknown)

They had one child:

2	i.	Lucas (Leuas) (1715-)

Second Generation

---

2. Lucas (Leuas) HAMMER. Born in 1715 in Bellheim.

On 29 Aug 1740 when Lucas (Leuas) was 25, he married Maria Ottilie PFISTER, daughter of Stephanus PFISTER & Rosina SCHWAB, in Neupotz Bavaria. Born on 9 Nov 1718 in Neupotz Bavaria. Maria Ottilie died in Neupotz Bavaria, on 16 Dec 1796; she was 78.

They had the following children:

3	i.	Salomon (1742-)
4	ii.	Joannes Adamus (1744-1811)
5	iii.	Margaretha (1746-1757)
6	iv.	Maria Barbara (1748-)
7	v.	Joannes Petrus (1752-1825)
8	vi.	Georgius Petrus (1755-1760)
9	vii.	Joannes Georgius (1757-1758)
10	viii.	Joannes Georgius(2) (1758-1758)
11	ix.	Georgius Adamu (1760-1768)

Third Generation

---

3. Salomon HAMMER. Born on 7 Jan 1742 in Neupfotz.

Salomon married Catherina GEHRLEIN, daughter of Joannes Georgius GEHRLEIN & Maria Barbara BURCK. Born on 27 Oct 1745 in Neupfotz.

They had the following children:

12	i.	Joannes (1768-)
13	ii.	Margretha (1771-)
14	iii.	Joannes Petrus (1773-)
15	iv.	Joannes Georgius (1775-)
16	v.	Regina (1778-)
17	vi.	Joannes Georgius (1781-)
18	vii.	Regina (1784-)

4. Joannes Adamus HAMMER. Born on 8 Sep 1744 in Neupotz Bavaria. Joannes Adamus died in Neupotz Bavaria, on 7 May 1811; he was 66.

On 2 Aug 1772 when Joannes Adamus was 27, he married Maria Regina SCHAAF, daughter of Joannes Jacobus SCHAAF & Maria Barbara WUNSCHEL, in Neupotz Bavaria. Born on 2 Feb 1753 in Neupotz Bavaria.

They had the following children:

19	i.	Joannes Salomon (1772-1787)
20	ii.	Joannes Georgius (1774-1851)
21	iii.	Eva Catharina (1776-)
22	iv.	Maria Apollonia (1778-1787)
23	v.	Maria Barbara (1780-1787)
24	vi.	Margaretha (1783-1786)
25	vii.	Georgius Adamus (1785-1789)
26	viii.	Solomon (1788-)
27	ix.	Maria Barbara (2) (1791-)

5. Margaretha HAMMER. Born on 3 Dec 1746 in Neupotz. Margaretha died in Neupotz on 25 Dec 1757; she was 11.

6. Maria Barbara HAMMER. Born on 21 Jan 1748 in Neupotz.

On 11 Feb 1771 when Maria Barbara was 23, she married Joannes William GEHRLEIN, in Neupfotz.

Third Generation

7. Joannes Petrus HAMMER. Born on 5 Jul 1752 in Neupotz. Joannes Petrus died in Neupotz on 5 Nov 1825; he was 73.

On 11 Nov 1776 when Joannes Petrus was 24, he first married Maria Anna BURCK, in Neupfotz. On 23 Feb 1784 when Joannes Petrus was 31, he second married Margaretha ANTONY.

8. Georgius Petrus HAMMER. Born on 23 Jan 1755 in Neupotz. Georgius Petrus died in Neupotz on 12 Feb 1760; he was 5.

9. Joannes Georgius HAMMER. Born on 29 Jul 1757 in Neupotz. Joannes Georgius died in Neupotz on 6 Jan 1758; he was <1.

10. Joannes Georgius(2) HAMMER. Born on 17 Oct 1758. Joannes Georgius(2) died on 17 Nov 1758; he was <1.

11. Georgius Adamus HAMMER. Born on 28 Dec 1760 in Neupfotz. Georgius Adamus died in Neupfotz on 12 May 1768; he was 7.

Fourth Generation

12. Joannes HAMMER. Born on 8 Dec 1768 in Neupfotz.

13. Margretha HAMMER. Born on 1 Apr 1771 in Neupfotz.

14. Joannes Petrus HAMMER. Born on 17 Sep 1773 in Neupfotz.

15. Joannes Georgius HAMMER. Born on 7 Oct 1775 in Neupfotz.

16. Regina HAMMER. Born on 16 Apr 1778 in Neupfotz.

17. Joannes Georgius HAMMER. Born on 18 Mar 1781 in Neupfotz.

In 1799 when Joannes Georgius was 17, he married Maria Catherine WUNSCHEL, in Neupfotz. Born in 1778 in Neupfotz.

They had the following children:

28	i.	Regina (1800-)
29	ii.	Georgius Michael (1802-1826)
30	iii.	Joannes Petrus (1803-)

18. Regina HAMMER. Born on 26 Mar 1784 in Neupfotz

19. **19.Joannes Salomon HAMMER.** Born on 15 Oct 1772. Joannes Salomon died on 7 Aug 1787; he was 14.

Fourth Generation

---

20. Joannes Georgius HAMMER. Born on 14 Sep 1774 in Neupotz. Joannes Georgius died in Neupotz on 25 Dec 1851; he was 77.

On 23 Jan 1798 when Joannes Georgius was 23, he married Maria Eva HEID (HEIDT), daughter of Joannes Adamus HEID & Maria Eva MALTHANER, in Neupotz Bavaria. Born on 17 Feb 1776 in Neupotz Bavaria. Maria Eva died in Neupotz Bavaria, on 21 Sep 1841; she was 65.

They had the following children:

31	i.	Georgius Petrus (1799-1835)
32	ii.	Maria
33	iii.	Eva Margretha (1805-)
34	iv.	Joannes Georgius (1808-1810)
35	v.	Otilia (1810-)
36	vi.	Johannes George (1812-1875)
37	vii.	Joannes Michael (1815-)
38	viii.	Laurentius (1818-)
39	ix.	Casparus (1821-)
40	x.	UNNAMED

21. Eva Catharina HAMMER. Born on 21 Jul 1776 in Neupfotz.

22. Maria Apollonia HAMMER. Born on 25 Dec 1778. Maria Apollonia died on 13 May 1787; she was 8.

23. Maria Barbara HAMMER. Born on 28 Oct 1780. Maria Barbara died on 13 May 1787; she was 6.

24. Margaretha HAMMER. Born on 10 May 1783. Margaretha died on 24 Jan 1786; she was 2.

25. Georgius Adamus HAMMER. Born on 24 Dec 1785. Georgius Adamus died on 1 Mar 1789; he was 3.

26. Solomon HAMMER. Born on 31 Mar 1788 in Leimersheim.

27. Maria Barbara (2) HAMMER. Born on 22 Feb 1791.

Fifth Generation

---

28. Regina HAMMER. Born on 19 Nov 1800 in Neupfotz.

29. Georgius Michael HAMMER. Born on 8 Sep 1802 in Neupfotz. Georgius Michael died in Neupfotz on 22 Nov 1826; he was 24.

30. Joannes Petrus HAMMER. Born on 10 Dec 1803 in Neupfotz.

31. Georgius Petrus HAMMER. Born on 2 Jun 1799 in Neupotz, Rheinland-Pfalz Bavaria. Georgius Petrus died in Neupotz Bavaria, on 28 Dec 1835; he was 36. Religion: Roman Catholic.

On 12 Oct 1824 when Georgius Petrus was 25, he married Eva Margaretha MALTHANER, daughter of Georgius Michael MALTHANER & Elisabetha Virginia GEHRLEIN, in Neupotz Bavaria. Born on 26 Feb 1803 in Neupotz, Rheinland-Pfalz Bavaria. Eva Margaretha died in Ft.Thomas KY, on 29 Dec 1876; she was 73.

They had the following children:

41	i.	Georgius Wendelenus (1826-1826)
42	ii.	Casparus (1828-1829)
43	iii.	Casper (1830-1874)
44	iv.	Maria Eva (1833-1916)
45	v.	Michael X. (1835-1912)

32. Maria Elisabetha HAMMER. Born on 6 Jan 1803.

On 31 Jan 1836 when Maria Elisabetha was 33, she married Salomon BEHR.

33. Eva Margretha HAMMER. Born on 20 Sep 1805 in Neupotz.

On 10 Nov 1832 when Eva Margretha was 27, she married Joannes Petrus BURCK.

34. Joannes Georgius HAMMER. Born on 19 Feb 1808. Joannes Georgius died on 30 Nov 1810; he was 2.

35. Otilia HAMMER. Born on 3 Mar 1810 in Neupotz.

Otilia married Joannes Georgius BECKER.

Fifth Generation

---

36. Johannes George HAMMER. Born on 25 Oct 1812 in Neupotz
Bavaria. Johannes George died in Newport KY, in April 1875 (78?); he was 62.
Buried in St. Stephens, Ft.Thomas KY.

On 24 Aug 1838 when Johannes George was 25, he married Eva Margaretha
MALTHANER, daughter of Georgius Michael MALTHANER & Elisabetha
Virginia GEHRLEIN, in Neupotz Bavaria. Born on 26 Feb 1803 in Neupotz,
Rheinland-Pfalz Bavaria. Eva Margaretha died in Ft.Thomas KY, on 29 Dec 1876;
she was 73.

They had the following children:

46	i.	Annie Eva (1839-1916)
47	ii.	Jacob (1841-1899)
48	iii.	Sophia (1847-1919)
49	iv.	Philippina (1847-1847)
50	v.	Ludovius (1850-1850)

37. Joannes Michael HAMMER. Born on 12 Nov 1815.

38.Laurentius HAMMER. Born on 10 Aug 1818 in Neupotz.

39.Casparus HAMMER. Born on 12 Jul 1821.

40. Unnamed.

41. Georgius Wendelenus HAMMER. Born on 13 May 1826 in Neupotz Bavaria.
Georgius Wendelenus died in Neupotz Bavaria, on 3 Aug 1826; he was <1.

42. Casparus HAMMER. Born on 8 Apr 1828 in Neupotz Bavaria. Casparus died
in Neupotz Bavaria, on 5 May 1829; he was 1.

Sixth Generation

---

43. Casper HAMMER. Born on 13 Nov 1830 in Neupotz Germany. Casper died in St Stephes/Ft. Thomas KY, on 9 Aug 1874; he was 43. Occupation: Laborer. Religion: Roman Catholic.

Casper first married Victoria Maragretha SCHNEIDER, daughter of John SCHNEIDER. Born on 6 Nov 1835 (abt) in France. Victoria Maragretha died in Ft. Thomas Campbell Co. KY, on 6 Dec 1920; she was 85.

They had the following children:

51	i.	Florentinus (1862-)
52	ii.	Lorenz (1863-)
53	iii.	Georgius Theodor (1865-1940)
54		

Casper second married Mary Marg.. Born in 1840 in France.

44. Maria Eva HAMMER. Born on 30 May 1833 in Neupotz Bavaria. Maria Eva died in Mt.Olive/St.Louis MO, on 12 Aug 1916; she was 83.

Maria Eva married Joseph SEVERIN. Born on 2 Apr 1831 in Germany. Joseph died in St Louis Mo, on 9 Apr 1893; he was 62.

They had one child:

55	i.	UNNAMED

Sixth Generation

---

45. Michael X. HAMMER. Born on 24 Sep 1835 in Leimersheim, Bavaria. Michael X. died in St. Louis, MO, on 11 Jan 1912; he was 76. Buried in Mt. Olive, St. Louis. Occupation: Cigar Manufacturer. Religion: Roman Catholic.

On 7 Apr 1870 when Michael X. was 34, he married Rosina SCHIRER, daughter of John SCHERER & Eva SCHLOSS, in Newport KY. Born on 17 Mar 1849 in Newport, KY. Rosina died in St. Louis, MO, on 27 Jan 1883; she was 33.

They had the following children:

56	i.	Drusilla Maria (1870-1958)
57	ii.	Margaret (1872-1961)
58	iii.	Mary Josephine (1878-1960)

46. Annie Eva HAMMER. Born on 6 May 1839 in Neupotz Bavaria. Annie Eva died in St. Louis, Missouri, in 1916; she was 76.

On 14 May 1859 when Annie Eva was 20, she married Ferdinand SPAETH (E), son of Klaus (Claus) SPAETH(E), in Cincinnatti OH. Ferdinand died in 1893.

They had one child:

59	i.	Mary J

47. Jacob HAMMER. Born on 19 Oct 1841 in Neupotz Bavaria. Jacob died in Ft.Thomas KY, on 4 Aug 1899; he was 57. Buried in St. Stephens, Ft.Thomas KY.

On 17 Aug 1886 when Jacob was 44, he married Mariam Ursula KRAEMER, in St Stephes/Newport KY.

48. Sophia HAMMER. Born 11 Nov 1847 in Neupotz Bavaria. Died in 1919; she was 71.

On 22 Feb 1870 when Sophia was 22, she married Michael SCHERRER, son of John SCHERER & Eva SCHLOSS, in Newport KY, St.Stephen's Church. Born on 25 Jul 1846 in Neupfotz. Michael died in Ft. Thomas KY, on 20 Jul 1920; he was 73.

They had the following children:

60	i.	Sophia Marie (1878-1943)
61	ii.	Ferd Fredericos (1871-<1897)
62	iii.	George John (1883-1960)
63	iv.	Jacob Joseph (1885-1960)

Sixth Generation

---

9. Philippina HAMMER. Born on 27 Jan 1847. Philippina died in 1847; she was <1.

50. Ludovius HAMMER. Born on 25 Aug 1850. Ludovius died on 10 Sep 1850; he was <1.

Seventh Generation

---

51. Florentinus HAMMER. Born on 21 Dec 1862 in Wilder, Campbell Co. KY.

52. Lorenz HAMMER. Born in 1863 in Kentucky.

53. Georgius Theodor HAMMER. Born on 18 Feb 1865 in Campbell County KY. Georgius Theodor died in Campbell Co. KY, on 13 Jan 1940; he was 74.

54. Margaretha HAMMER. Born in 1868 in Ohio.

55. UNNAMED.

56. Drusilla Maria HAMMER. Born on 26 Apr 1870 in Cincinnati, OH. Drusilla Maria died in St. Louis, MO, on 8 Dec 1958; she was 88. Buried on 11 Dec 1958 in Mt. Olive, St. Louis, Missouri. Religion: Roman Catholic.

On 29 Oct 1889 when Drusilla Maria was 19, she married Henry Xavier Thomas Louis BUCHMANN, son of Louis BUCHMANN & Marie Anne RICHERT, in St. Boniface, St.Louis,Missouri. Born on 18 Dec 1859 in Rosenwiller, Bas du Rhin, Alsace-Lorraine, France. Henry Xavier Thomas Louis died in St. Louis, MO, on 19 Feb 1948; he was 88.

They had the following children:

64	i.	Arthur Michael (1892-1967)
65	ii.	Florence Andrew (1895-1979)
66	iii.	EMILE HENRY (1899-1960)
67	iv.	Marie Elizabeth (1905-1989)

Seventh Generation

7. Margaret HAMMER. Born on 13 Feb 1872 in Lawrenceburg, TN. Margaret died in St. Louis Missouri, on 18 Sep 1961; she was 89.

Margaret married Henry FELDMEIER. Born on 10 Jan 1861 in St Louis Mo. Henry died in St. Louis Missouri, on 19 Jul 1940; he was 79.

They had the following children:

68	i.	Emile
69	ii.	Frank
70	iii.	Harry
71	iv.	Oscar
72	v.	Walter (1907-1995)

58. Mary Josephine HAMMER. Born on 2 Jan 1878 in St. Louis, Missouri. Mary Josephine died in St Louis Mo, on 13 Feb 1960; she was 82.

Mary Josephine married William HERTLING. He died on 6 Jan 1926 in St Louis Mo.

They had the following children:

73	i.	Adolph
74	ii.	Margaret (1910-)
75	iii.	Agnes
76	iv.	Lawrence

59. Mary J SPAETH.

Mary J married SEVERIN.

60. Sophia Marie SCHERRER. Born on 21 Nov 1878 in Ft. Thomas Campbell Co. KY. Sophia Marie died in Ft. Thomas Campbell Co. KY, on 27 Jan 1943; she was 64.

Sophia Marie first married Adrian WAGNER.They had one child:

77	i.	Lillian

Sophia Marie second married Fred WAGNER.

They had the following children:

78	i.	Arthur
79	ii.	Earl
80	iii.	Donald

Seventh Generation

61. Ferd Fredericos SCHERRER. Born on 6 Jul 1871 in Ft. Thomas Campbell Co. KY. Ferd Fredericos died in Ft. Thomas Campbell Co. KY, bef 1897; he was 25.

62. George John SCHERRER. Born on 15 Feb 1883 in Ft. Thomas Campbell Co. KY. George John died in Ft. Thomas Campbell Co. KY, on 10 Oct 1960; he was 77.

63. Jacob Joseph SCHERRER. Born on 15 Dec 1885 in Ft. Thomas Campbell Co. KY. Jacob Joseph died in Ft. Thomas Campbell Co. KY, on 4 Feb 1960; he was 74.

Eighth Generation

64. Arthur Michael BUCHMANN. Born on 28 Dec 1892 in St. Louis, MO. Arthur Michael died in Franklin, Missouri, on 15 Mar 1967; he was 74. Buried on 18 Mar 1967 in Mt. Olive/St.Louis MO.

On 26 Jun 1921 when Arthur Michael was 28, he married Marie Catherine RECK, daughter of Alois RECK & Ann Josephine NEKVINDA, in St. Wenceslaus/St.Louis MO. Born on 23 Mar 1901 in Vienna Austria. Marie Catherine died in Washington MO, on 17 Dec 1975; she was 74.

They had the following children:

81	i.	Herbert Alois (1922-)
82	ii.	Kenneth Henry (1929-)

65. Florence Andrew BUCHMANN. Born on 12 Jun 1895 in St. Louis, MO. Florence Andrew died in Veteran's Home, Danville, Illinois, on 28 Jul 1979; he was 84. Buried on 30 Jul 1979 in Mt.Olive Cemetery/St.LouisMO.

Eighth Generation

---

66. EMILE HENRY BUCHMANN. Born on 21 Aug 1899 in St. Louis, MO. EMILE HENRY died in San Francisco, CA, on 30 Jul 1960; he was 60. Buried on 2 Aug 1960 in Walnut Hill Cemetery/Belleville, IL. Occupation: Physical Education/ Dance/Youth Counselor. Education: Butler University. Religion: Christian Science.

On 30 Jun 1924 when EMILE HENRY was 25, he married LEOTA EMMA GROMBACH, daughter of Henry GROMBACH & Emma NEUTZLING, in Belleville,IL. Born on 13 Jun 1898 in Belleville, IL. LEOTA EMMA died in Belleville, IL, on 23 Aug 1984; she was 86.

They had the following children:

83	i.	Rose Marie (1927-)
84	ii.	Emmy Lee (1927-)
85	iii.	Lois Jean (1928-)
86	iv.	Carl Emile (1929-)

67. Marie Elizabeth BUCHMANN. Born on 25 Jan 1905 in St. Louis, MO. Marie Elizabeth died in St. Louis, MO, on 19 Mar 1989; she was 84. Buried on 22 Mar 1989 in Mt. Olive, St. Louis, MO. Occupation: Teacher. Education: St.Louis University St.Louis MO. Religion: Catholic.

68. Emile FELDMEIER.

69. Frank FELDMEIER.

70. Harry FELDMEIER.

71. Oscar FELDMEIER.

72. Walter FELDMEIER. Born on 16 Jun 1907. Walter died on 11 Feb 1995; he was 87.Walter married Willa. Born on 29 Nov 1906. Willa died in St Louis MO, on 8 Mar 1994; she was 87.

73. Adolph HERTLING.

Eighth Generation

---

74. Margaret HERTLING. Born in 1910 in St.Louis MO.

In 1950 when Margaret was 40, she married Edward BRANDT, in St.Louis MO. Born on 17 Aug 1900. Edward died in St. Louis MO, on 20 Aug 1983; he was 83.

They had the following children:

87	i.	Robert (1954-)
88	ii.	Donald (1956-)

75. Agnes HERTLING.

76, Lawrence HERTLING

77. Lillian Wagner

78. Arthur WAGNER

    child **89** i. **Joyce**

79,Earl WAGNER

80. Donald WAGNER

Ninth Generation

---

81. Herbert Alois BUCHMANN. Born on 27 Oct 1922 in St. Louis MO. Occupation: Bank Officer. Education: Washington U. St.Louis. Religion: Catholic.

On 30 Oct 1948 when Herbert Alois was 26, he married Catherine Marie HARMS, in St. Louis MO. Born on 9 Mar 1932 in St. Louis MO.

They had the following children:

90	i.	Herbert Alois II (1949-)
91	ii.	Gregory Michael (1951-)
92	iii.	Barth David (1955-)
93	iv.	Cynthia Marie (1962-)

Ninth Generation

---

82. Kenneth Henry BUCHMANN. Born on 31 Dec 1929 in St Louis MO. Occupation: Veterinarian. Education: U.of Missouri/Columbia. Religion: Catholic.

In 1956 when Kenneth Henry was 26, he first married Ann PERKINS. Born on 2 Aug 1936 in St Louis MO.

They had the following children:

94	i.	Diane Karen (1958-)
95	ii.	Eric William (1959-)
96	iii.	Brian Thomas (1961-)
97	iv.	Elaine Marie (1962-)
98	v.	David Andrew (1964-)
99	vi.	Neal Howard (1966-)
100	vii.	Kenneth Edward (1967-)

In Oct 1987 when Kenneth Henry was 57, he second married Cathy Jean KLOPPE.

83. Rose Marie BUCHMANN. Born on 3 Feb 1927 in Belleville, IL. Occupation: University Administrator. Education: Millikin, SSU, UIS, Illinois State. On 17 Jun 1950 when Rose Marie was 23, she first married Robert Corwine ROACH, son of Charles MILLER & Marie LOGAN, in Belleville,IL. Born on 21 Jan 1927 in Chicago, IL. Robert Corwine died in Springfield, IL, on 21 Nov 1978; he was 51.

They had the following children:

101	i.	Kimberly Ellen (1952-)
102	ii.	Robert Corwine, Jr. (1956-)
103	iii.	Andrew Thomas (1958-)
104	iv.	Phillip Matthew (1966-)

On 7 Nov 1981 when Rose Marie was 54, she second married Fred James MILLER Jr., son of Fred James MILLER & Lillian COOKE, in Springfield,Illinois. Born on 11 Sep 1926 in Thomas, OK.

Ninth Generation

84. Emmy Lee BUCHMANN. Born on 3 Feb 1927.

On 9 Oct 1948 when Emmy Lee was 21, she married James Edward WILLIAMS, in St.Paul's Evangelical /Belleville IL. Born on 31 Jan 1923 in Decatur Illinois.

They had the following children:

105	i.	Jill Diane (1951-)
106	ii.	Julia Moore (1954-)
107	iii.	James David (1961-)

85. Lois Jean BUCHMANN. Born on 25 Feb 1928 in Belleville IL.

On 2 Sep 1954 when Lois Jean was 26, she married John KLUGA, in Los Angeles CA. Born on 18 Dec 1924.

They had the following children:

| 108 | i. | Jon Christopher (1961-) |
| 109 | ii. | Kyra Lee (1963-) |

86. Carl Emile BUCHMANN. Born on 15 Sep 1929 in Belleville, IL.

On 22 Jun 1958 when Carl Emile was 28, he married Mary Carolyn CRAIG, daughter of Hugh MacGregor CRAIG & Mary Helen HAMILTON, in Linton,Indiana. Born on 5 Aug 1935 in Syracuse, NY.

They had the following children:

| 110 | i. | Craig Eric (1962-) |
| 111 | ii. | Caron Susann (1965-) |

87. Robert BRANDT. Born in 1954.

88. **Donald BRANDT.** Born in 1956.

89. **Joyce WAGNER.**

Hammer Surname Index

GEHRLEIN

Catherina	spouse of 3
Elisabetha Virginia	parent of spouse of 31
Elisabetha Virginia	parent of spouse of 36
Joannes Georgius	parent of spouse of 3
Joannes William	spouse of 6

GROMBACH

Henry	parent of spouse of 66
LEOTA EMMA	spouse of 66

HAMMER

Annie Eva	46
Casparus	42
Casparus	39
Casper	43
Drusilla Maria	56
Eva Catharina	21
Eva Margretha	33
Florentinus	51
Georgius Adamus	11
Georgius Adamus	25
Georgius Michael	29
Georgius Petrus	31
Georgius Petrus	8
Georgius Theodor	53
Georgius Wendelenus	41
Jacob	47
Joannes	12
Joannes Adamus	4
Joannes Georgius	20
Joannes Georgius	34
Joannes Georgius	9
Joannes Georgius	15
Joannes Georgius	17
Joannes Georgius(2)	10
Joannes Michael	37
Joannes Petrus	7
Joannes Petrus	14
Joannes Petrus	30
Joannes Salomon	19
Johannes George	36
Laurentius	38
Lorenz	52

HAMMER

Lucas (Leuas)	2
Ludovius	50
Margaret	57
Margaretha	54
Margaretha	5
Margaretha	24
Margretha	13
Maria Apollonia	22
Maria Barbara	6
Maria Barbara	23
Maria Barbara (2)	27
Maria Elisabetha	32
Maria Eva	44
Mary Josephine	58
Michael X.	45
Michaelis	1
Otilia	35
Philippina	49
Regina	16
Regina	18
Regina	28
Salomon	3
Solomon	26
Sophia	48

HEID

Joannes Adamus	parent of spouse of 20

HEID /HEIDT

Maria Eva	spouse of 20

HERTLING

Adolph	73
Agnes	75
Lawrence	76

HERTLING

Margaret	74
William	spouse of 58

KRAEMER

Mariam Ursula	spouse of 47

MALTHANER

Eva Margaretha	spouse of 31
Eva Margaretha	spouse of 36
Georgius Michael	parent of spouse of 31
Georgius Michael	parent of spouse of 36
Maria Eva	parent of spouse of 20

NEKVINDA

Ann Josephine	parent of spouse of 64

NEUTZLING
    Emma   parent of spouse of 66
PFISTER
    Maria Ottilie   spouse of 2
    Stephanus   parent of spouse of 2
RECK
    Alois   parent of spouse of 64
    Marie Catherine   spouse of 64
RICHERT
    Marie Anne   parent of spouse of 56
SCHAAF
    Joannes Jacobus   parent of spouse of 4
    Maria Regina   spouse of 4
SCHERER
    John   parent of spouse of 45
    John   parent of spouse of 48
SCHERRER
    Ferd Fredericos   61
    George John   62
    Jacob Joseph   63
    Michael   spouse of 48
    Sophia Marie   60
SCHIRER
    Rosina   spouse of 45
SCHLOSS
    Eva   parent of spouse of 45
    Eva   parent of spouse of 48
SCHNEIDER
    John   parent of spouse of 43
    Victoria Margaretha   spouse of 43
SCHWAB
    Rosina   parent of spouse of 2
SEVERIN
    UNNAMED   spouse of 59
    Joseph   spouse of 44
SPAETH
    Mary J   59
SPAETHE
    Ferdinand
    Klaus (Claus)   parent of spouse of 46

WAGNER
    Adrian   spouse of 60

Adrian	spouse of 60
Arthur	78
Donald	80
Earl	79
Fred	spouse of 60
Joyce	child of 78
Lillian	77

WUNSCHEL

Maria Barbara	parent of spouse of 4
Maria Catherine	spouse of 17

The HAMMER family lived in Neupfotz, Leimersheim and Bellheim, Germany. The earliest recorded ancestor in this line is Michaelis Hammer born in Bellheim in 1680.

Michael X. Hammer was born in 1835 in Leimersheim, Bavaria. He emigrated from LeHavre France on the ship *Carack* with his mother, Eva, and five younger siblings. The *Carack* docked in New York harbor on July 5, 1853. The family settled in Ft. Thomas, Kentucky. Michael later lived in Cincinnati Ohio and finally moved to St. Louis Missouri.

The Chronicle of Neupotz, "Vom Rheinübergang um das Jahr 275 zum Neuen-Potz. Familien- und Gebäudechronik der Gemeinde Neupotz von 1650 bis 1997", written by Albert Weigel.

The Chronicle of Neupotz, "Vom Rheinübergang um das Jahr 275 zum Neuen-Potz. Familien- und Gebäudechronik der Gemeinde Neupotz von 1650 bis 1997", written by Albert Weigel.

Pl.-Nr.: 197   Wohnhaus, Schupfe, Stall, Sauställe, Hof mit Brunnen

Eigentümer und Erwerber:
Gehrlein Hans Kilian / Heintz Anna Katharina – 1739
Gehrlein Hans Jakob / L. Liebel Maria Barbara, II. Avril Maria Eva – 1777
Antoni Johann Adam III. / Gehrlein Maria Barbara – 1821
Schwein Johann Michael / Gehrlein Maria Barbara – 1863
Schwein Jakob / Heid Maria Eva – 1863
Gehrlein Leonhard / Bellaire Pauline – 1900
Gehrlein Adam / Gehrlein Anna Barabara – 1904
Wünschel Karl III. / Gehrlein Anna Barbara – 1912
Wünschel Kuno Alfons / Kuhn Agathe Franziska – 1949
Wünschel Hubert / Antoni Kornelia Maria – 1990

1739   Haus erbaut
1821   Metzgerei und Gastwirtschaft
1900   Bäckerei
um 1905   Brückenwaage eingerichtet
1956   Umbau der Gastwirtschaft
1989   Modernisierung der Gastwirtschaft

Hauptstraße Nr. 7 – früher Vordergasse Nr. 40 a –

Pl.-Nr.: 107 a   Wohnhaus, Scheuer mit Stall, Sauställe und Hof
Pl.-Nr.: 107 b   Garten

Eigentümer und Erwerber:
Heid Nikolaus / Pfirmann Theresia Maria – 1810 – Hirschwirt – Haus-Neubau – 1840
Heid Dominik / Antoni Katharina Anna – 1841
Gehrlein Karl Peter / Heid Maria Eva – 1874
Burger Friedrich / Gehrlein Sophie – 1890
Kreger Franz Theodor / Schaaf Josephine – 1917
Kreger Pius / Gehrlein Paulina – 1934
Kreger Franz Theodor / Trapp Maria Antonia – 1960

1841   Metzgerei und Wirtschaft
1945   Schäden am Gebäude durch Kriegseinwirkung
1975   Anbau mit Pavillon und Fremdenzimmer
Wirtschaft "Zum Lamm" mit kunstvollem Wirtshausschild, gefertigt v. Persohn Elmar.
Über den Wirtsräumen war bis 1960 ein Tanzsaal, der wie folgt auch fremdgenutzt wurde.
1909   Unterkunft für deutsche Soldaten
1940–1941   Schulsaal, weil Schulräume in gemeindlichen Schulhaus zu wenig
1945   Unterkunft für franz. Besatzungstruppen
1956–1960   Filmsaal für Filmtheater Rodelsau
1960   Umbau in 4 Fremdenzimmer
1993   Umbau in Wohnung für die Wirtsfamilie Kreger

Hauptstraße Nr. 8 – früher Vordergasse Nr. 39 –

Pl.-Nr.: 198   Wohnhaus, Scheuer mit Stallung und Hof mit Brunnen

Eigentümer und Erwerber:
Malthaner Hans Peter L. / L. Anna Barbara, II. Freudenstein Anna Rosina – 1688
Malthaner Adam / Heid Anna Margaretha – 1720
Heid Johann Adam / Malthaner Maria Eva – 1767
Hammer Johann Georg / Heid Maria Eva – 1798
Hammer Johann Georg / Malthaner Eva Margartha – 1844
Gehrlein Kasimir, ledig – 1852
Gehrlein Franz Anton / Antoni Philippine – 1857
Gehrlein Ludwig / Zircker Maria Appollonia – 1865
Gehrlein Josef / Antoni Philippine – 1875

454

Heid Karl Otto / Gehrlein Katharina – 1915
Bellaire Herbert, Otto und Ernst – 1951
Thomas Franz Eugen / Fromm Anna Maria – 1970
Sand Gertried / Heid Waltraud
und
Heid Willi / Hauck Lieselotte – 1988

1690 erstes Haus erbaut davon sind noch Eichenbohlen vorhanden ferner guterhaltener Brunnen mit Ziegelsteinrand unter der Hoffläche
1989/90 Das Anwesen war sehr verwahrlost, die unbrauchbare Substanz wurde entfernt, das Grundstück erneuert und ein zweigeschossiges Wohn- und Geschäftshaus errichtet mit:
a) Wohnhaus mit Arztpraxis und Poststelle und 4 Wohneinheiten
b) Wohnhaus mit Blumenladen und 2 Wohneinheiten

1690 *The first house was built and of it are some oak-boards in good condition, further a well in good condition with brick-wall under the yard.*

1989/90 *The property was very neglected, the bad substance was taken away, the ground was improved and a new house with 2 floors was built for living and business.*
a) Dwelling-house with Doctor's Office and Post-Office
b) Dwelling with 2 residences and a Flower-Shop

Hauptstraße Nr. 9 – früher Vordergasse Nr. 36 –

Pl.-Nr.: 200   Wohnhaus mit Wagnerwerkstätte, Scheuer mit Stallung, Schupfe, Sauställe und Hof
Pl.-Nr.: 201   Garten

Eigentümer und Erwerber:
Hammer Lucas / Pfister Maria Odilia – 1740
Hausbau – 1764
Hammer Hans Peter / L. Burck Maria Anna, II. Antoni Margarethe – 1780
Antoni Johann Adam / Hammer Maria Anna – 1811
Antoni Nikolaus / Gehrlein Eva Katharina – 1847
Geißert Philipp Michael / Gehrlein Barbara – 1873
Geiger Mathäus / Gehrlein Maria Theresia – 1890
Heid Karl Theodor / Wünschel Anna – 1912
Heid Franz Alfons / Schindler Anna Maria – 1938
Heid Karl Günther
Burger Franz Herbert / Heid Maria Elfriede – 1956

1830 Wagnerwerkstätte erbaut
1890 Neubau Stallung, Saustall, Schlachtstäle und Abort
1954 Neubau Tabaktrockenschuppen
1962 Neubau der Scheuer und Anbau und Stall
1968 Wohnhaus aufgestockt
Jahreszahl an Scheuer "1764"

Heid Karl Theodor / Wünschel Anna – 1912
Heid Franz Alfons / Schindler Anna Maria – 1938
Heid Karl Günther
Burger Franz Herbert / Heid Maria Elfriede – 1956

1830 Wagnerwerkstätte erbaut
1890 Neubau Stallung, Saustall, Schlachtstäle und Abort
1954 Neubau Tabaktrockenschuppen
1962 Neubau der Scheuer und Anbau und Stall
1968 Wohnhaus aufgestockt

The Family Neighborhood in Neupfotz
1688 -1988

Hauptstraße 7 *Hauptstraße 12* *Hauptstraße 13* *Hauptstraße 14*

Hauptstraßße 8
1688 -Malthaner
1798 -Hammer
1875 -Gehrlein
1988 - Heid

Hauptstraßße 9
1740 - Hammer
1912 - Heid

Hauptstraßße 10
1859 - Heid
1875 - Burck
1886 - Heid
1921 - Wunschel

Hauptstraße 18 *Hauptstraße 19* *Hauptstraße 20*

Vessel name: **Ship Carack**
Port of departure: **Havre, France**
Port of arrival: **New York, New York**
Date of arrival: 5 July 1853
Source: National Archives and Records Administration
Film M237 , Reel 128

DISTRICT OF NEW-YORK...PORT OF NEW-YORK

There was no sworn Captain's statement with this manifest. List or Manifest of all the passengers on board the Ship Carack where of Wm J. Faler is Master, from Havre burthen 874 tons. Columns represent: Names, Age (years/months), Sex, Occupation, The Country to which they severally belong, The Country of which the intend to become inhabitants and Died on the voyage. The destination of all passengers was U. S. America, the occupation "Farmers and Mechanics" was written at the top of each page and there were no deaths on the voyage, so these three columns have been eliminated.

1 Kelsch Madelaine   18 f Germany
2 Kelsch Friederic   20 m Germany
3 Kuhn Elise   40   Germany
4 Kuhn Hieronyma   4 m Germany
5 Armbursted Franz   33 m Germany
6 Reiss Barbara   15 f Germany
7 Ingel Louis   21 m Germany
8 Stephang Geo   46   Germany
9 Stephang Cath   43   Germany
10 Stephang Sophia   16   Germany
11 Stephang Philippe   13 m German
12 Stephang Louise   9   Germany
13 Frey J Henri   22   Germany
14 Wisser Henri   30   Germany
15 <u>Hammer Caspar</u>   22   Germany
16 <u>Hammer Margaret</u>   48   Germany
17 ** <u>Hammer Michel</u>   18 Germany **(Drusilla's father)**
18 <u>Hammer Eva</u>   20   Germany
19 <u>Hammer Eva</u>   14   Germany
20 <u>Hammer Jacob</u>   10   Germany
21 <u>Hammer Sophia</u>   9   Germany

Genealogy of the Grombach Family

1800 to Emile and Leota

Henry Grombach & Emma Neutzling on their wedding day

The Grombach family lived in and around Mannheim
Germany. Phillip Grombach emigrated to the USA
from Mannheim in 1849 and settled in Belleville Illinois.
The earliest recorded ancestor in this line is Jacob
Grombach born in Mannheim (about) 1810.

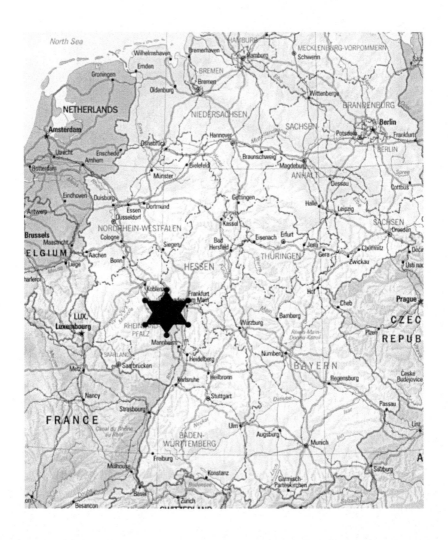

Jacob GROMBACH

Philip GROMBACH
b. 18 Jun 1832, Mannheim, Rheinland Pfalz, Bavaria
d. 11 Dec 1912, Belleville, IL
& Anna Maria WAHL
b. 20 Jul 1832, Niederkirchen, Deidesheim,Pfalz,Bayern
d. 24 Jun 1910, Belleville, IL
m. 25 Oct 1856, Belleville,Illinois

Jacob GROMBACH
b. 1857, Belleville, IL
d. 28 Jul 1939
& Johanna HAMMER
b. 1864, Belleville Illinois
d. 28 Apr 1939, Belleville Illinois
m. 21 Jul 1887, Belleville Illinois

Julius P. GROMBACH
b. 1889
d. 9 Feb 1948, Belleville Illinois

Jacob A GROMBACH
b. 1910
d. 11 Apr 1945

Emeline GROMBACH
& Robert SCHRAG

Stillborn Infant GROMBACH
b. 23 Apr 1897
d. 23 Apr 1897

Louisa GROMBACH
b. 18 Nov 1859, Belleville IL
d. 23 Dec 1930, Belleville IL
& Otto HARTMAN
b. 29 Jul 1859, Belleville IL
d. 9 May 1929, Belleville IL
m. 20 Jul 1886, Belleville IL

Edna HARTMAN
b. 21 Nov 1887

Henry HARTMAN
b. 3 Mar 1889

Emma HARTMAN
b. 29 Feb 1892

Otto HARTMAN
b. 10 Jul 1893, Belleville IL
d. 10 Aug 1894, Belleville IL

Hilda HARTMAN
b. 22 Feb 1895, Belleville IL

Ida HARTMAN
b. 18 Nov 1896

Pamelia HARTMAN
b. 21 Sep 1898

Bertha GROMBACH
b. 1862, Belleville Illinois

Henry GROMBACH
b. 24 Jul 1870, Belleville, IL
d. 21 May 1925, Belleville, IL
& Emma NEUTZLING
b. 17 Jul 1871, Belleville, IL
d. 13 Dec 1945, Belleville, IL
m. 6 Mar 1895, Belleville,Illinois

LEOTA EMMA GROMBACH
b. 13 Jun 1898, Belleville, IL
d. 23 Aug 1984, Belleville, IL
& EMILE HENRY BUCHMANN
b. 21 Aug 1899, St. Louis, MO
d. 30 Jul 1960, San Francisco, CA
m. 30 Jun 1925, Belleville,IL

First Generation

---

1. Jacob GROMBACH. About 1800
   Child:

2   i.   Philip (1832-1912)

Second Generation

---

2. Philip GROMBACH. Born on 18 Jun 1832 in Mannheim, Rheinland Pfalz, Bavaria. Philip died in Belleville, IL, on 11 Dec 1912; he was 80. Occupation: Coal Oil Inspector. On 25 Oct 1856 when Philip was 24, he married Anna Maria WAHL, daughter of Thomas WAHL & Barbara WEISBORD, in Belleville,Illinois. Born on 20 Jul 1832 in Niederkirchen, Deidesheim,Pfalz,Bayern. Anna Maria died in Belleville, IL, on 24 Jun 1910; she was 77.

They had the following children:

3   i.   Jacob (1857-1939)
4   ii.   Louisa (1859-1930)
5   iii.   Bertha (1862-)
6   iv.   Henry (1870-1925)
7   v.   August (1873-1936)

Third Generation

---

3. Jacob GROMBACH. Born in 1857 in Belleville, IL. Jacob died on 28 Jul 1939; he was 82.

On 21 Jul 1887 when Jacob was 30, he married Johanna HAMMER, daughter of HAMMER, in Belleville Illinois. Born in 1864 in Belleville Illinois. Johanna died in Belleville Illinois, on 28 Apr 1939; she was 75.

They had the following children:

8   i.   Julius P. (1889-1948)
9   ii.   Jacob A (1910-1945)
10   iii.   Emeline
11   iv.   Stillborn Infant (1897-1897)

Third Generation

4. Louisa GROMBACH. Born on 18 Nov 1859 in Belleville IL. Louisa died in Belleville IL, on 23 Dec 1930; she was 71. Buried in Walnut Hill Cemetery/ Belleville, IL.

On 20 Jul 1886 when Louisa was 26, she married Otto HARTMAN, in Belleville IL. Born on 29 Jul 1859 in Belleville IL. Otto died in Belleville IL, on 9 May 1929; he was 69.

They had the following children:

12	i.	Edna (1887-)
13	ii.	Henry (1889-)
14	iii.	Emma (1892-)
15	iv.	Otto (1893-1894)
16	v.	Hilda (1895-)
17	vi.	Ida (1896-)
18	vii.	Pamelia (1898-)

5. Bertha GROMBACH. Born in 1862 in Belleville Illinois.

6. Henry GROMBACH. Born on 24 Jul 1870 in Belleville, IL. Henry died in Belleville, IL, on 21 May 1925; he was 54. Occupation: Butcher. Religion: Presbyterian.

Henry Grombach 1870-1925

On 6 Mar 1895 when Henry was 24, he married Emma NEUTZLING, daughter of John(Johann) NEUTZLING & Margaretha Gretchen WEBER, in Belleville,Illinois. Born on 17 Jul 1871 in Belleville, IL. Emma died in Belleville, IL, on 13 Dec 1945; she was 74.

They had the following children:

19	i.Herbert August (1895-1955)
20	ii.LEOTA EMMA (1898-1984)
21	iii.Roma (1912-1989)

7.August GROMBACH.

Born on 1 Feb 1873. August died in Belleville Illinois, on 16 May 1936; he was 63. Buried in Walnut Hill, Belleville

Fourth Generation

---

8. Julius P. GROMBACH. Born in 1889. Julius P. died in Belleville Illinois, on 9 Feb 1948; he was 59.

9. Jacob A GROMBACH. Born in 1910. Jacob A died on 11 Apr 1945; he was 35.

10. Emeline GROMBACH.

Emeline married Robert SCHRAG.

11. Stillborn Infant GROMBACH. Born on 23 Apr 1897. Stillborn Infant died on 23 Apr 1897; he was <1.

12. Edna HARTMAN. Born on 21 Nov 1887.

13. Henry HARTMAN. Born on 3 Mar 1889.

14. Emma HARTMAN. Born on 29 Feb 1892.

15. Otto HARTMAN. Born on 10 Jul 1893 in Belleville IL. Otto died in Belleville IL, on 10 Aug 1894; he was 1. Buried in Messinger Cemetery,Belleville IL.

16. Hilda HARTMAN. Born on 22 Feb 1895 in Belleville IL.

17. Ida HARTMAN. Born on 18 Nov 1896.

18. Pamelia HARTMAN. Born on 21 Sep 1898.

19. LEOTA EMMA GROMBACH. Born on 13 Jun 1898 in Belleville, IL. LEOTA EMMA died in Belleville, IL, on 23 Aug 1984; she was 86. Buried in Walnut Hill, Belleville. Occupation: Teacher. Education: Illinois State Normal Univ. Religion: Christian Science.

On 30 Jun 1924 when LEOTA EMMA was 27, she married EMILE HENRY BUCHMANN, son of Henry Xavier Thomas Louis BUCHMANN & Drusilla Maria HAMMER, in Belleville,IL. Born on 21 Aug 1899 in St. Louis, MO.

EMILE HENRY died in San Francisco, CA, on 30 Jul 1960; he was 60.

They had the following children:

22	i.	Rose Marie (1927-)
23	ii.	Emmy Lee (1927-)
24	iii.	Lois Jean (1928-)
25	iv.	Carl Emile (1929-)

Fourth Generation

---

20. Herbert August GROMBACH. Herbert August died on 21 May 1955.

In 1927 Herbert August married Sada J. CHALMERS, in Belleville,IL. Born on 29 Oct 1903 in Bainbridge, IL. Sada J. died in Seattle, WA, on 11 Nov 1996; she was 93.

21. Roma GROMBACH. Born in 1912 in Belleville Illinois. Roma died in Belleville, IL, on 1 Jan 1989; she was 77.

Roma married Joseph BERGER. Joseph died in Apr 1983 in Belleville Illinois.

They had the following children:

26	i.	Richard Lee
27	ii.	Marlene
28	iii.	Sandra

Fifth Generation

---

22. Rose Marie BUCHMANN Ph.D. Born on 3 Feb 1927 in Belleville, IL. Occupation: University Administrator. Education: Millikin, SSU, UIS, Illinois State. Religion: Presbyterian.

On 17 Jun 1950 when Rose Marie was 23, she first married Robert Corwine ROACH, son of Charles MILLER & Marie LOGAN, in Belleville,IL. Born on 21 Jan 1927 in Chicago, IL. Robert Corwine died in Springfield, IL, on 21 Nov 1978; he was 51.

They had the following children:

i.	Kimberly Ellen (1952-)
ii.	Robert Corwine, Jr. (1956-)
iii.	Andrew Thomas (1958-)
iv.	Phillip Matthew (1966-)

On 7 Nov 1981 when Rose Marie was 54, she second married Fred James MILLER Jr., son of Fred James MILLER & Lillian COOKE, in Springfield,Illinois. Born on 11 Sep 1926 in Thomas, OK.

Fifth Generation

23. Emmy Lee BUCHMANN. Born on 3 Feb 1927.

On 9 Oct 1948 when Emmy Lee was 21, she married James Edward WILLIAMS, in St.Paul's Evangelical /Belleville IL. Born on 31 Jan 1923 in Decatur Illinois.

They had the following children:

i.	Jill Diane (1951-)
ii.	Julia Moore (1954-)
iii.	James David (1961-)

24. Lois Jean BUCHMANN. Born on 25 Feb 1928 in Belleville IL.

On 2 Sep 1954 when Lois Jean was 26, she married John KLUGA, in Los Angeles CA. Born on 18 Dec 1924.

They had the following children:

i.	Jon Christopher (1961-)
ii.	Kyra Lee (1963-)

25. Carl Emile BUCHMANN. Born on 15 Sep 1929 in Belleville, IL.

On 22 Jun 1958 when Carl Emile was 28, he married Mary Carolyn CRAIG, daughter of Hugh MacGregor CRAIG & Mary Helen HAMILTON, in Linton,Indiana. Born on 5 Aug 1935 in Syracuse, NY.

They had the following children:

i.	Craig Eric (1962-)
ii.	Caron Susann (1965-)

26. Richard Lee BERGER.

27. Marlene BERGER.

28. **Sandra BERGER**

Grombach Surname Index

BERGER

Joseph	spouse of 21
Marlene	27
Richard Lee	26
Sandra	28

BUCHMANN

Carl Emile	25
EMILE HENRY	spouse of 19
Emmy Lee	23
Henry Xavier Thomas Louis	parent of spouse of 19
Lois Jean	24
Rose Marie	22

CHALMERS

Sada J.	spouse of 20

GROMBACH

August	7
Bertha	5
Emeline	10
Henry	6
Herbert August	20
Jacob	3
Jacob	1
Jacob A	9
Julius P.	8
LEOTA EMMA	19
Louisa	4
Philip	2
Roma	21
Stillborn Infant	11
UNNAMED	parent of spouse of 3
Johanna	spouse of 3

HARTMAN

Edna	12
Emma	14
Henry	13
Hilda	16
Ida	17
Otto	spouse of 4
Otto	15
Pamelia	18

NEUTZLING
Emma   spouse of 6
John(Johann)   parent of spouse of 6

SCHRAG
Robert   spouse of 10

WAHL
Anna Maria   spouse of 2
Thomas   parent of spouse of 2

WEBER
Margaretha Gretchen   parent of spouse of 6
WEISBORD
Barbara   parent of spouse of 2

Anna Maria Wahl 1832-1910
(wife of Phillip Grombach)

Phillip Grombach   1832-1912

Grombach -Neutzling Wedding Party
March 6, 1895 in Belleville, Illinois

Leota (r) and friend about 1905

Herbert August Grombach 1896-1955

T. Reime BELLEVILLE, ILL.

Leota's 75th Surprise Party 1973

left to right:
Marlene Berger, Roma Berger,
Leota and Joe Berger

Herb in France during WWI   1918

Herb, the fisherman

Genealogy of the Neutzling Family

1710 to Emile and Leota

Wappenbrief

für

Familie Neutzling

First Generation

1. Johann NEUTZLING. Born in 1710 in Rotherhoh, Rheinland, Germany. Johann died in Sponheim, Germany, on 4 Apr 1779; he was 69. Occupation: Shepherd.

Johann married Maria Barbara UNKNOWN.

They had one child:

    2   i.   George Wilhelm (1741-1797)

Second Generation

2. George Wilhelm NEUTZLING. Born in 1741 in Sponheim, Germany. George Wilhelm died in Sponheim, Germany, on 10 May 1797; he was 56.

On 15 May 1778 when George Wilhelm was 37, he married Gertrude JUNG, daughter of Anton JUNG, in Sponheim,Germany. Born in 1755 in Sponheim Germany.

They had one child:

    3   i.   Johann Peter (1781-)

Third Generation

3. Johann Peter NEUTZLING. Born on 17 Oct 1781 in Sponheim, Germany.

On 6 Jan 1807 when Johann Peter was 25, he married Susanna JENEMANN, daughter of Johann Peter JENEMANN & Susanna SCHMITT, in Sponheim,Germany. Born on 10 Sep 1782 in Bockenau, Germany. Susanna died in Sponheim, Germany, on 22 Feb 1850; she was 67.

They had one child:

    4   i.   Peter (1810-1888)

The Buchmann Family

Fourth Generation

---

4. Peter NEUTZLING. Born on 22 Jul 1810 in Sponheim, Germany. Peter died in Pomeroy, Ohio, on 22 Oct 1888; he was 78.

On 17 Aug 1830 when Peter was 20, he married Anna Susanna KUSS, daughter of Nicholas KUSS & Barbara KARST, in Sponheim,Germany. Born on 25 Sep 1805 in Sponheim, Germany. Anna Susanna died in Pomeroy, Ohio, on 9 Mar 1886; she was 80.

They had the following children:

| 5 | i. | John(Johann) (1832-1901) |
| 6 | ii. | Anna Maria (1833-) |

Fifth Generation

---

5. John(Johann) NEUTZLING. Born on 5 Feb 1832 in Sponheim, Germany. John (Johann) died in Belleville, IL, on 1 Jan 1901; he was 68. Buried on 9 Jan 1901 in Walnut Hill, Belleville.

On 22 Mar 1856 when John(Johann) was 24, he married Margaretha Gretchen WEBER, daughter of Jacob WEBER & Catharina ARMBRUSTER, in Belleville,IL. Born on 13 Jul 1840 in Mandel, Germany. Margaretha Gretchen died in Belleville, IL, on 30 Dec 1913; she was 73.

They had the following children:

7	i.	Suzanne (1859-1920)
8	ii.	Ottillia (1861-1877)
9	iii.	Jacob (1863-1882)
10	iv.	Phillip (1865-1909)
11	v.	John (1867-1882)
12	vi.	Joseph Albert (1869-1927)
13	vii.	Emma (1871-1945)
14	viii.	Margaretha (1873-)
15	ix.	Anna (1874-)
16	x.	Anton (1877-1927)

Sixth Generation

---

6. Anna Maria NEUTZLING. Born on 26 Nov 1833 in Sponheim Germany. Anna Maria died on 23 Dec in Ironton OHIO.

On 4 Feb 1855 when Anna Maria was 21, she married Christian Jacob MEDINGER, in Pomeroy OH. Born in Oct 1831 in Germany. Christian Jacob died in Lawrence Co. OHIO, on 28 Feb 1907; he was 75.

7. Suzanne NEUTZLING. Born on 17 Nov 1859 in Belleville IL. Suzanne died in 1920; she was 60.

Suzanne married Anton DAEGNER.

8. Ottillia NEUTZLING. Born in 1861. Ottillia died in 1877; she was 16.

Ottillia married George (John) VOLLMAN.

9. Jacob NEUTZLING. Born on 15 Jan 1863. Buried on 4 Feb 1882 in West Belleville, IL. Jacob died in West Belleville, IL, on 4 Feb 1882; he was 19.

10. Phillip NEUTZLING. Born in 1865 in Belleville, IL. Phillip died in Belleville, IL, on 7 Oct 1909; he was 44. Occupation: Auditor/UMWA..coal Miner.

11. John NEUTZLING. Born on 2 Feb 1867 in West Belleville, IL. John died in Belleville, IL, on 12 Feb 1882; he was 15.

12. Joseph Albert NEUTZLING. Born in 1869 in Belleville, IL. Joseph Albert died in 1927; he was 58.

On 5 Sep 1891 when Joseph Albert was 22, he married Margaret LAMI, in Belleville,IL. Born in 1870. Margaret died in 1939; she was 69.

Sixth Generation

13. Emma NEUTZLING. Born on 17 Jul 1871 in Belleville, IL. Emma died in Belleville, IL, on 13 Dec 1945; she was 74. Buried in Walnut Hill, Belleville. Religion: Presbyterian.

On 6 Mar 1895 when Emma was 23, she married Henry GROMBACH, son of Philip GROMBACH & Anna Maria WAHL, in Belleville, Illinois. Born on 24 Jul 1870 in Belleville, IL. Henry died in Belleville, IL, on 21 May 1925; he was 54.

They had the following children:

17	*i.*Herbert August (1895-1955)
18	*ii.*LEOTA EMMA (1898-1984)
19	*iii.*Roma (1912-1989)

14. Margaretha NEUTZLING. Born in 1873.

Margaretha married Joseph STRAUB.

15. Anna NEUTZLING. Born in 1874 in Belleville, IL.

Anna married (unknown). EHRET.

16. Anton NEUTZLING. Born in 1877. Anton died in St. Louis Missouri, on 7 Feb 1927; he was 50.

Seventh Generation

---

17. LEOTA EMMA GROMBACH. Born on 13 Jun 1898 in Belleville, IL. LEOTA EMMA died in Belleville, IL, on 23 Aug 1984; she was 86. Buried in Walnut Hill, Belleville. Occupation: Teacher. Education: Illinois State Normal Univ. Religion: Christian Science.

On 30 Jun 1924 when LEOTA EMMA was 27, she married EMILE HENRY BUCHMANN, son of Henry Xavier Thomas Louis BUCHMANN & Drusilla Maria HAMMER, in Belleville,IL. Born on 21 Aug 1899 in St. Louis, MO. EMILE HENRY died in San Francisco, CA, on 30 Jul 1960; he was 60.

They had the following children:

i.	Rose Marie (1927-)
ii.	Emmy Lee (1927-)
iii.	Lois Jean (1928-)
iv.	Carl Emile (1929-)

18. Herbert August GROMBACH. Herbert August died on 21 May 1955.

In 1927 Herbert August married Sada J. CHALMERS, in Belleville,IL. Born on 29 Oct 1903 in Bainbridge, IL. Sada J. died in Seattle, WA, on 11 Nov 1996; she was 93.

19. Roma GROMBACH. Born in 1912 in Belleville Illinois. Roma died in Belleville, IL, on 1 Jan 1989; she was 77.

Roma married Joseph BERGER. Joseph died in Apr 1983 in Belleville Illinois.

They had the following children:

> *i. Richard Lee*
>
> *ii. Marlene*
>
> *iii. Sandra*

Neutzling Surname Index

LAMI
    Margaret   spouse of 12
MEDINGER
    Christian Jacob   spouse of 6
NEUTZLING
    Anna   15
    Anna Maria   6
    Anton   16
    Emma   13
    George Wilhelm   2
    Jacob   9
    Johann   1
    Johann Peter   3
NEUTZLING
    John   11
    John(Johann)   5
    Joseph Albert   12
    Margaretha   14
    Ottillia   8
NEUTZLING
    Peter   4
    Phillip   10
    Suzanne   7
SCHMITT
    Susanna   parent of spouse of 3
STRAUB
    Joseph   spouse of 14
UNKNOWN
    Maria Barbara   spouse of 1
VOLLMAN
    George (John)   spouse of 8
WAHL
    Anna Maria   parent of spouse of 13
WEBER
    Jacob   parent of spouse of 5
    Margaretha Gretchen   spouse of 5

Johann NEUTZLING
b. 1710, Rotherhoh, Rheinland, Germany
d. 4 Apr 1779, Sponheim, Germany
& Maria Barbara UNKNOWN

George Wilhelm NEUTZLING
b. 1741, Sponheim, Germany
d. 10 May 1797, Sponheim, Germany
& Gertrude JUNG
b. 1755, Sponheim Germany
m. 15 May 1778, Sponheim,Germany

Johann Peter NEUTZLING
b. 17 Oct 1781, Sponheim, Germany
& Susanna JENEMANN
b. 10 Sep 1782, Bockenau, Germany
d. 22 Feb 1850, Sponheim, Germany
m. 6 Jan 1807, Sponheim,Germany

Peter NEUTZLING
b. 22 Jul 1810, Sponheim, Germany
d. 22 Oct 1888, Pomeroy, Ohio
& Anna Susanna KUSS
b. 25 Sep 1805, Sponheim, Germany
d. 9 Mar 1886, Pomeroy, Ohio
m. 17 Aug 1830, Sponheim,Germany

John(Johann) NEUTZLING
b. 5 Feb 1832, Sponheim, Germany
d. 1 Jan 1901, Belleville, IL
& Margaretha Gretchen WEBER
b. 13 Jul 1840, Mandel, Germany
d. 30 Dec 1913, Belleville, IL
m. 22 Mar 1856, Belleville,IL

Suzanne NEUTZLING
b. 17 Nov 1859, Belleville IL
d. 1920
& Anton DAEGNER

Ottillia NEUTZLING
b. 1861
d. 1877
& George (John) VOLLMAN

Jacob NEUTZLING
b. 15 Jan 1863
d. 4 Feb 1882, West Belleville, IL

Phillip NEUTZLING
b. 1865, Belleville, IL
d. 7 Oct 1909, Belleville, IL

John NEUTZLING
b. 2 Feb 1867, West Belleville, IL
d. 12 Feb 1882, Belleville, IL

Joseph Albert NEUTZLING
b. 1869, Belleville, IL
d. 1927
& Margaret LAMI
b. 1870
d. 1939
m. 5 Sep 1891, Belleville,IL

Emma NEUTZLING
b. 17 Jul 1871, Belleville, IL
d. 13 Dec 1945, Belleville, IL
& Henry GROMBACH
b. 24 Jul 1870, Belleville, IL
d. 21 May 1925, Belleville, IL
m. 6 Mar 1895, Belleville,Illinois

LEOTA EMMA GROMBACH
b. 13 Jun 1898, Belleville, IL
d. 23 Aug 1984, Belleville, IL
& EMILE HENRY BUCHMANN
b. 21 Aug 1899, St. Louis, MO
d. 30 Jul 1960, San Francisco, CA
m. 30 Jun 1925, Belleville,IL

Herbert August GROMBACH
d. 21 May 1955
& Sada J CHALMERS
b. 29 Oct 1903, Bainbridge, IL
d. 11 Nov 1996, Seattle, WA
m. 1927, Belleville,IL

Roma GROMBACH
b. 1912, Belleville Illinois
d. 1 Jan 1989, Belleville, IL
& Joseph BERGER
d. Apr 1983, Belleville Illinois

Margaretha NEUTZLING
b. 1873
& Joseph STRAUB

Anna NEUTZLING
b. 1874, Belleville, IL
& EHRET

Anton NEUTZLING
b. 1877
d. 7 Feb 1927, St. Louis Missouri

Anna Maria NEUTZLING
b. 26 Nov 1833, Sponheim Germany
d. 23 Dec , Ironton OHIO
& Christian Jacob MEDINGER
b. Oct 1831, Germany
d. 28 Feb 1907, Lawrence Co. OHIO
m. 4 Feb 1855, Pomeroy OH

"Howdy, I'm your third cousin, twice removed,"

Relationship Terms   Sometimes, especially when working on your family history, it's handy to know how to describe your family relationships more exactly. The definitions below should help you out.

Cousin (a.k.a "first cousin")
Your first cousins are the people in your family who have two of the same grandparents as you. In other words, they are the children of your aunts and uncles.

Second Cousin
Your second cousins are the people in your family who have the same great-grandparents as you., but not the same grandparents.

Third, Fourth, and Fifth Cousins
Your third cousins have the same great-great-grandparents, fourth cousins have the same great-great-great-grandparents, and so on.

Removed
When the word **"removed"** is used to describe a relationship, it indicates that the two people are from different generations. You and your first cousins are in the same generation (two generations younger than your grandparents), so the word "removed" is *not* used to describe your relationship. The words **"once removed"** mean that there is a difference of one generation. For example, your mother's first cousin is your first cousin, once removed. This is because your mother's first cousin is one generation younger than your grandparents and you are two generations younger than your grandparents. This one-generation difference equals "once removed. **"Twice removed"** means that there is a two-generation difference. You are two generations younger than a first cousin of your grandmother, so you and your grandmother's first cousin are first cousins, twice removed.

Relationship Charts Simplify Everything

Now that you have an idea of what these different words mean, take a look at the chart below. It's called a relationship chart, and it can help you figure out how different people in your family are related. It's much simpler than it looks, just follow the instructions.

Instructions for Using a Relationship Chart

1. Pick two people in your family and figure out which ancestor they have in common. For example, if you chose yourself and a cousin, you would have a grandparent in common.
2. Look at the top row of the chart and find the first person's relationship to the common ancestor.
3. Look at the far left column of the chart and find the second person's relationship to the common ancestor.
   Determine where the row and column containing those two relationships meet.

Common Ancestor	Child	Grandchild	Great grandchild	Great-great grandchild
Child	Sister or Brother	Nephew or Niece	Grand-nephew or niece	G-grand-nephew or niece
Grandchild	Nephew or Niece	First cousin	First cousin, once removed	First cousin, twice removed
G-grandchild	Grand-nephew or niece	First cousin, once removed	Second cousin	Second cousin, once removed
G-g-grandchild	G-grand-nephew or niece	First cousin, twice removed	Second cousin, once removed	Third cousin

Birth Years

1636 -
HERTLING   Anselm Casimir

1642 -
GEHRLEIN   Jacobus

1643 -
MALTHANER   Joannes

1652 -
BURCK   Johann Barthel

1654 -
BAUER   Appolonia

1668 -
BURCK ??   Joannes

1669 -
GEHRLEIN   Laurentius
SCHAAF   Joannes

1671 -
BURCK   Joannes

1672 -
HOFFMAN   Anna
WOLFF   Anna Barbara

1673 -
RUNCK   Margartha
GEHRLEIN   Georgius

1675 -
GOETZ   Anna Marie

1680 -
HAMMER   Michaelis

1687 -
BURCK   Eva

1689 -
MALTHANER   Anna Elisabetha

1691 -
PFISTER   Stephanus
BURCK   Anna Catharina
MALTHANER   Anna Catharina
BURCK

1693 -
MALTHANER   Christopher

1694 -
MEYER   Andreas
GEHRLEIN   Joannes Jacobus
BURCK   Maria Barbara

1695 -
SCHWAB   Rosina
MALTHANER   Johannes A.
MALTHANER   Antonius
SCHAAF   Joannes
SCHAAF   Joannes (2)

1696 -
BURCK   Peter

1698 -
FRIEDENSTEIN   Anna Rosina
WOLFF   Maria Barbara
HEID   Anna
HERTLING   Maria Barbara

Birth Years

1699 -
WUNSCHEL   Joannes
WUNSCHEL   Joannes

1700 -
WOLFF   Anna Catharina
GEHRLEIN   Joannes Jacobus
MALTHANER   Anna Catharina
SCHAAF   Joannes Petrus

1702 -
SCHAAF   Justus
GEHRLEIN   Joannes

1703 -
WUNSCHEL   Elisabetha

1704 -
SCHAAF   Maria Otilia

1705 -
MALTHANER   Joannes C.

1706 -
SCHAAF   Anna Eva

1707 -
GEHRLEIN   Joannes
GEHRLEIN   Georgius
BURCK   Maria Barbara

1708 -
MALTHANER   Joannes

1710 -
NEUTZLING   Johann
FRANCK   Lorenz

1711 -
MALTHANER   Maria Barbara

1712 -
GEHRLEIN   Joannes Petrus
SCHAAF   Joannes Jacobus

1713 -
GEHRLEIN   JoannesP.

1714 -
GEHRLEIN   Joannes
SCHAAF   Joannes Jacob

1715 -
HAMMER   Lucas (Leuas)
HOFFMANN   Maria Barbara

1716 -
WUNSCHEL   Maria
SCHAAF   Joannes

1717 -
PFISTER   Maria Barbara
GEHRLEIN   Catharina
GEHRLEIN   Maria Barbara

1718 -
BURCK   Maria Eva
PFISTER   Maria Ottilie

1719 -
MEYER   Anna Maria

1720 -
GRAUSS   Anne Marie
GEHRLEIN   Johann
PFISTER   Margretha
HEID   Joannes
SCHAAF   Joannes Petrus
BURCK   Johann

1722 -
STEYER   Jean
HUCK   Mathieu
SCHAAF   Laurentius

1723 -
SCHAAF   Maria Eva
PFISTER   Eva Elisabetha
BURCK   Anna

1724 -
WUNSCHEL   Margretha
SCHAAF   Laurentius

1725 -
BURCK   Anna
HUCK   Jacobi

1726 -
SCHAAF   Joannes
SCHAAF   Jacobus

Birth Years

1727 -
GEHRLEIN — Petrus
BURCK — MariaApollonia

1728 -
PFISTER — Wendelinus
MALTHANER — Anna Catharina

1729 -
GEHRLEIN — Barbara
BURCK — Anna Christina
GEHRLEIN — Maria Barbara

1730 -
WUNSCHEL — Maria
SCHAAF — Maria E.
PFISTER — Georgius
MALTHANER — Joannes A.
GEHRLEIN — Maria Prea

1732 -
BURCK — Barthel
GEHRLEIN — Eva Catharine

1733 -
BURCK — Laurentius
BURCK — Heinrich Joseph
MALTHANER — Joannes
GEHRLEIN — Maria Anna
GEHRLEIN — Joannes

1734 -
BRONNER — Jean
PFISTER — Joannes P.
BURCK — Johann Peter
SCHLINDWEIN — Anna
GEHRLEIN — Joannes Petrus

1735 -
BURCK — Maria Barbara
REIS — Anna Eva
FINK — Anna Eva

1736 -
PFISTER — Joannes
SCHAAF — Joannes
GEHRLEIN — Joannes Petrus
MALTHANER — Maria Eva
GEHRLEIN — Maria Rosina
GEHRLEIN — Maria Barbara

1738 -
WUNSCHEL — Margretha
MALTHANER — Margretha
SCHAAF — Margretha
BURCK — Maria Apollonia

1739 -
FUGER — Odile
GEHRLEIN — Josephus
GEHRLEIN — Joannes

1740 -
WANTZ — Barbe
SCHAAF — Joannes
UHL — Anna Mariam
GEHRLEIN — Georgius

1741 -
NEUTZLING — George
ANTONY — Joannes Petrus
GEHRLEIN — Georgius
MALTHANER — Joannes s
BURCK — Maria Eva

1742 -
GOETZ — Joannes
HAMMER — Salomon
GEHRLEIN — Joannes
SCHAAF — Joannes

1743 -
BUCHMANN — Phillipe
SCHEIDT — Gertrude
MEYER — Jean
FREY — Mathieu
GEHRLEIN — Joannes
HUCK — Bernard
MALTHANER — Maria Regina
SCHAAF — Dominicus

1744 -
GEHRLEIN — Maria Barbara
HAMMER — Joannes
GEHRLEIN — Margretha

Birth Years

1745 -
SCHAAF   Maria
GEHRLEIN   Catherina
HUCK   Jean Adam

1746 -
BURCK   Maria E.
HAMMER   Margaretha

1747 -
GEHRLEIN   Joannes

1748 -
HAMMER   Maria Barbara

1749 -
RUDOLFF   Louis
HAMMER   Maria
ZECHIN   Anna Maria

1750 -
WAHL   Jacobo
GEHRLEIN   Joannes

1752 -
HAMMER   Joannes Petrus

1753 -
SCHAAF   Maria Regina
GEHRLEIN   Anna Catharina

1754 -
STEYER   Francois Joseph
SCHAAF   Andreas
GEHRLEIN   Joannes

1755 -
JUNG   Gertrude
HAMMER   Georgius Petrus

1756 -
SCHAAF   Georgius

1757 -
GEHRLEIN   Andreas
HAMMER   Joannes G.

1758 -
HEID   Maria Apollonia
HAMMER   Joannes(2)
GEHRLEIN   Maria Eva

1760 -
GEHRLEIN   Eva C.

HAMMER   Georgius

1761 -
GEHRLEIN   Eva Margretha

1763 -
GEHRLEIN   Maria

1767 -
ADERS   Michael
HAMMER   Salomon
MEYER   Odile

1768 -
HAMMER   Joannes

1769 -
WAHL   Jacobus

1771 -
ADERS(IN)   Barbara
HAMMER   Margretha

1772 -
BRONNER   Gertrude
HAMMER   Joannes

1773 -
Aders   Joannes
Wilhelmus   MALTHANER
HAMMER   Joannes Petrus

1774 -
RICHERT   Charles
HAMMER   Joannes

1775 -
ADERS   Maria Anna
HAMMER   Joannes
MALTHANER   Joannes Petrus

1776 -
HEID (HEIDT)   Maria Eva
HAMMER   Eva Catharina
RUDOLFF   Denis

1777 -
ADERS   Apollonia
MALTHANER   Christophorus

Birth Years

1778 -
WUNSCHEL	Maria Catherine
KARST	Barbara
HAMMER	Regina
MALTHANER	Georgius
HAMMER	Maria

1779 -
KUSS	Nicholas
FREY	Madeline

1780 -
Aders	Michael (#2)
HAMMER	Maria
Barbara	

1781 -
HAMMER	Joannes
GEHRLEIN	Georgius
NEUTZLING	Johann Peter

1782 -
JENEMANN	Susanna

1783 -
GEHRLEIN	Georgius
HAMMER	Margaretha

1784 -
GEHRLEIN	Elisabetha
HAMMER	Regina

1785 -
HAMMER	Georgius

1787 -
HUCK	Julienne
GEHRLEIN	Eva Margaretha

1788 -
BUCHMANN	Phillippe
HAMMER	Solomon
GEHRLEIN	Georgius

1791 -
HAMMER   Maria Barbara (2)

1794 -
GEHRLEIN	Joannes

1795 -
BELLAIRE	Karl Jakob

1799 -
WEBER	Jacob
ARMBRUSTER	Catharina
HAMMER	Georgius Petrus

1800 -
HAMMER	Regina
WAHL	Thomas
RICHERT	Francois Joseph

1802 -
HAMMER	Georgius M.

1803 -
HAMMER	Maria
MALTHANER	Eva
WEISBORD	Barbara
STEYER	Scholastique
HAMMER	Joannes Petrus

1805 -
WAHL	Catharina
HAMMER	Eva Margretha
KUSS	Anna Susanna

1806 -
MALTHANER	Catharina

1807 -
WAHL	Catharina (2)
WAHL	MariaAnna
HERTLING	William

1808 -
HERTLING	Anna
HAMMER	Joannes P.
MALTHANER	Joannes

1810 -
HAMMER	Otilia
MALTHANER	Joannes P.(2)
NEUTZLING	Peter

1811 -
SCHERER	John

Birth Years

1812 -	
RUDOLFF	Brigitte
WAHL	JoannesW,(2)
HAMMER	Johannes
MALTHANER	Joannes
BUCHMANN	Xavier

1813 -	
SCHLOSS	Eva

1815 -	
MALTHANER	Georgius
HAMMER	Joannes

1817 -	
RICHERT	Marie Anne
MALTHANER	Joannes

1818 -	
HOFFMAN	Eva Barbara
HAMMER	Laurentius

1819 -	
RICHERT	Madeleine

1820 -	
PUDERER	Jacob

1821 -	
BUCHMANN	Caroline
HAMMER	Casparus

1824 -	
WEBER	Margaretha

1825 -	
WEBER	Ottillia

1826 -	
HAMMER	Georgius

1828 -	
WAHL	Elizabetha
HAMMER	Casparus

1829 -	
WEBER	Phillip
RICHERT	Charles

1830 -	
HAMMER	Casper

1831 -	
SEVERIN	Joseph
WEBER	Eva (Eve)
MEDINGER	Christian Jacob

1832 -	
NEUTZLING	John(Johann)
RICHERT	Caroline
GROMBACH	Philip
WAHL	Anna Maria

1833 -	
HAMMER	Maria Eva
WEBER	Johann S.
NEUTZLING	Anna Maria

1834 -	
LAUFF	Johannes
BUCHMANN	Louis
RICHERT	Marie Anne

1835 -	
WEBER	Franz (Frank)
HAMMER	Michael X.
SCHNEIDER	Victoria

1837 -	
WEBER	Catharina
RICHERT	Aloise

1839 -	
SCHERER	Elisabeth
SCHALL	Maria
HAMMER	Annie Eva
RICHERT	Joseph

1840 -	
WEBER	Margaretha

1841 -	
HAMMER	Jacob

1843 -	
SCHERER	Margaretha
WEBER	Heinreich

1844 -	
MALTHANER	Ottilie
BELLAIRE	Theresia

1846 -	
SCHERRER	Michael
NEUTZLING	Elizabeth

Birth Years

1847 -	
HAMMER	Philippina
HAMMER	Sophia

1848 -	
MALTHANER	Ludwig

1849 -	
SCHIRER	Rosina

1850 -	
HAMMER	Ludovius

1851 -	
PUDERER	Emma

1852 -	
MALTHANER	Jakob

1853 -	
PUDERER	Julius

1856 -	
MALTHANER	Karl

1857 -	
GROMBACH	Jacob
PUDERER	Frank
LAUFF	Amelia

1858 -	
MALTHANER	Johannes

1859 -	
PUDERER	Philipp
HARTMAN	Otto
NEUTZLING	Suzanne
GROMBACH	Louisa
BUCHMANN	Henry Xavier

1861 -	
NEUTZLING	Ottillia
FELDMEIER	Henry
BUCHMANN	Edouard Xavier

1862 -	
GROMBACH	Bertha
PUDERER	Louise
HAMMER	Florentinus

1863 -	
HAMMER	Lorenz
PUDERER	Anna M.
NEUTZLING	Jacob
WEBER	Jacob John
BUCHMANN	Marie Brigitte

1864 -	
HAMMER	Johanna
BUCHMANN	Elisabeth

1865 -	
NEUTZLING	Phillip
HAMMER	Georgius

1866 -	
PUDERER	William Jacob
BUCHMANN	Charles

1867 -	
NEUTZLING	John

1868 -	
HAMMER	Margaretha
PUDERER	Louisa
KESSLER	Eva
BUCHMANN	Marie Louise

1869 -	
NEUTZLING	Joseph Albert
BUCHMANN	Charles

1870 -	
LAMI	Margaret
HAMMER	Drusilla Maria
GROMBACH	Henry

1871 -	
SCHOELLKOPF	Carolina Rosina
SCHERRER	Ferd Fredericos
NEUTZLING	Emma
BUCHMANN	MarieMadeline

1872 -	
DOEMKER	Mary Louise
HAMMER	Margaret

1873 -	
NEUTZLING	Margaretha
GROMBACH	August

Birth Years

1874 -		1899 -	
NEUTZLING	Anna	PUDERER	Petronilla
NEUTZLING	Kattie	PUDERER	Irma
		MILLER	Charles
1877 -		STAYNOR	Anthony
NEUTZLING	Anton	BUCHMANN	EMILE HENRY
NEKVINDA	Ann Josephine		
		1900 -	
1878 -		BUCHMANN	Louie
HAMMER	Mary Josephine	CRAIG	Hugh
SCHERRER	Sophia Marie	HAMILTON	Mary Helen
		BRANDT	Edward
1883 -			
SCHERRER	George John	**1901 -**	
		LOGAN	Marie
1885 -		RECK	Marie Catherine
SCHERRER	Jacob		
		1902 -	
1887 -		ANGEVINE	Merrill Louis
HARTMAN	Edna		
		1903 -	
1889 -		CHALMERS	Sada J.
GROMBACH	Julius		
GROMBACH	Julius P.	**1904 -**	
HARTMAN	Henry	COOKE	Lillian
		1905 -	
1892 -		BUCHMANN	Marie Elizabeth
HARTMAN	Emma		
GROMBACH	Henrietta	**1906 -**	
BUCHMANN	Arthur Michael	NEUTZLING	Lester
		BUCHMANN	Josephine
1893 -			
HARTMAN	Otto	**1907 -**	
		FELDMEIER	Walter
1895 -			
HARTMAN	Hilda	**1910 -**	
BUCHMANN	Florence	HERTLING	Margaret
		GROMBACH	Jacob A
1896 -		BUCHMANN	Edward
HARTMAN	Ida		
		1911 -	
1897 -		DOXSIE	Louis E.
GROMBACH	Stillborn		
		1912 -	
1898 -		GROMBACH	Roma
BUCHMANN	EMMA		
GROMBACH	LEOTA EMMA	**1913 -**	
HARTMAN	Pamelia	BUCHMANN	Jerome
		1914 -	
		-----------	Beryl Leah

Birth Years

1922 -
BUCHMANN   Herbert Alois

1923 -
WILLIAMS   James Edward

1924 -
KLUGA   John

1925 -
ANDERSON   Charles Albert

1926 -
ROBERTSON   Horace
MILLER   Fred James

1927 -
ROACH   Robert Corwine
BUCHMANN   Rose Marie
BUCHMANN   Emmy Lee

1928 -
BUCHMANN   Lois Jean

1929 -
JACKSON   Sally Ann
BUCHMANN   Carl Emile
CRAIG   Emylie Susann
BUCHMANN   Kenneth Henry

1930 -
BAUER   Barbara Jane

1931 -
ANGEVINE   Jack Merrill

1932 -
HARMS   Catherine Marie

1933 -
MILLER   Karl

1935 -
CRAIG   Mary Carolyn

1936 -
GRETHER   Marie Therese
PERKINS   Ann

1940 -
EZELLE   Travis Kirk

1945 -
DUPELECHAIN   Donna Gail
POTEET   David

1948 -
DeMichele   Daniel

1949 -
DOXSIE   Susan Marie
BUCHMANN   Herbert

1950 -
ROBERTSON   Kurtis Lex

1951 -
BUCHMANN   Gregory
WILLIAMS   Jill Diane
McPHERSEN   Marno

1952 -
ROSEMANN   Sherryl Denise
GOSNEY   Katherine
ROACH   Kimberly Ellen
ROBERTSON   Mary Elisa

1953 -
DOXSIE   John Robert
MILLER   Dale Wilson

1954 -
BRANDT   Robert
WILLIAMS   Julia Moore

1955 -
BUCHMANN   Barth David

1956 -
BRANDT   Donald
ANDERSON   Marilyn Jean
ROACH   Robert C., Jr.

1957 -
KUNDERER   Joann Elizabeth
MILLER   Alan James

1958 -
ROACH   Andrew Thomas
BUCHMANN   Diane Karen

1959 -
BUCHMANN   Eric

Birth Years

1960 -
SISSUM — Teresa
RILEY — Patrick Lynn
MURABITO — Donald Patrick
MILLER — Chris

1961 -
SERVATIUS — Mary
OVERLIN — Amber
BUCHMANN — Brian Thomas
KLUGA — Jon Christopher
WILLIAMS — James David

1962 -
MILLER — Karen Jean
BUCHMANN — Craig Eric
BUCHMANN — Cynthia Marie
BUCHMANN — Elaine Marie

1963 -
WHITE — Kurt
KLUGA — Kyra Lee
BREZ — Anita

1964 -
BUCHMANN — David Andrew
LOMMEN — Barbara Katrin
EZELLE — Kayla Maurissa
RUSSELL — Jana Dee

1965 -
BUCHMANN — Caron Susann
MILLER — Kathy Louise

1966 -
ROACH — Phillip Matthew
BUCHMANN — Neal Howard
SCHANTZ — Amy

1967 -
BUCHMANN — KennethE.

1968 -
BUICK — Michelle Grace
EZELLE — Kammie Nicole

1969 -
BUCHMANN — Heather Renee

1971 -
GUMMINGER — Amy

1974 -
BUCHMANN — Norma

1977 -
BUCHMANN — Amanda
BUCHMANN — Kyra Anne

1978 -
BUCHMANN — Brett Alois
BUCHMANN — Alesia Marie

1979 -
BUCHMANN — Miranda

1981 -
BUCHMANN — Tiffany Marie

1983 -
DOXSIE — Jill Suzanne
MILLER — Laura Kristin

1985 -
DeMichele — Daniel
BUCHMANN — Arikka

1986 -
MILLER — Rachel
WHITE — Jeffrey Alan

1987 -
MILLER — Sarah
MILLER — Douglas James
BUCHMANN — Emily Allison
DOXSIE — Jeffrey Thomas

1988 -
WHITE — Lynn Marie
DeMichele — Thomas Daniel

1991 -
DeMichele — Joseph
Daniel
BUCHMANN — Abby
Elizabeth
MURABITO — Drusilla Marie
BUCHMANN — Bryce

1992 -
BUCHMANN — Gregory II

1993 -
BUCHMANN — Maggie Elise
BUCHMANN — Connor

Birth Years

1994 -
MURABITO   Madeline Marie

1995 -
CZAPALA   Kayla Christine

1996 -
BUCHMANN   Andrea
CZAPALA   Karissa

1997 -
RILEY   Stuart Michael
CZAPALA   Madeline

1998 -
WILLIAMS   Parker James
1999 -
BUCHMANN   Alexis K.
Roach-LOMMEN   Jack Henry

2000 -
WILLIAMS   Carter Davidson
BUCHMANN   Alayna Nadine
BROOKS   Sawyer Carl
KLUGA   Catherine Jeane

2001 -
BUCHMANN   Claire Marie

2002 -
BROOKS   Camryn
Roach-LOMMEN   Charles Emile
BUCHMANN   Jack William
WILLIAMS   Windsor Nichole

2004 -
BUCHMANN   Jonah David

2005

2006

2007

2008

2009

2010

We do not choose to be born.
We do not choose our parents,
Or our times or country of birth,
Or the circumstances of our upbringing.
We do not – most of us – choose to die
But within all this realm of choicelessness
We do choose how we shall live –
Courageously or in cowardice,
Honorably or dishonorably,
With purpose or adrift.
We decide what is important and what is trivial,
What makes us significant is what we do,
Or refuse to do.
We decide and we choose
And so we give definition to ourselves.

--Joseph Epstein
from <u>*Ambition*</u> *(E. P. Dutton,1980)*

Additions, corrections, new information

Made in the USA
Las Vegas, NV
13 September 2021